Published by Macmillan in association with the International Institute for Strategic Studies

Studies in International Security

Hedley Bull: THE CONTROL OF THE ARMS RACE
James Cable: GUNBOAT DIPLOMACY, 1919–1979
Donald C. Daniel: ANTI-SUBMARINE WARFARE AND SUPERPOWER STRATEGIC STABILITY
Paul Dibb: THE SOVIET UNION: The Incomplete Superpower
Lawrence Freedman: THE EVOLUTION OF NUCLEAR STRATEGY
Gwyn Harries-Jenkins (*editor*): ARMED FORCES AND THE WELFARE SOCIETIES: Challenges in the 1980s
Robert Jackson: SOUTH ASIAN CRISIS
J.M. Lee: AFRICAN ARMIES AND CIVIL ORDER
Hanns W. Maull: RAW MATERIALS, ENERGY AND WESTERN SECURITY
Adam Roberts: NATIONS IN ARMS
Robert Thompson: DEFEATING COMMUNIST INSURGENCY

International Institute for Strategic Studies conference papers

Christoph Bertram (*editor*):
  NEW CONVENTIONAL WEAPONS AND EAST–WEST SECURITY
  PROSPECTS OF SOVIET POWER IN THE 1980s
  THE FUTURE OF STRATEGIC DETERRENCE
  THIRD-WORLD CONFLICT AND INTERNATIONAL SECURITY
  AMERICA'S SECURITY IN THE 1980s
  DEFENCE AND CONSENSUS

Robert O'Neill (*editor*):
  THE CONDUCT OF EAST-WEST RELATIONS IN THE 1980s
  NEW TECHNOLOGY AND WESTERN SECURITY POLICY

François de Rose:
  EUROPEAN SECURITY AND FRANCE

Series Standing Order

If you would like to receive future titles in this series as they are published, you can make use of our standing order facility. To place a standing order please contact your bookseller or, in case of difficulty, write to us at the address below with your name and address and the name of the series. Please state with which title you wish to begin your standing order. (If you live outside the U.K. we may not have the rights for your area, in which case we will forward your order to the publisher concerned.)

Standing Order Service, Macmillan Distribution Ltd,
Houndmills, Basingstoke, Hants, RG21 2XS, England.

ANTI-SUBMARINE WARFARE AND SUPERPOWER STRATEGIC STABILITY

Donald C. Daniel

©International Institute for Strategic Studies 1986

All rights reserved. No reproduction, copy or transmission of this publication may be made without written permission.

No paragraph of this publication may be reproduced, copied or transmitted save with written permission or in accordance with the provisions of the Copyright Act 1956 (as amended).

Any person who does any unauthorised act in relation to this publication may be liable to criminal prosecution and civil claims for damages.

First published 1986

Published by
THE MACMILLAN PRESS LTD
Houndmills, Basingstoke, Hampshire RG21 2XS
and London
Companies and representatives
throughout the world

Printed in Hong Kong

British Library Cataloguing in Publication Data
Daniel, Donald C.
Anti-submarine warfare and superpower strategic
stability.—(Studies in international security)
1. Anti-submarine warfare
I. Title II. Series
359.4   V214
ISBN 0–333–39750–9

Contents

List of Tables and Figures   viii
Acknowledgements   ix
List of Abbreviations   x

Introduction   1

PART I   GENERIC CONSIDERATIONS

1 ASW Process and Operations   19
    Barrage   20
    Trailing   22

2 Submarine Observables and Indicators   27
    Acoustic indicators   28
    Non-acoustic indicators   36
    Potential indicators: summary remarks   49

3 ASW Sensors and their Deployment   59
    Deployment modes and platforms   59
    Sensors   65
    Actual and potential sensors: summary remarks   84

PART II   US ASW AND SOVIET SSBNs

4 Soviet SSBN Forces and Operations   97
    Trends in the number and composition of the Soviet SSBN fleet   97
    The primacy of SSBN and SSBN-support missions   101
    SSBN and SSBN support operations   102

5 US ASW Developments — **117**
- Background — 117
- The US effort in long-range passive acoustic detection — 118
- US efforts with alternative technologies for wide-area search — 126
- ASW attack platforms — 130
- ASW weapons — 134
- The US ASW effort as a unified system — 136

6 US ASW and Soviet SSBNs: Conclusions — **145**
- Factors enhancing America's anti-SSBN potential — 145
- Factors degrading America's anti-SSBN potential — 147
- Net assessment and conclusions — 151

PART III SOVIET ASW AND US SSBNs

7 US SSBN Forces and Operations — **161**
- Trends in the number and composition of the US SSBN fleet — 161
- SSBN and SSBN support operations — 165

8 Soviet ASW Developments — **175**
- Background — 175
- Detection systems — 177
- Soviet attack platforms and weapons systems — 182

9 Soviet ASW and US SSBNs: Conclusions — **189**
- Factors enhancing the USSR's anti-SSBN potential — 189
- Factors degrading the USSR's anti-SSBN potential — 190
- Net assessment and conclusions — 193

PART IV CONCLUSION

10 Conclusions — **201**
- Findings concerning stability — 201

Negotiated ASW arms control: an additional measure? 206
Soviet ASW and the SSBN forces of Britain and France 211
Closing Observations 211

Index 215

List of Tables and Figures

TABLES

1.1	Estimated MTEs per submarine variant and missile mod	14
2.1	Potential indicators	50
3.1	Estimated potential uses of actual or potential sensors	85
4.1	Characteristics of Soviet SSBNs and SLBMs	98
6.1	Summary of factors enhancing and degrading the US's anti-SSBN potential	152
7.1	Characteristics of US SSBNs and SLBMs	162
9.1	Summary of factors enhancing and degrading the USSR's anti-SSBN potential	194

FIGURES

3.1	Ground track of radar search satellite	64
7.1	SLBM launcher levels	164

Acknowledgements

I am very happy to express strong appreciation to the IISS where I was a Research Associate in 1983, to the Ford Foundation for funding support in 1981, to the Brookings Institution where I was a Visiting Scholar in 1981, and the Naval Postgraduate School for allowing me leave-time to complete this work.

I am no less appreciative of those individuals who commented on portions of the manuscript or otherwise provided support. Among the former are Robert O'Neill, Jonathan Alford, Robert Nurick, Philip Zelikow, Michael MccGwire, Richard Garwin, Robert Bourke, James Eagle, Paolo Cotta-Ramusino, Worth Bagley, Michael McCune and Gael Donelan-Tarleton. Among the latter are John Baker, Christoph Bertram, Sherman Blandin, Robert Elliot, Patrick Parker, Albertine Potter, John Steinbruner, Carol Wilkins, and the administrative and library staffs of the IISS and Brookings. I remain, of course, solely responsible for errors.

Monterey, California   D.C.D.

List of Abbreviations

ABM	anti-ballistic missile
ACDA	Arms Control and Disarmament Agency
ASW	anti-submarine warfare
BAR	barrier
BMEWS	Ballistic Missile Early Warning System
CBG	carrier battle group
CBM	confidence-building measure
CNO	Chief of Naval Operations
DARPA	Defense Advanced Research Projects Agency
DoD	Department of Defense
ELF	extremely low frequency
EM	electromagnetic
FLIR	forward-looking infra-red
FWA	floating wire antenna
FY	fiscal year
GAO	General Accounting Office
IEEE	Institute of Electrical and Electronic Engineers
IFF	identification, friend or foe
INF	intermediate nuclear force
IR	infra-red
IRR	infra-red radiometer
IUSS	Integrated Undersea Surveillance System
K	kelvin
KT	kiloton
LLLII	low-light-level image intensifier
LOC	localisation
MAD	magnetic anomaly detector
MCM	mine countermeasures
MHD	magnetohydrodynamics

MIRV	multiple independently-targetable re-entry vehicle(s)
MRV	multiple re-entry vehicle(s)
MT	megaton
MTE	megaton equivalent
NM	nautical mile
NROSS	Navy Remote Oceanographic Sensing System
OTA	Office of Technology Assessment
OTH-B	over-the-horizon backscatter
PD	probability of detection
PFA	probability of false alarm
PK	probability of kill
PMR	passive microwave radiometer
PSI	pounds per square inch
RAR	real aperture radar
RDSS	Rapidly-Deployable Surveillance System
RV	re-entry vehicle(s)
SACEUR	Supreme Allied Commander, Europe
SALT	Strategic Arms Limitation Talks
SAR	synthetic aperture radar
SIAM	self-initiating anti-air missile
SIGINT	signals intelligence
SINS	submarine inertial navigation system
SIPRI	Stockholm International Peace Research Institute
SLBM	submarine-launched ballistic missile
SLMM	submarine-launched mobile mine
SOFAR	sound fixing and ranging
SOSUS	Sound Surveillance System
SOW	stand-off weapon
SQUID	superconducting quantum interference device
SSBN	nuclear-powered ballistic missile submarine
SSN	nuclear-powered general-purpose submarine
START	Strategic Arms Reduction Talks
SUBROC	rocket-assisted depth charge with nuclear warhead

List of Abbreviations

SURTASS	Surveillance Towed Array Sensor System
TLAM-N	Tomahawk Nuclear land attack cruise missile
TRK	tracking
TRL	trailing
VD	variable depth
VMF	*Voyenno-Morskoy Flot* (Soviet Navy)
WAS	wide-area search
WEU	West European Union
WIG	wing-in-ground

Introduction

For the purposes of this study, the superpower strategic relationship can be regarded as stable as long as both remain deterred from utilising nuclear weapons against the other's homeland. The fundamental basis for deterrence has been the belief that the victim of a nuclear attack could respond to an attack causing damage unacceptable to the attacker however fierce the initial strike. Such a response obviously puts a premium on survivable nuclear forces, and the consensus is that the most survivable today are deployed ballistic missile submarines (or SSBNs). They are regarded – in the West and probably also in the USSR – as the ultimate guarantors of stability, and, conversely, threats to their survivability are considered destabilising if deterrence can no longer be assured.

Since the first deployment of SSBNs more than two decades ago, it has been the practice of many Western (and presumably also Soviet) policy-makers and observers to be prudently sceptical about the survivability of the submarines in the long term. The expression of such views was usually linked with allusions to prospective anti-submarine (ASW) developments but, except possibly in the last few years, such assertions had no significant or lasting effect on the consensus that the submarines would remain survivable. What differentiates the period since the late 1970s is a seemingly greater willingness to be genuinely rather than just prudently sceptical. In other words, in an age where change and technological progress (at least in weapons systems) often seem the only constants, there appears to be a small but growing group of people who believe or sincerely fear that advances in anti-submarine warfare (ASW) capabilities are eroding the invulnerability of the SSBN.

The International Institute for Strategic Studies (IISS), for example, addressed ASW in the 1970, 1975, 1977, and 1980–1 issues of its annual *Strategic Survey*, and only in the last did the editors conclude that 'individual SSBNs are becoming vulnerable to detection and attack'.[1] They saw the oceans as offering modern submarines 'much less protective cover than they have enjoyed for the two decades since the advent of the strategic SSBN'. They also acknowledged, however, that new SSBN developments could 'partly offset' ASW gains and that the vulnerability of ballistic missile submarines was a 'slow' and 'creeping' affair.

Similarly, the Stockholm International Peace Research Institute (SIPRI) also addressed ASW developments in its *Yearbooks* for 1969–70, 1974 and 1979 and in a separate 1974 monograph.[2] The thrust of the pre-1979 publications was that SSBNs should remain survivable for the foreseeable future, but the 1979 *Yearbook* contained a strong shift in position, articulated by Owen Wilkes:

> A significant evolution in ASW now seems imminent. Combined developments may soon make it possible to detect, locate, and destroy all adversary missile submarines within a time so short as to effectively eliminate the adversary's sea-based retaliatory capability. In a military sense, the oceans will soon be transparent.
>
> It seems the USA will soon be able to implement these technologies[3]

While SIPRI raised the spectre of an American threat to Soviet submarines, other highly respected analysts have argued the opposite. In a paper responding to Wilkes's arguments, Michael MccGwire offered: 'Concern about the destabilising effects of strategic ASW [i.e., against SSBNs] is usually directed at the Western advantage in acoustic detection methods . . . [T]his concern is misplaced'.[4] Rather, he goes on, 'within the terms of nuclear deterrence theory, the emerging Soviet capability [against US missile submarines] will be destabilising, in that it weakens the US's assured response and hence increases the Soviet temptations to attack and pressures on the West to launch these missiles while they are still available'.

These citations make it obvious that those who do see an anti-SSBN threat do not always agree about whose submarines are most threatened. One highly placed official in the Carter Administration stressed the potential vulnerability of both. This was William Perry, then Under Secretary of Defense for Research and Engineering. He firmly believed that the US deterrent posture should be based on a mix of nuclear retaliatory forces, and he supported deployment of the MX missile, retention of a strategic bomber capability, and the purchase of both *Trident* missiles and new submarines for carrying them. When asked in 1980 why he supported both the land-based MX and the sea-based *Trident*, as opposed to the latter only, he argued that the invulnerability of sea-based systems could not be fully assured in the 1990s, and he emphasised then and on numerous other occasions the possibility that the US or the USSR might indeed achieve a capability to put the other's sea-based deterrent in hazard.[5] While offering few details, he also spoke of the possibility of the oceans becoming transparent, and he offered scenarios of deployed SSBNs being simultaneously tracked and then barraged with warheads from land-based missiles. While he was careful to stress that any SSBN survivability problems would probably not occur before the next decade, his public statements almost certainly contributed to the heightening of general concern evident since the early 1980s.[6]

This study addresses that general concern. It is intended to serve as a primer on the complexities of anti-SSBN warfare and also on the broad features of superpower ASW and SSBN developments as described in public sources. The ultimate aim is to assess whether foreseeable ASW developments will indeed pose a destabilising threat to the SSBNs as a result of either 'out-of-the-blue' surprise strikes or conventional war attrition. In the former, the issue is whether either superpower's ASW potential will be good enough to tempt it (in conjunction with attacks on silo-based intercontinental ballistic missiles (ICBM) to initiate a surprise attack against the other's land *and* sea-based strategic forces. In conventional war, the issue is whether either superpower will suffer so much attrition of its SSBNs that it considers using, as opposed to possibly losing, its remaining sea-based missiles.

As an aid to the judgements made in this study, it is essential to estimate how many submarines must survive either to deter surprise nuclear attack or to forestall a use of missiles triggered by fear of future attrition. Of course, any estimate of the necessary number of submarines is dependent upon the presumed survivability prospects of all retaliatory forces, but, for the purposes of argument, it will be assumed that SSBNs would be the only systems remaining available for use against the other superpower.

DETERRING A SURPRISE ATTACK

How many submarines are enough to deter a surprise attack? Probably very few for, as Quanbeck and Blechman put it: 'the price [to the attacker] of missing even one submarine could be extraordinarily high'.[7] President Carter drove the point home in his 1979 State of the Union address when he said 'Just one of our relatively invulnerable Poseidon [missile] submarines – comprising less than 2 per cent of our total nuclear force of submarines, aircraft, and land-based missiles – carries enough warheads to destroy every large and medium-size city in the Soviet Union'.[8] Because of the Moscow anti-ballistic missile (ABM) system, the geographic dispersion of Soviet cities, the range of American submarine-launched ballistic missiles (SLBMs), and the probability that not all warheads would penetrate to their targets, it might actually take two submarines to hit these cities and more than two to destroy them totally because of the rather small missile yields but, since most Soviet cities, peoples and industry are concentrated in the western USSR, one submarine should suffice to do so much damage there as effectively to devastate the Soviet economy. A warhead on a Poseidon missile has 50 kilotons (KT) of destructive power – roughly two-and-a-half-to-four times that of the Hiroshima bomb, and one Poseidon missile submarine alone carries 160 of these.[9] If one assumes that 15 per cent do not reach target, this leaves an effective inventory of 136 weapons on one submarine. By virtue of its sixteen missile tubes, a former *Poseidon* submarine converted to carry the *Trident* missile accounts for 128 warheads (or an effective inventory of 108 if 15 per cent are discounted) and new twenty-four tube Ohio-class submarines designed to carry the *Trident* each have some 192 warheads and, for the purposes of this study, an assumed effective inventory of 163 deliverable weapons.

Should the US be the perpetrator rather than the victim of a surprise disarming attack, the retaliatory threat from Soviet submarines would vary depending on type. The more modern have multiple independently-targetable re-entry vehicles (MIRV) and the most recent of these probably carry from 140 to 200 warheads, each with a possible yield in the low hundreds of kilotons (KT) and at least ten-to-sixteen times more powerful than the Hiroshima weapon.[10] Again discounting 15 per cent, this results in about 119 to 170 or so deliverable warheads. Over 50 per cent of US industrial production is concentrated in the north-east, middle Atlantic and east-central sections of the US, and to threaten these areas with over 100 nuclear warheads from one surviving submarine should surely be enough to deter, especially when one considers the interdependent nature of the US economy and the long-term effects of any nuclear attack.[11]

What about lesser threats? From the latest *Military Balance*, one finds that only about 25 per cent of the Soviet SSBN fleet have missiles with MIRV.[12] While the proportion should rise to at least half (and possibly much more) by the mid-1990s, there will still be single warhead missiles, or multiple warhead missiles that are not independently targetable, in the fleet for many years to come. Some submarines carry twelve-to-sixteen 1 megaton (MT) warhead missiles or sixteen missiles with three 200 KT MRV whose combined yield is slightly over 1 megaton equivalent (MTE) per missile due to more effective spreading of the explosive power. An 85 per cent reliability rate would mean ten-to-thirteen missiles arriving on target. Would the threat of their being directed against important national decision-making and commercial centres be enough to deter a US President? It has been estimated that a single 1 MT weapon striking Washington, DC, would cause 624000 immediate fatalities and another 1.4m casualties. If the target were New York City, there would be 1.7m and 4.5m immediate fatalities and casualties respectively.[13] If the warheads were to hit 10–13 such centres, the combined immediate fatalities and casualties could easily run into the low tens of millions for one surviving submarine.[14] This possibility should be enough to deter. McGeorge Bundy has observed:

> Think-tank analysts can set levels of acceptable damage well up in the tens of millions of lives. They can assume that the loss of dozens of great cities is somehow a real choice for sane men. They are in an unreal world. In the real world of political thinkers – whether here or in the Soviet Union – a decision that would bring one hydrogen bomb on one's own country would be recognized in advance as a catastrophic blunder; ten bombs on ten cities would be a disaster beyond history; and a hundred bombs on a hundred cities are unthinkable.[15]

FORESTALLING THE USE OF NUCLEAR WEAPONS

These calculations assumed that a nation subjected to surprise nuclear attack would retaliate with its surviving SLBMs. What if that nation were instead engaged in a conventional war and were suffering SSBN losses? When might it consider using the missiles on surviving SSBNs for fear that delaying could mean the total loss of its sea-based deterrent capability? How many submarines might it feel were needed to ensure deterrence?

While it has already been argued that a nation contemplating a surprise nuclear attack would be deterred if only one or at most two enemy submarines retaliated, a nation wishing to continue to deter in the course of a conventional war might contemplate using its missiles before it estimated that only one or two SSBNs would be left. It might adopt a worst-case perspective on the amount of punishment an opponent is willing to take, and it might also wish to have some SLBMs in reserve for deterring third parties in possession of nuclear weapons or for post-conflict negotiations should it seem sensible to contemplate them.

How many submarines are enough for all these aims? The answer adopted for this study is keyed to each superpower retaining about 200MTE available from SLBMs. The prospect of being able to deliver about 100MTE (or nearly 5000–8000 times the yield of the Hiroshima bomb) against an opponent's industrial base should be enough to give each superpower confidence that it could continue to deter the other. The additional 100MTE would compensate for expected warhead and missile reliability problems and for potential communication problems between national command authorities and some SSBNs. It could also deter third parties and affect post-war negotiations.

Arthur Katz estimates that a 100MTE attack against the US's seventy-one largest metropolitan areas would immediately destroy 25–35 per cent of American industry.[16] He characterises these percentages as misleadingly low, however, since they are based on a measure – termed 'manufacturing value added' – which 'seriously understates the true scope and magnitude of all economic effects that result from widespread and, for some industries, high levels of destruction'.[17] Should a 100MTE attack, furthermore, be carried out with large numbers of weapons in the KT range, such as those on Soviet multiple warhead SLBMs, rather than only with 1MT weapons, the destruction would be greater because of the greater number of impact points. For example, Katz shows how 631 50KT weapons directed against fifty selected cities can be calculated to have the same destructive effect as 144 1MT warheads even though the total MTE of the 50KT strike is only 86, that is, 60 per cent that of the 1MT strikes.[18] In other words, the effect of a 100MTE attack with low kiloton weapons could well be far worse than the 'understate[d]' 25–35 per cent calculated to be destroyed if 1MT warheads were used. That amount of destructive power should give the USSR confidence that it could deter the US.

As for deterring the Soviet Union, the US should feel confident if they can subject the 103 largest Soviet cities (those with populations of 300 000 or more in the 1970 census) to a 5 psi (pounds per square inch) overpressure over the area of the cities.[19] These cities account for more than 52 per cent of Soviet industrial production,[20] and 5 psi would cause 'severe damage to industrial capacity'.[21] US SLBMs have either 50 or 100KT warheads. 627 of the former and 369 of the latter would be needed to cover the areas of each city with the requisite overpressure.[22] Adding an additional forty-three warheads to deal with the Moscow ABM system (sixty-four interceptors arbitrarily assumed to have a probability of destroying an incoming warhead (PK) of 0.67 gives a requirement for 670 50KT and 412 100KT warheads with 94 and 91MTE respectively. While accuracy problems should limit the requisite distribution of the warheads in each target area, such attacks should nevertheless greatly impair the bulk of the industries in those cities and thus destroy a very large portion of the entire nation's industrial capacity.

It seems reasonable to accept, then, that a capability to deliver 90–100MTE against opposing industrial targets should give each superpower the confidence that it can deter the other. With a total of 200MTE, each should feel additionally confident that it can compensate for uncertainties and problems as well as maintain an adequate strategic reserve in conjunction with intermediate nuclear force (INF) systems. In order to have 200MTE with SLBMs in 1985, the United States would have needed an average of eight submarines within a range which ran from a low of seven and a high of nine units.[23] The Soviet Union would have needed an average of twelve submarines within a range of eight to eighteen submarines.[24]

Some may regard the foregoing totals as too low; hence it is worth pointing out that whatever numbers one accepts for 1985 should actually become smaller in the future as each superpower modernises its SSBN fleet with boats which carry more and, for the US at least, larger warheads. These more modern boats, furthermore, would probably also be the most survivable. Two other factors work against setting higher totals. One is that both superpowers certainly realise the awesome implications of using SSBNs simply to avoid losing more in a conventional war. The consequences will obviously include immediate escalation to the nuclear level and the probable triggering of what may become a mutually suicidal exchange. It merely hastens the onset of that process to set a high minimum number of SSBNs which must survive conventional attrition. A second factor is that, prior to the use of the SSBNs, both superpowers would still have available their full complements of land-based intercontinental nuclear forces (ICBM) and, it might be presumed, most of their strategic bombers. This means that, on the one hand, each can afford to lose some (perhaps many) SSBNs and, on the other, that its adversary still has ample warheads with which to respond.

Finally, it must be emphasised that the significance of the numbers offered here as hedges against both surprise strike and conventional war attrition lies not in their specificity, for, as will be seen, judgements about each superpower's anti-SSBN potential will be highly qualitative. Nevertheless, without a general sense of how many SSBNs must survive to ensure stability, it would be impossible to make reasoned judgements about the stability consequences of ASW developments.

CONTENTS OF THIS STUDY

This study has four parts. The first focuses on generic features of ASW independent of specific American or Soviet activities. It concentrates on the complexities of the ASW process and on the natural phenomena, suggested means and physical laws which provide scope for, and limit, what can be done. The conclusions from that section will be important for estimating the stability consequences of US and Soviet efforts in ASW. Based on information readily available in the public literature, Parts II and III describe the broad trends and main features of superpower SSBN and ASW developments in order to assess the destabilising potential of the latter. Part II concentrates on America's potential and Part III on that of the USSR. Overall conclusions and the prospects for ASW arms control are reserved for Part IV, and they provide the backdrop for assessing ASW arms-control prospects and for offering some general thoughts on the survivability of British and French SSBNs, sparse though information in the open literature concerning them undoubtedly is.

NOTES

1. In 1970, see pp. 12–17; 1975 edn, p. 24; 1977 edn, p. 118; and 1980–1 edn, pp. 31–36. Citations are from the 1980–1 edn, p. 36. See also P. Nailor and J. Alford, *The Future of Britain's Deterrent Force*, Adelphi Paper no. 156; (London: IISS, 1980) p. 23.
2. See SIPRI, *Yearbook of World Armaments and Disarmament 1969/70* (New York: Humanities Press, 1970) Chap. 3; *Yearbook . . . 1974* (Cambridge: MIT Press, 1974) Chap. 10; *Yearbook . . . 1979* (New York: Crane, Russak, 1979) Chap. 8; and K. Tsipis and R. Forsberg, *Tactical and Strategic Anti-submarine Warfare*: *A SIPRI Monograph* (Cambridge: MIT Press, 1974).
3. Wilkes, in SIPRI, *Yearbook*, 1979. (cf. note 2), p. 427. See also Statement of Dr G. H. Heilmeier, Director, US Defense Advanced Research Projects Agency, in US Senate Appropriations Committee, *Department of Defense Appropriations FY 1978*, 95th Congress, 1st Session (1977) Pt 5, pp. 44–6; B. Blair, 'Arms Control Implications of Anti-submarine Warfare (ASW) Programs' in Congressional Research Service *Evaluation of FY 79 Arms Control Impact Statements: Report Prepared for the Subcommittee on International Security and Scientific Affairs of the House Committee on International Relations*, 95th Congress, 2nd Session (1978) pp. 103–9; H. B. Silverstein, 'Caesar, SOSUS, and Submarines: Economic and Institutional Implications of ASW Technologies' in the Marine Technology Society and the Institute of Electrical and Electronics Engineers, *Oceans '78* (Washington: The Marine Technology Society, 1978) pp. 406–10; H. Rowen, 'New Weapons Technologies and East–West Security in the 1980s' in *New Conventional Weapons and East–West Security: Part II –*

Papers from the IISS Nineteenth Annual Conference, Adelphi Paper no. 145 (London: IISS, 1978) p. 2; J. Wit, 'Advances in Anti-submarine Warfare', *Scientific American* (February 1981) pp. 31–41; I. Mather, 'The Most Secret Service', *The Observer Magazine* (22 May 1983) pp. 33–41; L. Gelb, 'Nuclear Bargaining', *The New York Times Magazine* (27 June 1982) p. 17; R. Aldridge, *The Counterforce Syndrome: A Guide to US Nuclear Weapons and Strategic Doctrine* (Washington: Institute for Policy Studies, 1978) pp. 45–61; M. O. Hatfield, 'The Age of Anxiety: Emerging Nuclear Tensions in the 1980s', *AEI Foreign Policy and Defense Review*, no. 6 (1980) pp. 14–15.

4. MccGwire, 'Technological and Operational Trends in the Field of Strategic ASW and Countermeasures' (paper prepared for SIPRI: December 1979) pp. 54–6. See also R. Speed, *Strategic Deterrence in the 1980s* (Stanford: Hoover Institution Press, 1979) pp. 56–63; K. J. Moore, 'Anti-submarine Warfare' in M. MccGwire (ed.) *Soviet Naval Influence: Domestic and Foreign Dimensions* (New York: Praeger, 1977) chap. 8; H. Bradsher, 'Vulnerability Growing for US Sub-Based Missiles?' *Washington Star* (12 December 1977) p. 1; B. F. Raynes, 'USSR *vs.* USA: The Coming Window of a First Strike', *Government Executive* (October 1980) pp. 37–41; B. Knickerbocker, '"Star Wars" and Ocean Wars Tactics: Good Defense or Not?', *Christian Science Monitor* (1 August 1983) p. 3; R. Toth, 'US Reliance on Nuclear Subs Being Debated', *Los Angeles Times* (22 May 1983) p. 1; S. Gibert and L. B. Thompson, 'Our Underwater Fleet is Vulnerable', *Wall Street Journal* (19 September 1983) p. 32; J. Garn, 'Soviet Superiority: A Question for National Debate', *International Security Review* (Spring 1979) p. 19; W. Van Cleave, 'Strategy and the Navy's 1983–87 Program: Skepticism's Warranted', *Armed Forces Journal International* (April 1982) pp. 50–1; J. Fialka, 'MX Push Based on Feeling Subs Vulnerable', *Washington Star* (19 April 1980) p. 1; 'ASW: Is the US Lead Slipping as Russia Begins to Challenge the Last Frontier of US Naval Superiority?', *Armed Forces Journal International* (April 1980) pp. 46–7; N. Polmar, 'Soviet ASW: Highly Capable or Irrelevant?', *International Defense Review*, no. 5 (1979) pp. 721–8; T. C. Reed, 'News Briefing by Mr T. C. Reed, Director, Telecommunications and Command and Control Systems at the Pentagon, March 4, 1975' (copy of transcript) pp. 2, 5, 8 and 9.

5. Testimony of William Perry in US Senate Armed Services

Committee, *Department of Defense Authorization for Appropriations for FY 1981*, 96th Congress, 2nd Session (1980) Pt 6, pp. 3473–4; '"Can't Miss Weapons" – Revolution in Warfare: Interview with W. J. Perry, Under-secretary of Defense', *US News and World Report* (8 September 1980) p. 61. See also J. C. Barton, III, 'Quietly Conventional', *Defense and Foreign Affairs* (November 1980) pp. 19–20; R. J. Smith, 'An Alternative to the MX,' *Science* (21 May 1982) p. 828; E. Ulsamer, 'In Focus', *Air Force Magazine* (June 1980) p. 17; J. Wit, 'Are Our Boomers Vulnerable', *US Naval Institute Proceedings* (November 1981) pp. 62 and 69; T. Burns, *The Secret War for the Ocean Depths* (New York: Rawson Associates Publishers, 1978) pp. 33 and 42; F. Barnaby, 'Death Beneath the Waves', *New Scientist* (27 September 1979) pp. 958–60. Testimony of Admiral S. Turner in US House Budget Committee, *Budget Issues for FY 1983*, 97th Congress, 2nd Session (1982) vol. 2 p. 97; J. Tierney, 'The Invisible Force', *Science* (November 1983) p. 76; and W. H. Bagley, *Sea Power and Western Security: The Next Decade*, Adelphi Paper no. 139 (London: IISS, 1977) p. 34; and R. Wohl, 'Ocean Transparency: Impossible or Inevitable', *Defense Science 2002+* (February 1984) pp. 20–8.
6. See, in particular, the Wit and Ulsamer references in note 5.
7. A. Quanbeck and B. M. Blechman, *Strategic Forces: Issues for the Mid-Seventies* (Washington: Brookings, 1971) p. 80.
8. As quoted in 'A Submarine That Can Destroy Russia', *US News and World Report* (12 February 1979) p. 30.
9. For data on US submarines, see Chapter 7.
10. For data on Soviet submarines, see Chapter 4.
11. A. M. Katz, *Life after Nuclear War* (Cambridge: Ballinger, 1981) p. 109.
12. Percentage calculated by author from information in IISS, *The Military Balance 1983–1984* (London: IISS, 1983) pp. 14 and 119.
13. Katz, *Life after Nuclear War*, pp. 397–408.
14. Ibid, pp. 379–410, where data on expected fatalities and casualties are presented for 199 cities.
15. McG. Bundy, 'To Cap the Volcano', *Foreign Affairs* (October 1969) pp. 9–10.
16. Katz, *Life after Nuclear War*, p. 116. Katz notes (p. 115) that his estimates are consistent with those of a separate study done for the US Arms Control and Disarmament Agency (ACDA) in 1974.
17. Ibid, p. 117. See also p. 99. On p. 79, footnote 13, Katz

defines manufacturing value added as 'the dollar difference between the value of a raw material or semi-finished product and the final manufactured product'.
18. Ibid. p. 316, Table 10.2. Katz's example is that of an attack on Soviet cities.
19. As found in G. Kemp, *Nuclear Forces for Medium Powers – Parts II and III: Strategic Requirements and Options*, Adelphi Paper no. 167 (London: IISS, 1974) Appendix A.
20. See H. Brown, *Department of Defense Annual Report FY 1981* (Washington: GPO, 1980) p. 79.
21. Katz, *Life after Nuclear War*, p. 99.
22. Calculated by the author from data contained in Kemp, *Nuclear Forces*, Appendix A.
23. The rationale is relatively simple. For each of the basic categories of US SSBNs, if one multiplies the number of missiles per boat by the number of warheads per missile and by the MTE for each warhead, one can arrive at a total MTE carried by each boat. For 16-tube Poseidon submarines with an assumed ten warheads per missile, the MTE total was 22.4; for 16-tube boats converted to carry Trident with an assumed 8 warheads per missile, the MTE total was 28.16. For 24-tube Trident boats, it was 42.24. After accounting for the number of boats per category, the estimated average MTE per submarine for the entire force is 28.27. This leads to a requirement for 7.07 (or 8) 'average' boats to have at least 200 MTE.

The low end of the range was derived by assuming that the two 24-tube Trident missile boats would survive and by adding to them the number of 16-tube Trident missile submarines which would also have to survive in order to meet the 200 MTE total. The number for the two categories was 6.1 (or 7) boats. The high end of the range was derived by dividing the smallest MTE for the three basic categories into 200 for a total of 8.92 (or 9) submarines. See Chapter 7.
24. The rationale for the Soviet numbers is more complex than that for the US because of the wide variety of combinations potentially available. As will be seen in Chapter 4, the USSR has 62 first-line boats spread over six variants: Yankee 1 and 2, Delta 1, 2, and 3, and Typhoon. There are in turn five types of missiles on these boats with some types having different configurations or 'mods'. While the general missile type carried on board a particular variant is known, there is no information as to which mod of the missile is on board, whether boats carry a mixed load of modified missiles or whether there is a standard loading.

TABLE I.1 *Estimated MTEs per submarine variant and missile mod*

Variant	Mod	MTE	Averaged MTE
Yankee 1	SS-N-6 mod 1 or 2	16.00 MTE	16.64
Yankee 1	SS-N-6 mod 3	17.28 MTE	
Yankee 2	SS-N-17	12.00 MTE	12.00
Delta 1	SS-N-8 mod 1	12.00 MTE	11.16
Delta 1	SS-N-8 mod 2	10.32 MTE	
Delta 2	SS-N-8 mod 1	16.00 MTE	14.88
Delta 2	SS-N-8 mod 2	13.76 MTE	
Delta 3	SS-N-18 mod 1	17.28 MTE	21.60
Delta 3	SS-N-18 mod 2	9.44 MTE	
Delta 3	SS-N-18 mod 3	38.08 MTE	
Typhoon	SS-NX-20	61.20 MTE	61.20

Information on warhead numbers and possible yields drawn from IISS, *The Military Balance 1983–84*, p. 119 and US Department of Defense, *Soviet Military Power*, 2nd edn (Washington: GPO, 1983) pp. 22–3. For the SS-N-6 mod 3 it was assumed the missile carried three warheads, and for the SS-NX-20, nine warheads.

Table I.1 lists the estimated MTEs for each of the variants of submarines if one assumes that the submarines do not carry mixed loads but rather only one missile mod per SSBN. Thus, for example, there are three estimated MTEs for the Delta III. In order to have only one estimated MTE per variant, the MTEs for variants with multiple MTEs were averaged. For example, potential Delta III MTEs were 17.28, 9.44, and 38.08, and the simple average is 21.60 for Delta IIIs as a group. After accounting for the number in each variant, the fleet's average MTE per submarine was found to be 16.69, which means in turn that 11.90 (or 12) 'average' submarines would be needed to meet the 200-MTE standard. The low end of the range was derived by assuming the survival of the one Typhoon in the fleet as of 1983 and 6.40 (or 7) Delta IIIs. The high end assumes the survival of Delta Is only, with 17.9 (or 18) accounting for 200MTE.

Part I
Generic Considerations

1 ASW Process and Operations

Anti-submarine warfare (ASW) is a multi-step process with its own terminology. After *searching* for and *detecting* or *acquiring* a possible submarine, ASW forces strive to *hold* the contact and *classify* it as a false alarm or a true submarine, determining its specific type if possible. They would *prosecute* a valid contact by *localising* (that is, pinpointing) its position to an area small enough for staging an *attack*.

These activities occur within the context of overlapping and analytically distinguishable operations, only five of which need be specifically identified. *Area search* is the simultaneous or rapid sensing of tens of thousands to millions of square miles. Area-search sensors generally serve to 'cue' or 'vector' the means of destruction (such as æroplanes) to where they can find, localise and destroy a target. Should an area-search sensor be able to localise the target on its own, however, then an attack could immediately follow with rapidly delivered weapons such as land-based missiles.

After finding a target, area-search systems can also be used to track it. For the purposes of this study, *tracking* will mean knowing a target's general position well enough to enable follow-up action to be taken to localise it. It does not mean, however, that the target must be held continuously; rather, contact can be intermittent as long as the target can be reacquired in a predictable period or in some planned-for fashion.

If no area-search system is available, tracking could be done by units mounting trail on SSBNs. Generally viewed as a task for anti-submarine submarines (usually SSN), *trailing* can be overt or covert, with the trailer falling in behind its quarry as it leaves port, passes a choke point, or moves through a predictable area.

These locations are also appropriate sites for *barrier* or blockade operations. An area-search system might provide initial detection information to the blockading forces, or they might engage in their own individual search operations within assigned sectors. Mines are very cost-effective barrier instruments, but once sown they may constrain the movement of friendly units.

A final operational category is *barrage*, the saturation of an SSBN deployment region with nuclear explosions. These would generate hydrodynamic over-pressures which would rupture the hull of any submarine close enough to the point of detonation. The weapons would have to be of the 'plunging' type, that is, specially fused to explode under water, since 'normal' surface or air bursts would result in most of the released energy dissipating into the atmosphere.[1]

The possibility of barrage is considered particularly destabilising when linked to an area-search operation which could simultaneously detect, track, and localise all deployed SSBNs.[2] Trailing every missile submarine is viewed as equally destabilising since it too offers the possibility of wiping out an enemy's sea-based deterrent at a stroke.[3] Hence it is appropriate to consider here some factors conditioning barrage and trailing while other factors, especially as they relate more directly to area search, tracking, and barrier operations, are best left for future chapters.

BARRAGE

A complex amalgam of factors affect the success of barrage beyond a need for specially-fused nuclear warheads. One is the submarine's depth at the time of impact, shallow submarines (paradoxically) being more survivable. Other factors are obviously the number and yield of available nuclear warheads, the number of real and suspected SSBNs to be barraged, and the extent to which the latter are localised. Harold Brown has argued, for example, that a 1MT weapon would destroy all submarines within a five-mile radius and that 10 000 such warheads would destroy twenty-five submarines if each were localised within a circle of 100-mile radius.[4] A similar analysis by William Perry has twenty submarines destroyed by 8000 warheads if each submarine is localised to 50 NM (nautical miles) and each warhead has a lethal radius of about 3.5 NM.[5]

As will be seen, neither superpower has the numbers of warheads available to conduct attacks such as those illustrated, and most of the nuclear warheads they do possess have less than 1MT yields used in Brown's and probably also in Perry's calculations.[6] Very important for reducing required warhead numbers or yields would be a lessening of the radius of location uncertainty around each target. This is naturally because the area to be saturated increases in proportion to the square of the radius. Perry shows, for instance, that a radius half that assumed in the above case (that is, down to 25 from 50 NM) allows a 75 per cent drop (to 2000) in the number of warheads needed.

In the final analysis, however, two requirements still remain. One is detecting, continuously tracking, and simultaneously localising all deployed enemy missile submarines. The other is filtering out the false alarms (not the least of which will be all submarines other than SSBNs) which would push up the number of aim points and, therefore, the number of nuclear warheads needed for an all-out attack. For example, if (as was done by the US Congress's Office of Technology Assessment (OTA)) one accepts an SSBN deployment area of 2 to 3 million sq. NM and only one false alarm per 100 000 square miles, this would still result in twenty to thirty false alarms.[7] Such a small number would, by itself, mean a doubling (or more) of the number of warheads that Brown and Perry estimated were needed to destroy their postulated twenty to twenty-five SSBNs – that is, to about 20 000 warheads for Brown's instance and 8000 to 16 000 warheads for Perry's instances cited above. Forthcoming chapters will address the prospects of being able simultaneously to localise all SSBN's while filtering out false alarms. Suffice it to say here that this is very difficult to do.

TRAILING

Compared with barrage, trailing may seem a less demanding task, for it posits an ASW unit maintaining its own contact with the target as opposed to placing reliance on an 'outside' area-search system which may or may not be able to find, localise and single out all opposing SSBNs. In addition, should war occur, a trailer could presumably dispose of his quarry with a few tactical weapons instead of drawing down his nation's strategic warhead inventory. Nevertheless, trailing has its difficulties and these are substantial. It is, as one US official put it, more an art than a science, and requires not only acquiring the target but also holding it, often for weeks.[8] The predominant view in published sources is that in the case of submarine trailing, at least two or three anti-submarine submarines (SSN) are needed per SSBN – though not necessarily simultaneously – if there is to be any hope of maintaining long-term contact.[9] Beyond the submarines needed to trail contacts, additional units would be necessary to cover all possible routes to the open sea from enemy bases in order to catch those SSBNs which might leave at random times and with little or no warning or in unexpected directions.

Once a target is acquired, the trailing can be covert or overt, with the former being the more difficult. A submarine sensitive to the possibility of being covertly trailed could run back down its track or could tow detection devices in order to search for trailers. It can also pass through areas where friendly 'gatekeeper' or 'delousing' ASW forces could find the trailers, confuse or decoy them, jam their sensors, or otherwise prevent them from continuing the trail. Even without gatekeepers, SSBNs could themselves release large numbers of quite inexpensive devices which can generate SSBN signals and so draw off trailers.[10] The SSBN could also gradually pay out behind itself a decoy which makes it seem to the trailer that the SSBN is moving more slowly than it really is. The trailer would then be forced to slow down, increasing the range to the target, and would risk losing it altogether should the tow be dropped or the device shut off. Trailers would also have to contend with naturally-produced conditions. As will be shown in the next two chapters, the environmental factors which can both mask and mimic the presence of an SSBN are numerous.

A major problem for the covert trailer is that it is severely restricted as to how close it can approach or manœuvre about the target as well as how vigorously it can respond to target manœuvres, countermeasures, or environmental conditions without giving itself away to its quarry. If two or more trailers are working together, the requirement for covertness further restricts their communicating directly both in order to avoid mutual interference while keeping contact with the quarry and to avoid being overheard.

Overt trailing should be less difficult. The most simple type (and the one most likely to be used) would involve the trailer 'illuminating' the target with bursts of acoustic energy from a sonar, much as a radar illuminates an æroplane with microwave energy. If the trailer remains close to the target and has a speed and depth advantage, the quarry could find it difficult to elude the hunter. Yet the very overtness of the trail also simplifies the application of countermeasures. One of these is to have the submarine that knows it is being trailed generate a 'dense underwater cloud of bubbles' such that the sonar 'could mistake the cloud for a submarine or could not observe the submarine manœuvring behind the screen to escape'.[11] A second measure is analogous to the Quail device carried by American B-52 bombers during the 1960s to counter radars. It was a self-powered decoy which, after release by the aircraft, would 'retransmit the radar signal . . . in a way that would make the plane and the decoy indistinguishable to the radar'. Presumably the same kind of device could be devised to deceive sonars.[12] A third measure, one also practised against radars, would be simply to jam the trailing sonar. This might be done either by the SSBN or by the forces acting in support of it, and the latter could do so in the context of acting as 'gatekeepers' or 'delousers'. Alternatively several friendly submarines might join together to confuse and, if necessary, to harass the trailers. Yet another measure is obviously to have friendly submarines trail the trailers and be ready to take instant action against them should it be deemed necessary, although communicating the orders to attack before the enemy can sink the SSBN may prove difficult.

Possibly the most important measure, however, may be to prevent an overt or covert trailer from acquiring the target in the first place, especially as it moves from port to the open sea. Potential trailers waiting for SSBNs to leave port could be kept in turmoil by deliberately-generated false alarms, some of which could be produced by '[s]imple, inexpensive, and recoverable devices using either battery or fuel-cell technology to simulate submarines egressing from port'.[13] Deploying SSBNs could leave in pairs and later separate (one possibly returning to port after a few days) so as to divide trailing forces. The SSBNs could also leave in company with friendly decoying submarines or with escorting forces which jam enemy sensors, 'sanitise' routes of advance, or otherwise block the trailer's efforts to latch on to its quarry. An SSBN might even pass through a mined area within its own territorial waters. It would do so through channels which are changed periodically (especially if the mines can be remotely controlled, that is, armed/disarmed) and known only to itself. The mines might also be programmed with an 'identification friend or foe' (IFF) system allowing free passage to the SSBN but not to trailers.

In short, there are numerous sets of factors which are likely to affect the success of trailing. These include the number of units available for trailing, naturally-produced environmental conditions, countermeasures by SSBNs and allied forces, and the requirements imposed by the overt or covert nature of the attempt. Of these sets of factors, that most under the trailer's own control is the number of units; for instance, a nation determined on trailing could ensure that it always has two to three trailers per opposing SSBN. As for the last three sets, the trailer does not so much control them as continually readjust to deal with the constraints they impose on him. This section has reviewed the constraints imposed by the last two sets only, but it does suggest that trailing can be made extremely difficult. In other words, a vigilant and determined effort by SSBN and support units should ensure that most of the submarines are free of this threat most of the time.

It is now appropriate to turn to consideration of environmental and other factors affecting not only barrage and trailing but also area search, tracking, and blockade.

NOTES

1. See Testimony of Vice Admiral R. Y. Kaufmann in US Senate, Armed Services Committee, *Department of Defense Authorization for Appropriations FY 1980*, 96th Congress, 1st Session (1979) Pt 6, p. 3320.
2. See, *inter alia*, MccGwire, 'Technological and Operational Trends', p. 56; Tsipis and Forsberg, *Tactical and Strategic ASW*, in Introduction, note 2, pp. 41–6; and Testimony of Norman Polmar in US Senate Armed Services Committee, *Fiscal Year 1974 Authorization for Military Procurement, Research and Development, Construction Authorization for the ABM, and Active Duty and Selected Reserve Strengths*, 93rd Congress, 1st Session (1973) Pt 8, p. 6054.
3. See, *inter alia*, Tsipis and Forsberg, *Tactical and Strategic ASW*, in Introduction, note 2, pp. 41–6; testimony of Norman Polmar note 2 above, p. 6054; G. R. Lindsey, 'The Future of Anti-Submarine Warfare and Its Impact on Naval Activities in the North Atlantic and Arctic Regions' in C. Bertram and J. Holst (eds) *New Strategic Factors in the North Atlantic* (Guildford: IPC Science and Technology Press, 1977) p. 150.
4. 'ICBMs *vs*. Subs', *Aerospace Daily* (6 December 1982) p. 178; L. Gay, 'Brown Cites N-Sub Peril by 1990s', *Pittsburgh Press* (8 December 1982) p. 11; H. Brown, *Thinking About National Security: Defense and Foreign Policy in a Dangerous World* (Boulder, Colorado: Westview, 1983) pp. 63–4.
5. Perry, *Testimony* pp. 3473–3475 (see Introduction, note 5).
6. See Ulsamer, 'In Focus . . . ', p. 17 (see Introduction, note 5).
7. US Congress, Office of Technology Assessment (OTA), *M-X Missile Basing* (Washington: GPO, 1981) p. 178. As will be seen, some SSBNs can patrol tens of millions of square miles and still be within target range.
8. Testimony of Assistant Secretary of Defense G. P. Dineen, in

US Senate Armed Services Committee, *Department of Defense Authorization for Appropriations FY 1980*, 96th Congress, 2nd Session (1979) Pt 6, p. 3355.
9. See, for example, R. L. Garwin, 'Will Strategic Submarines be Vulnerable?' *International Security* (Fall, 1983) p. 56; Assembly of the Western European Union, 'Anti-Submarine Warfare: Report Submitted on Behalf of the Committee on Defense Questions and Armaments by Mr Roper, Rapporteur', Document 725, (29 November 1976) pp. 9–10; Tsipis and Forsberg, *Tactical and Strategic ASW*, pp. 41–3; Nailor and Alford, *Future of Britain's Deterrent Force*, pp. 23–4.
10. OTA, *M-X Missile Basing*, p. 196. Much of the information in this paragraph is drawn from this source, p. 193–6.
11. Ibid, p. 196.
12. Ibid.
13. Ibid, p. 194. See also US Congressional Budget Office, *The US Sea-Based Strategic Force: Costs of the Trident Submarine and Missile Programs and Alternatives* (Washington: February 1980) p. 48.

2 Submarine Observables and Indicators

Submarine *observables* consist of the submarine itself and detectable changes in the environment caused by its presence or activities. From an area-search perspective, the environmental changes may be easier to deal with since a submarine by itself is a relatively small object, hard to detect against its background. In contrast, some environmental changes cover a much wider area or volume than the submarine, either because they propagate outward from the boat or because they leave a detectable effect behind for seconds or even many hours after being produced.

An *indicator* or *signal* is any evidence of a submarine's location which enters a detection system or sensor. With passive detection systems, the observables themselves constitute the indicators since the sensor is intended to detect them directly. In other words, the sensor, once positioned, passively awaits the signal. With active detection systems, bursts of energy are transmitted which spread out and bounce against the object or some trace of its presence. The echo or return constitutes the indicator.

A long-accepted convention distinguishes acoustic from non-acoustic indicators, and this division is applied below. Acoustic signals are dealt with first, followed by enquiry into the many non-acoustic phenomena suggested in the literature as potential indicators.[1] For observables presumed to be detectable through passive means, a description will be followed by enquiry into how far the signal might spread, how long it might persist, and what effect the environment and submarine countermeasures can have on its being detected. For indicators which result from the use of active sensors, the questions of spreading, environmental effects, and countermeasures remain relevant, but that of persistence does not since it is the ASW hunter who himself generates and transmits the bursts of energy which indicate the presence of a submarine.

ACOUSTIC INDICATORS

Acoustic indicators have figured so prominently in ASW research and operations since the Second World War that they merit initial and separate attention. The investment in acoustic systems is built on the fact that water is a relatively good transmitter of sound energy. As far back as the fifteenth century Leonardo da Vinci was able to write 'If you cause your ship to stop and place the head of a long tube in the water and the other extremity to your ear, you will hear ships at great distance from you'.[2] Under admittedly highly favourable circumstances, acoustic energy can propagate up to 10 or 15 000Km in the water and, at those distances, the signal may be two to three hours old.[3] By contrast, water is also generally an extremely poor transmitter of those other energy forms (especially in the electromagnetic spectrum, such as light and radio waves) relied upon for detecting and tracking targets in the atmosphere.

Consistent with what was said earlier, one can distinguish between reflected and radiated acoustic signals. Reflected signals are acoustic energy bounced against a submarine's hull or some other observable such as the submarine's wake. Sonars work on this principle and consist of a sound transmitter (or *transducer*) and a receiver (or *hydrophone*). The transmitter and receiver can be co-located, as on the same ship, or placed some distance apart, as on separate ships. Though capable of being used actively, sonars can also be employed in a strictly passive mode in order to detect radiated submarine noise. This noise can include deliberate acoustic equipment emissions as well as any incidental sounds produced in the course of the submarine's operations. A deliberate emission would occur should the submarine activate its own sonar. This is the type of activity that SSBNs would generally avoid except in guarded ways or in unusual circumstances since enemy ASW forces might also pick up the sonar transmission on their own hydrophones. Hence, only those signals incidental to a submarine's operations generally provide the bases for passive detection.

The sources of incidental radiated signals are hydrodynamic disturbances outside the submarine, and machinery operations inside. As a submerged submarine moves forward and overcomes the resistance of surrounding water pressing against the hull, turbulence arises in the layer of water closest to the hull as well as in the boat's wake. In addition vortices are formed and thrown off as water flows against discontinuities, protuberances, and rough spots along the submarine's surface. These hydrodynamic disturbances generate what are termed 'flow' and, in some cases, 'singing' noises, and they are often accompanied by another hydrodynamic effect termed 'cavitation'. It results when the rapid turning of the submarine's propellor at shallow depths forms cavities or voids along the face of each blade. The onrush of surrounding water filling each void causes detectable popping sounds.

The signals from hydrodynamic disturbances tend to be *broadband*, that is, spread over a spectrum of frequencies.[4] They increase in intensity the faster a submarine travels and the more shallow its depth. At high speeds particularly they will tend to dominate the incidental sounds radiating outward from a submarine.

Internal machinery noises are usually monochromatic or *narrowband* and tend to dominate when the submarine is moving slowly and especially when it is moving slowly in deep water.[5] Responsible for these noises are propulsion and auxiliary equipment such as turbines, motors, gears, steam engines, electrical generators, compressors, blowers, pumps, and hydraulic systems. These machines generate acoustic energy which is transmitted to the water through excitation of the submarine's hull.

Different types of submarines will usually produce hydrodynamic and internal sounds peculiar to their own type. In other words, they can have an acoustic 'signature' which can be used to identify the class or group to which the submarine belongs.[6]

In order to appreciate fully what is involved in relying upon acoustic indicators for detection, tracking, or localisation, it is necessary to understand some features of acoustic signal propagation in sea-water. Some are associated with the signal itself and others with the characteristics of the ocean medium through which the signal travels.

Two closely related features are the initial intensity and the spreading of a signal. Signals of the same frequency can be detected at distances which vary with the intensity of each signal's source. A signal will spread or diverge as it propagates from the source and the spreading loss will vary with environmental conditions. The variation is highly complex and generally could range from $1/r$ to $1/r^2$ where r is the distance from the source when none of the signal is absorbed. At $1/r$, a tenfold increase in distance equates to a tenfold decrease in intensity. At $1/r^2$ it equates to a hundredfold decrease.

The loss of intensity is especially significant for active sonars since the signal must travel the distance from the transmitter to the submarine, and it must then travel the distance back. The result is that the intensity of the reflected sound will vary inversely roughly between the second and fourth power of the range as the sound makes the two-way trip. At worst a signal which had decreased by a factor of 100 in intensity on the outward leg would have decreased by a factor of ten thousand by the time it returned to the sonar source.[7]

Spreading is only one reason for intensity or propagation loss. Another is absorption because sea-water molecules convert into heat the acoustic energy which strikes against them. At any given frequency, a constant fraction of each signal's energy is absorbed per unit distance travelled, and the percentage absorbed over any given distance varies directly with a signal's frequency. Lower-frequency sounds propagate farther than higher-frequency sounds. For example, it is estimated that, for two signals of the same initial intensity transmitted in the western Mediterranean in winter, that of 100 hertz (or cycles per second) could propagate nearly 150 miles while a 2000 hertz signal could propagate only one-third that distance – with both undergoing the same loss of intensity.[8]

The direction and intensity of sound is also affected by factors which vary markedly depending on geographic location and, for some places, on time of year and time of day as well. These include: the condition of the ocean bottom – muddy and absorptive or hard and reflective; the concentration of sedimentary inorganic particles, tiny sea organisms, detritus, schools of fish, gas bubbles, and any other such objects or phenomena which can scatter or absorb sound; and last but no means least, horizontal or vertical boundaries in the water column which can duct, refract, block or attenuate sound.

The most significant of the horizontal boundaries, other than the sea surface and bottom, are the separations between water-layers differing sharply in temperature profile. A highly simplified picture of much of the oceans would show three layers whose depths and extent vary with latitude, season, and time of day. These are: a surface isothermal layer, ranging from a few tens to a few hundred metres, where temperature is relatively constant because of the mixing of water by wind and wave action; a middle or 'main thermocline' layer, up to about 1000m wide, where temperature drops rapidly and is little affected by variations in surface conditions; and a deep isothermal layer where temperature is again nearly constant. The discontinuities represented by the boundaries between each layer, coupled with the effect on sound direction of the pressure and temperature characteristics of each layer, can cause some of the sound to be ducted or channelled between the boundaries. This can mean that the transmission and reception of reflected signals and the hearing of submarine-radiated noise can be excellent within a duct. It also means, however, that submarine detection can be greatly hampered if the target is in one layer while the detection devices are in another.

Some sound, however, travels steeply enough to penetrate from one layer to another. It will undergo related attenuation and refraction (bending), but if it should penetrate into the deep isothermal layer, it may then travel horizontally very great distances with relatively little attenuation except for spreading and absorption. It is particularly within this layer – also termed the deep sound or SOFAR (sound fixing and ranging) channel – that sound propagates for many thousands of kilometres.

Cutting across horizontal boundaries in the water column are vertical boundaries associated with ocean eddies, fronts, the interfaces between two currents, and the presence of underwater mountains and ridges. Such boundaries can stretch for hundreds to thousands of miles, and, as with horizontal boundaries, can affect submarine detection if the boat is on one side and the acoustic sensor on the other. For example, a submarine detected in the Labrador Current but crossing into the Gulfstream has been compared to a person going from an open field and 'disappearing into an adjoining wood'.[9]

No less important for submarine detection and tracking is the interweaving effect on sound velocity of the water's temperature, pressure, and salinity. Decreases in each of these contribute to a decrease in velocity, and sound waves will bend or refract as much as 15° towards those water areas which permit slower speed. While salinity, for the most part, remains relatively uniform in most oceans, temperature and pressure do not. Changes in them can make for highly complex sound propagation paths, especially where temperature decreases with depth (as it normally does), while pressure invariably increases.

The bending of sound waves can give rise to 'shadow zones', that is, areas where sound does not penetrate. This means that a hydrophone might not hear a submarine even though both were quite close and in the same temperature layer. Similarly, active sonar emissions might be bent away from, and thus not reflect against, a target even when the latter is near the sonar and again in the same layer.

In addition to shadow zones, the bending of sound waves can cause the formation of 'convergence zones', and these can be beneficial to the detection of shallow submarines by sensors placed near the surface many kilometres away. Convergence zones result when sound generated by a shallow submarine propagates downward into deep water and then, because of pressure changes, refracts upward until it approaches the surface where it again propagates downward to repeat the process until the sound is dissipated. Every time the sound approaches the surface, there is formed an area, roughly 5km wide according to Tsipis, where the sound converges, that is, becomes compressed or focused.[10] Being more intense there, the sound is thus more easily detectable by a shallow sensor, such as on a surface ship. If convergence zones occur, as they tend to, roughly 50km apart in the mid-latitudes, this means that a sensor could detect the submarine 50, 100, 150km or more away even though it might not be able to sense it (or do so as easily) in the intervals between the convergence zones.

From this it should be clear that the propagation and attenuation of acoustic indicators can vary widely depending on place, season, and time of day. Some sense of the variation is given by Cox when he writes that the capability of a sonar 'can vary . . . from one-half to more than six times any given range simply because the sound transmission capabilities of the ocean vary through a similar spread of values'.[11]

Yet, if a submarine is to be detected, ASW forces must contend with more than the variable sound transmission qualities of sea-water. It is also a fact that the world's oceans are themselves rather noisy. Ocean life, the actions of wind upon the surface, human uses and exploitation of the ocean and seabeds – all contribute to the generation of background or ambient noise which can mask or cover what one is trying to hear. American officials have noted that, for purposes of ASW, the ambient noise problem has worsened because of the greater frequency of ocean drilling and, until recently, a rise in the number of very large tankers and bulk carriers plying the ocean.[12]

Ambient noise is further problematic because it can be a source of false signals which mimic those desired. For the purposes of anti-SSBN warfare, any submarine not an SSBN can constitute a false target. There are nearly 800 non-SSBN submarines on active service worldwide and, of these, slightly over 200 are nuclear-powered.[13] Besnault has estimated that at any given time there would be deployed on the high seas one hundred or so submarines of which three-fourths could be nuclear-powered and no more than two-fifths (including French and British) would be ballistic-missile armed.[14] In times of crisis, he adds, numbers of submarines so deployed could grow greatly, further complicating the SSBN detection problem especially if, as should be expected, the proportion of tactical submarines at sea increases. Apart from other submarines, surface ships and marine life may generate acoustic signals and, in the case of marine life, cause acoustic reflections similar to those of submarines.[15]

In sum, the propagation of sound in sea-water is affected by the characteristics of acoustic indicators themselves, the condition of the bottom and surface, the concentration of living and non-living substances, horizontal and vertical boundaries, and the water's temperature, pressure and salinity at specific times and places. The detection of sound, furthermore, is conditioned by the level of ambient noise, which can mask desired signals, as well as the presence of non-SSBN submarines and marine life which can mimic ballistic missile submarines. Hence, it should not be surprising, as Kosta Tsipis put it, that 'in spite of the enormous efforts devoted to developing submarine-detection equipment of exquisite sophistication and manageable size, [acoustic] ASW operations contain a large amount of uncertainty and are critically affected by topical conditions'.[16] Yet Tsipis also reminds us: 'Despite the dependence of sound on oceanographic variables, temperatures, salinity, bottom characteristics, and marine life, it remains the only form of energy that can penetrate the water-mass of the ocean over any distance'. For that reason, one can expect submarine forces to make themselves aware of countermeasures to acoustic detection.

Countermeasures

Most of what there is to be said about countermeasures flows logically and obviously from the foregoing discussion of acoustic phenomena. In the area of submarine design, streamlining the flow of water along the ship's hull (by doing away with appendages, rough surfaces and the like) and installing large slow-turning propellors can serve to reduce flow noise, singing, and cavitation. Making machinery quieter and shock-mounting it (so that its noise is not transmitted to the hull and thence to the water) will reduce equipment-radiated noise. Even reflected noise can be minimised by coating hulls with sound-absorbing materials and making submarines as small as is reasonably possible to reduce their acoustic cross-section.[17]

Several operational countermeasures have already been mentioned in this and the previous chapter. These include employing decoys, jamming enemy hydrophones or sonars, and the abstinence by SSBNs of active acoustic transmissions detectable by hostile forces. In addition, because new submarine-launched missiles can fly 4000 or more nautical miles, some modern SSBNs now have very wide latitude to seek out areas where enemy acoustic platforms and devices are judged to be few or absent or where sonar conditions are known to be difficult. Should an SSBN commander feel that he must enter a potentially hostile region, doing so at slow speeds – less than 5 knots – would reduce his ship's hydrodynamic radiated noise. A slow submarine, especially if efforts have been made to quieten its machinery, could 'possibly . . . take itself out of the range of . . . passive sonar' or hydrophone.[18] In addition, if the submariner knows the condition of his ocean environment, he can take advantage of it. He could hide in areas of high ambient noise, which can vary as much as 40db from one place to another.[19] (Such a difference was compared to the noise heard on a 'busy Chicago Street' with that of an 'Iowa cornfield'.) A submariner who believed enemy hydrophones or sonars were in the surface isothermal layer might stay in the thermocline. Conversely, he might remain shallow if he believed there were listening devices in a lower layer. He might also hide in an eddy or keep enemy ASW systems on the other side of a front or ridge.

Measures to lessen active sonar returns could include manœuvring the SSBN directly away from or toward the sonar echo so as to reduce sonar cross-section. A submariner might also seek out shallow water where reverberations against the bottom would interfere with the sonar's ability to select returns which had reflected off the submarine's hull. He might go under pack ice to take advantage of the marked irregularities of the lower ice surfaces.

Other countermeasures will be more appropriately addressed later, but it should be said here that the extent to which any measure is implemented is a matter of judgement for submarine designers and operators. Silencing and shock-mounting machinery, for example, can be extremely costly in money and construction time, and these considerations together with decisions as to how one will operate one's own SSBNs can determine just how much quietness will be bought. Similarly questions such as whether to operate shallow or deep may involve judgements not only as to the acoustic detection threat which an enemy may pose, but also the non-acoustic threat. These judgements may centre on the trade-offs to be made about minimising one threat at the expense of another. To get a better sense of the trade-offs which may be made, some understanding of possible non-acoustic indicators is in order.

NON-ACOUSTIC INDICATORS

Potential non-acoustic indicators are many and varied and, as with their acoustic counterparts, they consist of reflected and submarine-generated phenomena. Unlike their acoustic counterparts, however, information concerning them tends to be diffuse, and for some phenomena at least the extent to which they truly constitute indicators in any practical sense remains a matter of speculation.

Reflected indicators

Portions of a submarine on the surface can be observed optically and, with radar, at ranges up to many hundreds of kilometres, much as any surface ship could be. Radar waves, however, do not penetrate into the water column and will not directly detect a submarine if it is entirely submerged.

Light rays do penetrate to an extent, and, according to William Perry, a blue-green laser 'can penetrate water down to submarine depths and reflect the energy back to the surface'.[20] A laser beam might also reflect against the submarine's underwater wake. Estimates of beam penetration vary from less than one hundred up to a few hundred metres for blue-green lasers, but any one general depth estimate is nominal since local water turbidity and weather conditions will determine how far a laser beam will actually penetrate to strike a target below the surface and return to the source.[21] As a result, a submarine which cruised deep enough could avoid detection of its hull altogether and possibly also of any wake it produced. Whatever the laser's depth penetration, furthermore, its swath width would probably be limited since the beam would have to be thin, highly parallel and 'at near-perpendicular incidence to the sea surface' for effective penetration.[22]

In short, non-acoustic reflected indicators have great potential utility for submarine detection when the submarine or a portion of it broaches the surface, but only reflected light has any utility when the target is fully submerged. As will be seen, this does not mean that a sensor such as a radar has no potential role to play in helping to find submerged submarines. It is simply that a radar cannot detect them directly.

Submarine-generated indicators

When it is operating, a submarine generates electro-magnetic, thermal, biological, contaminant, and hydrodynamic displacement effects. A submarine, furthermore, deliberately generates signals when it communicates, activates its radars or launches its missiles. The latter group will be dealt with first.

Deliberately-generated signals

As with surface ships, any submarine which emits radio or radar signals runs the risk of being detected by electronic or signal intelligence collectors. During the Second World War, Admiral Karl Doenitz sought to plan for the optimal utilisation of his deployed submarines by insisting that they radio back to headquarters on a regular basis. The transmissions were instrumental in helping the Allied forces to find and either to destroy or to avoid German U-boats. It is expected that, just as SSBNs under normal circumstances would avoid active acoustic transmissions in the water, so they would also avoid detectable radio or radar transmissions in the atmosphere.

Should a submarine launch its missiles, an over-the-horizon radar could detect them while they were still thousands of kilometres away, and an infra-red sensor on a satellite could detect their heat exhaust.[23] If the submarine fires all its strategic weapons and is not in a position to reload, then the fact that it may have revealed its presence in a particular area may be of no great consequence. Nevertheless, it would still want to leave the area of launch as fast as prudence allowed. Where this consideration has greatest relevance is in the case of a submarine which fires only some of its missiles. Whether and to what extent it is then vulnerable to attack is the subject of some debate.

Electromagnetic (EM) effects

EM effects are an incidental observable, and they result from a submarine's generation of extremely low frequency (ELF) electric fields and magnetic anomalies. One EM effect is a galvanic current running between a submarine's ferrous hull and its brass propellor. The current is produced because the hull and propellor have different electrical potentials and thus act like the terminals of a battery with sea-water being the conductor of electricity between them. The current modulates at a frequency related to the shaft r.p.m. (revolutions per minute) and the number of blades of the propellor.[24] A second EM effect results when water displaced by the submarine moves across the earth's magnetic field and generates an electric field. This 'little understood' phenomenon is termed magnetohydrodynamics (MHD).[25] A third, closely related, effect is a detectable disturbance in the earth's magnetic field caused by the passage of a ferrous metal object such as a submarine.

The propagation of each of the above phenomena is relatively short-ranged. The magnetic disturbances would be very narrowly circumscribed to the submarine's immediate area, but the MHD effect can be expected to remain in the general vicinity of the submarine's track.[26] The effect of the galvanic current would probably propagate the farthest if, as MccGwire suggests, it is detectable to a 'distance of several miles'.[27] He adds, however, that at those ranges, only highly sensitive bottom-mounted instruments could sense it, an impractical alternative if the aim is a wide-area search.

Whatever the exact distances, highly sensitive detectors would be needed for all the phenomena since the intensity of each should fall off quickly from the source. Some analyses, for example, have accepted the inverse cube law in calculations measuring electric and magnetic fields.[28] That is, for every doubling of distance the signal is assumed to fall to one-eighth of its strength.

Except for the magnetohydrodynamic effect, the signals would not persist for any appreciable length of time after generation. MHD signals persist because the moving submarine causes internal waves. The latter, which will be further described later, are vertical oscillations of the water column. They can contribute to the formation of the MHD effect and can possibly persist for quite a long time. Naturally-produced internal waves can certainly last for many hours or days, but there is no information available as to whether submarine-generated waves, which might tend to have shorter oscillatory periods, would last as long. If they do last for hours, then there could well be an effect remaining in the submarine's wake for a considerable distance – possibly tens of kilometres or more depending on the submarine's speed. Podney and Sager show, however, that fluctuating magnetic gradients originating from naturally-produced internal waves are 'minute' and measurable only with extremely sensitive sensors.[29] Presumably the same conclusions would apply to gradients produced by submarine-generated waves, and this suggests that they would not be easily detectable.

Among the systems which could possibly be used to detect EM effects are fixed magnetometers or gradiometers (large electric coils on the ocean floor) and magnetometers towed from a ship or submarine.[30] In addition, magnetic anomaly detectors are regularly carried today on aircraft. The possibility has also been raised of an airborne magnetic gradiometer for detection of low-strength ELF signals such as associated with internal wave backgrounds.[31]

One difficulty in detecting submarine-generated electric and magnetic effects is that they occur in an environment where naturally-produced EM effects can be frequent.[32] Surface and naturally-produced internal waves, winds, currents, solar events (which can cause magnetic 'storms'), the passage of surface ships, whales, schools of fish, pressure changes in general and wrecks on the ocean floor might all cause one or more of the EM effects mentioned above and complicate any submarine search based on them. Problems of magnetic anomaly detection are further complicated if submarines were to be partially demagnetised or to be built of a material (such as titanium) whose magnetic value is low.

Thermal scarring

Thermal anomalies on the surface of the ocean constitute a second type of incidental observable. These can arise from the upwelling of deeper cooler water pushed up to the surface by submarine hydrodynamic displacement effects. Such upwellings, however, would occur within the context of an even greater, and possibly opposing, thermal effect produced by great volumes of warm sea-water left in a nuclear submarine's wake. The effect arises because nuclear-powered submarines take in and then expel large quantities of sea-water used to cool the reactor spaces. Since the discharged water is warmer and consequently less dense than its surroundings, it rises and can potentially cause a thermal scar on the sea surface detectable with either infrared or passive microwave radiometers. One Soviet study has suggested that a thermal scar anomaly on the surface could be of the order of $0.005°C$.[33] If produced, a scar of this kind would remain in the vicinity of the submarine's wake for some time. Its persistence would depend on the sea state and could range from minutes to hours.[34]

A thermal scar may not necessarily appear on the surface. One reason is that the cooling water could become entrapped in the submarine's turbulent wake. It would rise no higher than the wake itself, which normally does not reach the surface, and the turbulence of the wake, furthermore, would serve to dissipate and mix the heated water with ambient water to the point that its thermal distinctiveness would be quickly lost. A second reason is that 'the temperature rise of the water in a [thermal] plume decreases rapidly with the increasing height above the source'.[35] Thus rising warm water could cool to its surrounding temperature prior to reaching the surface. A third reason is that a thermal plume of water rising upward can be trapped at boundaries between temperature and density layers, especially those at the thermocline where the discontinuities are greatest.[36] A fourth possible reason is related to the speed of the submarine: the greater the speed, the less time there is for warmer water to remain concentrated in one place. This effect, however, may be counteracted somewhat since the faster the submarine the more power must be generated by the reactor and the greater the volume of heated water it produces.

Beyond the fact that a thermal scar may not rise to the surface, those who would rely on surface scarring must contend with an additional 'serious problem'. This is the 'enormous number of "false alarms" that . . . result from local temperature differences on the ocean's surface that are generated by a myriad of mechanisms other than a submarine'.[37] Natural currents, for example, can certainly produce turbulence in the water which gives rise to temperature differentials on the surface.

Biological luminescence

A submarine's passage disrupts biological life in the vicinity of its track. For ASW purposes, the biological effect of greatest interest is marine bioluminescence. A moving submarine can mechanically disturb plants and animals and stimulate them to glow or emit visible light. According to a chief of US naval research in the early 1960s, 'This phenomenon has made surface vessels, submarines, and mine fields detectable from the air. In fact, during World War Two a number of ships and torpedo boats were detected and attacked as a result of their bioluminescent wakes'.[38]

The luminescent glow is confined to the immediate vicinity of the submarine and its wake, and the glowing wakes of a ship have sometimes been observed to 'extend a distance equal to several times the ship's length'.[39] The length of time any one organism will emit light ranges from microseconds to a few seconds, but the overall luminescent wake may well persist from seconds to minutes if it can remain glowing to a distance 'several times a ship's length'.[40]

Biological luminescence can be observed with the human eye or with optical instruments such as bathyphotometers and low-light-level image intensifiers (LLLII). Bathyphotometers placed as deep as 1000m have confirmed that bioluminescence does occur at those depths, but any effect produced by a deep-running submarine would probably not be visible at the surface because of the difficulties of light transmission in water.[41] A submarine at shallower depths might well cause a visible surface effect, but its observation would be limited to night-time and, even with LLLII, 'moonlight . . . tends to mask bioluminescence by decreasing the contrast between the luminescent area and the background'.[42]

As an observable, bioluminescence is also subject to mimicking in that it is readily produced by the passage of schools of fish, whales, and by seismic and other disturbances. Indeed, in areas where bioluminescence has been readily observed, its extent has generally been so widespread as to raise questions about being regularly able to distinguish submarine produced effects from naturally occurring background.[43] It seems to be generally agreed that an 'ability to use marine bioluminescence as a detection method . . . depends on knowing the distribution of various luminescent organisms . . . [O]ur knowledge of this area is inadequate'.[44] Marine scientists 'presently understand surprisingly little of the causes, distribution, and importance of background luminescence'.[45]

Contaminants

A nuclear submarine introduces a variety of products into the ocean. These result from the leeching of anti-fouling paint, the leaking of lubricants from propellor shafts, retractable masts or control surfaces, the dumping of various types of wastes, the corrosion and pitting of the submarine's outer surface and propellors, and the formation of radio-isotopes following the escape of neutrons from the nuclear reactor into the sea-water.[46]

Most contaminants could persist from minutes to hours, but the extent to which a contaminant remains concentrated determines its detectability. The spreading which occurs by virtue of the submarine's movement and the action of winds, waves, underwater flows, currents, and the like contribute to mixing and dilution. Most contaminants would probably mix too rapidly and reduce themselves to background levels before they could spread far as a detectable phenomenon. Furthermore contaminants discharged into the submarine's wake would be confined to the wake which in turn usually remains at the general depth stratum of the submarine. Observing these contaminants before they dissipated would necessitate placing a sensor at that depth.

Waste products are probably the contaminants with the greatest concentration when released. That their release is controllable is important because it allows submarine personnel to do so only periodically and at times, in places, and in such ways that their release would pose the least hazard.[47] Because the trace element detectors used to find most contaminants must be brought into the vicinity of the submarine's track by ship or æroplane to be effective, a submarine could release waste products when no ship was about and when weather or intelligence information suggested that aircraft would not be present at the time of release.

Hydrodynamic displacement effects

There are five hydrodynamic displacement effects of interest, and they interact with one another. One, the magnetohydrodynamic phenomenon, has already been mentioned. A second and third are the formation of a hump and a 'Kelvin wake' along a submarine's track. The fourth is wake turbulence. The fifth is the formation of 'internal' waves.

As a submarine moves forward, it pushes water away from itself in all directions. Since water is nearly incompressible, the entire water column above the submarine will rise by some potentially measurable amount. The hump will move with the submarine, and it may generate a surface wave, termed a 'Kelvin wake'. The latter is the same V-shaped type wake produced by surface ships. While the hump advances with the submarine and does not persist behind it, a Kelvin wake could persist many minutes under favourable conditions.

The generation of both phenomena is highly dependent upon the depth and speed of the submarine. On the one hand, a submarine moving fast and shallow could produce a pronounced hump and surface wake.[48] On the other, because the lifting of the wake above the submarine attenuates rapidly because of sideways flow, a submarine moving slowly and at depth would produce such small effects – for example, a hump of a few ångströms – as to be virtually undetectable in the midst of other ocean surface displacements such as those caused by winds, waves, whales, and other natural causes.[49]

Turbulent wakes are a fourth hydrodynamic effect. One obvious source of marine turbulence is the turning of the propellors. Another is the tendency of sea-water to resist being pushed out of the submarine's way. This resistance causes both turbulence in the layer of water immediately adjacent to the hull and an associated shedding of vortices from the edges of rough spots, such as the sail and other appendages to the hull. The wake resulting from all these effects can potentially propagate to 'several kilometres astern of the submarine' and persist for many minutes or even hours.[50]

A number of factors affect the degree of turbulence and its continuity. One is the extent to which the submarine's designers have streamlined its shape so as to facilitate water flow around the submarine. Submarine size, depth, and speed can also be significant: the greater the value of each, the greater the turbulence. Finally, the continuity of a wake is conditioned by the strength and direction of underwater currents and flows which act upon it.

An important factor affecting the passive detection of the wake (as opposed to active detection by means of a laser, already discussed) is that, as noted earlier, it remains confined in the general vicinity of the submarine's depth stratum.[51] Hence, it can be passively observed only if a sensor is inserted at about the same depth as the submarine – a rather impractical measure if the aim is large open-ocean search.

A wake-sensor could be a passive optical or pressure/temperature-sensitive instrument or one which measures variations in sea-water electrical conductivity associated with turbulence. These sensors could be attached to a stationary buoy, affixed to the hull of a submarine, or towed by a surface ship or submarine.[52]

While turbulent wakes are passively detectable only within the water column, they also contribute to the formation of potentially detectable surface effects. Of particular significance is the role of wake turbulence in the generation of internal waves. These are the last of the hydrodynamic displacement effects of interest here, and they are the 'best known examples of internal [ocean] motions showing up in sea surface imagery'.[53] As stated earlier, an internal wave is an internal oscillation of the water column.

There are two main contributants to its formation.[54] One is the upward displacement of water which causes the hump identified earlier. The vertical column of water pushed up by the submarine falls again as the latter passes. As it does so, it drops below its own density level, gets forced upward again by the more dense water beneath it, and repeats the cycle. The second contributant is wake turbulence, for it also causes waters of different densities to mix. Water at the submarine's depth is thrust both upward, where it is heavier than its surrounding, and downward where it is lighter. A conical wake forms whose diameter expands as the submarine moves away. The cone eventually collapses as the displaced water ceases its outbound movement and returns to the density level from whence it sprang. As with the falling hump, the collapsed wake oscillates above and below its density equilibrium point until its energy is expended.

For naturally-produced internal waves, usually observed above the continental shelf, 'vertical displacements on the order of ten meters are typical' as are 'associated . . . horizontal displacements of about one kilometre'.[55] Their periods – that is, time for a complete oscillation – can range from many minutes to many hours, and oscillations can persist not only for hours but even for days.

While it is known that a 'moving submarine leaves behind it a wake of internal waves', there is little information about their propagation or persistence.[56] If they do last for hours, then the wake of waves could easily stretch tens of kilometres, but the amplitude of the waves would probably be significant only in the region limited to the track of the submarine.[57] In addition, 'internal waves have their greatest height at the interface between two [density] layers and their amplitude diminishes rapidly above and below it'.[58]

There are various means for detecting internal waves, some of which necessitate placing numerous point sensors in the water column. The sensors can be current meters or pressure/temperature-sensitive instruments (such as thermistors or bathythermographs) which are stationary, free-floating, hanging from buoys, or towed from waterborne platforms. A superconducting magnetic gradiometer has the advantage of being able to remain above the water. Its possible utility builds on a fact previously noted in the magnetohydrodynamics discussion – that is, internal waves affect magnetic force fields and sea-water electrical conductivity flows. As a result, some scientists have speculated that 'If magnetic measurements of acceptable quality can be made by aircraft, high-sweep-rate mapping of the surface and internal wave spectra of an entire ocean basin could be seriously contemplated'.[59] Before such measurements could be made, however, superconducting magnetic gradiometers would have to be designed to have wide coverage and to handle very serious magnetic signal-to-noise problems. In other words, they must be able to select the desired signals from the totality of the input entering the gradiometer.[60] The possibility of designing such a sensor is addressed in the next chapter.

Among those interested in advancing general oceanographic knowledge about internal waves, widespread interest has centred on the use of air- and especially space-borne microwave systems which detect surface manifestations of internal waves. It is believed that these manifestations result from mechanisms which affect surface reflectivity by modulating the short capillary waves superimposed on the ocean's swell or longer gravity waves.[61] One hypothesised mechanism is that internal waves produce surface currents which sweep together oils and materials in surface water convergence zones. The result is a damping of capillary waves and the forming of slicks or areas of increased surface reflectivity or sun glitter. A second hypothesised mechanism is that internal waves cause surface stress which focuses capillary wave energy in convergence zones. The result is an enhancement of small-scale roughness and an associated decrease in capillary wave reflectivity.

Some knowledgeable observers remain highly sceptical about the potential utility of internal wave phenomena for submarine detection. Those who focus on the area of greatest interest – surface manifestations of internal waves – agree that reliance on such manifestations is not at present feasible and remains 'an open question'.[62] William Perry has stated, for example, that while one could conceptually describe how such manifestations might be observed, turning such a capability into an operational system would be 'exceedingly difficult', and Perry did not anticipate broad ocean-search systems becoming effective in the foreseeable future.[63]

The bases for these judgements relate to the characteristics of internal waves themselves, to our knowledge about them, and to limitations on sensors for observing them. Questions of sensor limitations are best left to later discussions. What can be said now is that internal waves are 'a ubiquitous phenomenon in the ocean' and that 'it remains a major oceanographic problem to determine the dominant sources of internal waves, evaluate their interaction with each other and with motions of other scales and unravel the mechanisms and secondary effects of their dissipation'.[64] No single model has yet been devised which can account for observed internal wave features and effects.[65]

That 'there is no shortage of proposed mechanisms' for generating internal waves helps to account for their ubiquity.[66] These include surface ships, winds, surface waves, atmospheric pressure fluctuations, the movements of currents and tides over an irregular seabed, and the action of currents at the interface between ocean density and temperature layers. In short, it is not surprising that a 'very high false alarm rate' could attend reliance upon internal wave manifestations as submarine observables.[67]

Potentially detectable surface effects, not well understood in themselves, also seem very dependent upon local conditions.[68] Among these are rain, large-scale circulation patterns, shear currents, thermal layer depths and the water's density gradient, all of which interact to accentuate or minimise surface manifestations. Wind conditions are also important, because it is wind which excites capillary waves. Internal waves of large amplitude, for example, produce no detectable effects if there is too little wind. Similarly, too much wind – that is, above speeds which produce whitecaps – will cause slicks formed by the convergence of surface oils and materials to lose their integrity. In contrast, however, whitecaps seem to have little effect on surface stress manifestations – those resulting in increased roughness and lessened reflectivity. Rather they seem conditioned by the direction and velocity of internal and surface waves. For example, it is said that the effects are most pronounced when both wave sets are travelling in the same general direction.[69]

From the foregoing, it would seem that the surface effects of submarine-generated waves would be very dependent on the conditions in the area in which the submarine found itself and on the submarine's depth and mode of operations.[70] In addition, since falling hump and wake collapse are probably the main agents of submarine-produced internal waves, factors identified earlier as affecting the extent of these must presumably also influence internal wave outcomes. For instance, it may be that deep operations by a slow-moving submarine in waters with an appropriate thermal-density profile might mute both the generation of internal waves and their observable surface effects.[71]

POTENTIAL INDICATORS: SUMMARY REMARKS

Table 2.1 summarises features of potential indicators. As can be seen they vary widely as to their propagation and persistence, and in nearly all cases their detection is subject to substantial environmental limitations as well as to countermeasures.

Among signals which might propagate the farthest are those whose utility seems unrealistic or improbable because they require the submarine either to be on the surface or deliberately to emit detectable electromagnetic signals. Only low-frequency acoustic signals, turbulent wake, internal wave and related MHD effects may propagate any significant distance or persist for any significant time. The remaining signals either propagate only short distances or persist only for short periods or both.

Especially with mobile sensors, that an indicator may persist for some time in the submarine's track may be more important than how far it propagates, but it should be emphasised that the fact that a signal may persist for many hours or even days is not wholly useful unless a detector can expeditiously follow the signal down to its source. Otherwise an indicator of long persistence could be too old to be of much use since the submarine could have moved a great distance away from where it was when it first generated the detectable signal. This situation can be especially problematic if the submarine moves from where an indicator is detectable to where it is not. In addition, it could be difficult to know in which direction a detector should go to find the source. Unless two sensor platforms are employed, the

TABLE 2.1 *Potential indicators*

Indicator	Possible spatial or temporal extent	Remarks
Acoustics	Low frequency signals can propagate thousands of kilometres and, at those distances, be two to three hours old	Strongly subject to masking, mimicking, countermeasures and complexities of underwater sound propagation
Optical hull reflectivity	Lasers could possibly detect surfaced submarine hundreds of kilometres away, and blue-green laser could, under proper conditions, penetrate a few hundred metres of water to detect submerged submarine	Not very probable that submarine would remain on surface. Easily countered by deep running to avoid submerged detection. Also strongly affected by turbidity
Radar hull reflectivity	Radar could possibly detect surfaced submarine hundreds of kilometres away and launched missile thousands of kilometres away, but could not directly detect submerged submarine or missile before it broached the surface	Not very probable that submarine would remain on surface
Deliberate EM emission	Emissions can propagate thousands of kilometres	Unrealistic to expect submarine to communicate or radiate in detectable manner
Missile launch heat exhaust	Exhaust can be detected by satellite sensor hundreds of kilometres in space	May have little relevance if all missiles loosed

ELF galvanic current	Effect possibly detectable out to 'several miles'	Naturally-produced EM effects can be frequent. Intensity of all signals would fall off quickly from the source, requiring highly sensitive instruments for detection.
MHD	Phenomenon would probably remain in general vicinity of track, but possibly for long distance behind submarine if effect persists hours or more	Magnetic anomaly detection can be countered by measures which lower submarine's magnetic effect. MHD effect related to internal wave generation. (See below)
Magnetic anomaly	Effect is restricted to immediate vicinity of submarine	
Thermal scarring	Indicator would probably remain in general vicinity of track to a distance behind submarine which depends on how long effect persists. This could be minutes to hours	Subject to enormous number of 'false alarms' and local conditions. Countermeasures can ensure that thermal distinctiveness never rises to surface
Biological luminescence	Glow would remain in general vicinity of track to a distance behind submarine equal to 'several times [its] length'	Relevant only in darkness. Strongly subject to mimicking and masking. Deep operations easily negate surface observation
Contaminants	Contaminants would probably remain in general vicinity of track and persist from minutes to hours	Degree of concentration is critical. Release of some contaminants is controllable
Hump	Effect would be confined to area above hull	Easily countered through submarine design and operation to ensure surface effect is so small as to be undetectable
Kelvin wake	Effect would be confined to general vicinity of track and could persist for many minutes or more	See remarks under 'Hump'

continued on page 52

TABLE 2.1 continued

Indicator	Possible spatial or temporal extent	Remarks
Turbulent wakes	Effect would remain in general vicinity of track to 'several kilometres astern' and persist for many minutes or more	Can be lessened through submarine design and operations. Detectable only in water column
Internal waves	Naturally-produced waves can persist for hours or days. If submarine-generated waves persist for hours, then the 'wake of internal waves' behind a submarine could stretch a very considerable distance	Complex phenomenon whose utility as observable remains strongly questionable. Subject to 'very high false alarm rate' and to countermeasures

possibility arises that the submarine could be lost by virtue of going the wrong way down the track, that is, away from the submarine rather than towards it.

NOTES

1. For a listing of indicators, see, *inter alia*, OTA, *M-X Missile Basing*, p. 177; R. J. Starkey, 'Anti-Submarine Warfare Oceanography', *Military Electronics/Countermeasures* (April 1981) p. 40. See also discussion of indicators and ASW methods in Testimony of Vice Admiral K. McKee in US House Armed Services Committee, *Hearings on Military Posture and HR 2970 Department of Defense Authorization for Appropriations for FY 1982*, 97th Congress, 1st Session (1981) Pt 4, pp. 825–9 and B. I. Rodionov, *Anti-submarine Forces and Systems in Navies* (Moscow: Voyenizdat, 1977) chap. 3, section 7.
2. As cited in Government Data Publications, *Anti-Submarine Warfare* (Washington: Government Data Publications, 1963) p. 3.
3. See, *inter alia*, R. Garwin, 'Anti-submarine Warfare and National Security', in H. York (ed.) *Arms control: Readings from Scientific American* (San Francisco: W. H. Freeman, 1973) p. 250.
4. Ibid.
5. Ibid.
6. See G. Sundaram, 'ASW: The Key to Sea Control', *International Defense Review*, no. 3 (1980) p. 369 and T. B. Allen and N. Polmar, 'The Silent Chase', *The New York Times Magazine* (1 January 1984) p. 16.
7. For an excellent discussion of this point, see OTA, *M-X Missile Basing*, p. 186.
8. A. W. Cox, *Sonar and Underwater Sound* (Lexington, Massachusetts: D. C. Heath, 1974) p. 60.
9. D. C. Honhart, 'Navy Requirements for Space-Sensed Oceanographic Data', in Marine Technology Society and IEEE Council on Oceanic Engineering, *Oceans 82 Conference Record* (Washington, DC: 20–2 September 1982) p. 481.

10. K. Tsipis, 'Underwater Acoustic Detection', in Tsipis, A. Cahn and B. Feld, *The Future of the Sea-Based Deterrent* (Cambridge: MIT Press, 1973) pp. 174–5.
11. Cox, *Sonar and Underwater Sound*, p. 6.
12. See, for example, testimony of Dr D. Mann, in US Senate Armed Services Committee, *Department of Defense Authorization for Appropriations for FY 1980*, 96th Congress, 1st Session (1979) Pt 6, p. 2970.
13. See J. Moore (ed.) *Jane's Fighting Ships 1983–84* (London: Jane's, 1983) pp. 172–3.
14. R. Besnault, *'Genèse, Vie et Survie de SNLE'*, *Stratégique*, no. 3 (1979) p. 87.
15. OTA, *M-X Missile Basing*, p. 184.
16. Tsipis and Forsberg, *Tactical and Strategic ASW*, p. 20.
17. Ibid, p. 31; Allen and Polmar, *The Silent Chase*, p. 27.
18. 'Summary of Discussion of Papers on Ocean Technology', in B. Feld, *et al.* (eds) *Impact of New Technologies on the Arms Race* (Cambridge: MIT Press, 1971) p. 222.
19. V. Anderson, 'Ocean Technology', in *Impact of New Technologies*, p. 205.
20. W. Perry, 'Technological Prospects', in B. Blechman (ed.) *Rethinking the US Strategic Posture* (Cambridge: Ballinger Publications, 1982) p. 138.
21. Ibid.
22. Wilkes, in SIPRI, *Yearbook, 1979*, p. 443. Cf. K. Tsipis, 'Anti-submarine Warfare – Fact and Fiction', *New Scientist* (18 January 1975) p. 145.
23. See D. Ball, *Can Nuclear War Be Controlled?*, Adelphi Paper no. 169 (London: IISS, 1981) pp. 39–40.
24. G. Tacconi, 'Fundamentals of ELF Communications and Detection', in Advisory Group for Ærospace Research and Development (AGARD), *Applications of Remote Sensing to Ocean Surveillance*, AGARD Lecture Series no. 88 (London: Technical Editing and Reproduction Limited, 1977) pp. 9–17.
25. McKee, *Hearings On Military Posture FY 1982*, Pt. 4, p. 828.
26. See discussion on internal waves, in Chap. 2 under 'Hydrodynamic Displacement Effects'.
27. MccGwire, 'Technological and Operational Trends', p. 15
28. See Tacconi, 'Fundamentals of ELF', p. 9–21; F. Chilton, L. Wood, and R. Buntzen, 'Electric and Magnetic Sensing Systems Applications', in AGARD, *Applications*, p. 10–16; D. G. Polvani, 'Current and Future Underwater Magnetic Sensing', in Marine Technology Society and Institute of Electrical and IEEE Electronics Engineers, *Oceans 81 Conference*

Record (Boston, Massachusetts: 16–18 September 1981) vol. I, p. 443.
29. W. Podney and R. Sager, 'Measurement of Fluctuating Magnetic Gradients Originating from Oceanic Internal Waves', *Science* (28 September 1979) pp. 1381–2.
30. These are discussed in Tacconi, 'Fundamentals of ELF', Chap. 9 and in Chilton, Wood, and Buntzen, 'Electric and Magnetic Sensing Systems', Chap. 10.
31. Chilton, Wood, and Buntzen, 'Electric and Magnetic Sensing Systems', p. 10–1.
32. See, for example, Polvani, 'Current And Future Underwater Magnetic Sensing', p. 445 and P. Cohen, *The Realm of the Submarine* (London: Collier-Macmillan, 1969) p. 222.
33. Rodionov, *Anti-Submarine Forces and Systems*, Chap. 3, section 7.
34. Ibid.
35. W. P. Schimmel and W. N. Sullivan, *Experimental Study of Thermally Induced Buoyant Plumes in Water* (Albuquerque, New Mexico: Sandia Laboratories, 1975) p. 10.
36. B. Gebhardt, D. Hilder, and M. Kelleher, 'The Diffusion of Thermal Buoyant Jets', in T. F. Irvine and J. Hartnett (eds) *Advances in Heat Transfer*, vol. 16 (New York: Academic Press, 1984) in press.
37. Tsipis, 'Anti-Submarine Warfare', p. 176. See also I. Lobanov, 'Sea Watchers in Space', *Oceans* (November 1981) p. 40 and Feld *et al.* (eds) *Impact of New Technologies*, p. 221.
38. Rear Admiral L. D. Coates as quoted in V. F. Callahan, Jr, *Underwater Defense Handbook* (Washington: Callahan Publications, 1963) p. 12.
39. R. V. Lynch III, *The Occurrence and Distribution of Surface Bioluminescence in the Oceans During 1966 Through 1977* (Washington: Naval Research Laboratory, 1978) p. 2.
40. M. G. Kelly and P. Tett, 'Bioluminescence in the Ocean' in P. J. Herring (ed.) *Bioluminescence in Action* (London: Academic Press, 1978) p. 401 and R. J. Starkey, 'Antisubmarine Warfare Oceanography: Part III', *Military Electronics/Countermeasures* (July 1981) pp. 67–8.
41. Kelly and Tett, 'Bioluminescence in the Ocean,' p. 400.
42. Lynch, *Surface Bioluminiscence*, p. 6.
43. Kelly and Tett, 'Bioluminiscence in the Ocean', p. 400.
44. Lynch, *Surface Bioluminiscence*, p. 6.
45. Kelly and Tett, 'Bioluminiscence in the Ocean', p. 417.
46. Speed, *Strategic Deterrence*, p. 60–1; Allen and Polmar, *The Silent Chase*, pp. 26–7.

47. See Mather, 'The Most Secret Service', p. 37.
48. McKee, *Hearings On Military Posture FY 1982*, Pt. 4, p. 827.
49. Statement of Robert Morse in Harvard University, Program for Science and International Affairs, *Summary of a Workshop in Anti-submarine Warfare* (Cambridge: Program for Science and International Affairs, 1974) p. 16.
50. MccGwire, 'Technological and Operational Trends', p. 14.
51. See L. D. Landau and E. M. Lefohitz, *Fluid Mechanics* (Reading, Massachusetts: Addison-Wesley, 1959) p. 25.
52. See Speed, *Strategic Deterrence*, p. 60; McKee, Testimony, *Hearings On Military Posture FY 1982*, Pt. 4, p. 827; Moore, '*ASW*' p. 192; Ye. Buzov, 'Trends in The Development of Non-acoustic Means of Detection', *Morskoy Sbornik*, no. 9 (1974) pp. 6–8.
53. E. Mollo-Christensen, 'Surface Signs of Internal Ocean Dynamics', in R. C. Beal *et al.*, *Spaceborne Synthetic Aperture Radar for Oceanography* (Baltimore: Johns Hopkins 1981) p. 140.
54. See A. H. Schooley and R. W. Stewart, 'Experiments with a Self-Propelled Body Submerged in a Fluid with a Vertical Density Gradient', *Journal of Fluid Mechanics*, vol. 15 (1963) pp. 83–96; Schooley, 'Wake Collapse in a Stratified Fluid: Experimental Exploration of Scaling Characteristics', *Science*, vol. 160 (1968) pp. 763–4; Schooley and B. A. Hughes, 'An Experimental and Theoretical Study of Internal Waves Generated by the Collapse of a Two-Dimensional Mixed Region in a Density Gradient', *Journal of Fluid Mechanics*, vol. 51, Pt 1 (1972) pp. 159–75; and J. Wu, 'Mixed Region Collapse with Internal Wave Generation in a Density-stratified Medium', *Journal of Fluid Mechanics*, vol. 35, Pt 3 (1969) pp. 531–44; T. H. Bell, Jr, *Internal Wave Generation by Submerged Bodies* (Washington: Naval Research Laboratory, 1973).
55. C. Garrett and W. Munk, 'Internal Waves in the Ocean', in M. Van Dyke, J. V. Wehausen and J. L. Lumley (eds), *Annual Review of Fluid Mechanics*, vol. 11 (Palo Alto: Annual Reviews 1979) p. 340.
56. Ibid, p. 343.
57. J. M. Bergin, *The Wake of a Source in a Two-Layered Fluid* (Washington: Naval Research Laboratory, 1971) p. ii and Bergin, *Internal Wave Generation Caused by the Growth and Collapse of a Mixed Region* (Washington: Naval Research Laboratory, 1973) p. 43.

58. US National Defense Research Committee, *The Application of Oceanography to Subsurface Warfare* (Washington: GPO 1946) p. 73.
59. Chilton, Wood and Buntzen, 'Electric and Magnetic Sensing Systems', p. 10–11.
60. Ibid, pp. 10–7 to 10–9.
61. J. R. Apel *et al.*, 'Observations of Oceanic Internal and Surface Waves from the Earth Resources Technology Satellite', *Journal of Geophysical Research*, vol. 80, no. 6 (1975) p. 865; and L. L. Fu and B. Holt, *SEASAT Views Oceans and Sea Ice with Synthetic Aperture Radar* (Pasadena: Jet Propulsion Laboratory, 1982) p. 26.
62. W. O. Nierenberg, 'The United States Navy and Satellite Oceanography: The Charles H. Davis Lecture Presentation at the Naval Postgraduate School, Monterey, CA, November 17, 1981', p. 15. See also Tsipis, *Antisubmarine Warfare*, 22 above, pp. 145–6; and Morse, *Summary of a Workshop*, p. 16.
63. Perry, 'Technological Prospects', pp. 137–8.
64. Garrett and Munk, 'Internal Waves', pp. 339 and 357. See also Charles Elachi, 'Radar Images of the Earth from Space', *Scientific American* (December 1982) p. 61; H. N. Kritikos and J. Shiue, 'Microwave Sensing from Orbit', *IEEE Spectrum* (August 1979) pp. 40–1.
65. Garrett and Munk, 'Internal Waves', p. 271 and L. M. Brekhovskikh *et al.*, 'Short Period Internal Waves in the Sea', *Journal of Geophysical Research*, vol. 80, no. 6 (1975) p. 863.
66. Garrett and Munk, 'Internal Waves', p. 359.
67. OTA, *M-X Missile Basing*, p. 188.
68. See J. W. Miles, 'Internal Waves Generated by a Horizontally Moving Source', *Geophysical Fluid Dynamics*, vol. 2 (1971) pp. 63–87; O. M. Phillips, *The Dynamics of The Upper Ocean* (Cambridge: Cambridge University Press, 1977) pp. 211–17; J. R. Booker and F. P. Bretherton, 'The Critical Layer for Internal Gravity Waves in a Shear Flow', *Journal of Fluid Mechanics*, vol. 27 (1967); S. Kitaigorodskii, Statement in Panel Discussion, in R. C. Beal *et al.*, *Spaceborne*, p. 187; Apel *et al.*, 'Observations', p. 874; T. H. Bell, Jr, *Distortion of Internal Wave Patterns by Background Shear: A Case Study* (Washington: Naval Research Laboratory, 1979); Fu and Holt, *SEASAT Views*, p. 99.
69. O. M. Philips, 'The Structure of Short Gravity Waves in the Ocean Surface', in Beal *et al.*, *Spaceborne*, p. 34 and J. F. Vesecky and R. H. Stewart, 'The Observation of Ocean

Surface Phenomena Using Imagery from the SEASAT Synthetic Aperture Radar: An Assessment', *Journal of Geophysical Research*, vol. 87, no. C5 (1982) p. 3423.
70. Nierenberg, 'US Navy and Satellite Oceanography', p. 15 and Miles, 'Internal Waves'.
71. J. P. Craven, 'Ocean Technology and Submarine Warfare', in *The Implications of Military Technology in the 1970s*, Adelphi Paper no. 64 (London: IISS, 1968) p. 42.

3 ASW Sensors and their Deployment

This chapter looks at actual and potential ASW sensors and at ways to deploy them. It will simplify the evaluation of the utility of sensor possibilities if discussion first centres on the relative merits of deployment modes and platforms.

DEPLOYMENT MODES AND PLATFORMS

There are three basic deployment modes: stationary; mobile; and dual – the last combining features of the first two. Stationary sensors can be anchored within the water column, be placed on a platform above the water (similar to an oil rig), or be on land. When employed passively, they rely entirely on indicators coming to them and are generally useful only with respect to signals which propagate great distances or against submarines which must cross a barrier. Whether used passively or actively, they can be distinctly susceptible to destruction should an enemy know their location; active stationary sensors are especially vulnerable since their energy transmissions act as a beacon.

Mobile and dual-mode sensors do not wait for signals to come to them; water, air or space platforms transport these sensors to where signals may be found. The mobile sensors are those which can operate while their carrying platform is moving. The dual-mode sensors are of two types. One requires the ship or helicopter platform to become stationary when the sensor operates. The other type is jettisoned from its transporting craft into the water, either to float freely or to anchor itself to the ocean floor.

As with stationary platforms, ships and submarines are rather poor for searching wide areas unless the sought-for signals propagate over long distances. This is because waterborne craft normally have maximum speeds of 30–40 knots, and they may carry sensors which are effective only at much slower speeds. While publicists speculate about 70-knot submarines and hull-out-of-water surface ships capable of over 100 knots, there is no indication that such craft will enter ASW use in either superpower navy in the foreseeable future.

Submarines are the best of the mobile platforms for trailing. This is because of their endurance and ability to stay with an SSBN and to operate at comparable speeds. Unlike aircraft, furthermore, they are less affected by weather. Nuclear submarines are especially good since they need never break off to refuel, can avoid heavy weather altogether by remaining submerged, and can react better should an SSBN attempt to hide or break trail by changing depth. Submarines are also less restricted as to where they go; they can survive in waters where surface ships or aircraft might not.

Surface ships would appear now to be the most vulnerable of mobile platforms. Surveillance techniques against them are sophisticated, and, as the Falkland War has shown, it can be difficult for them to defend themselves against cruise missiles or other forms of ærial or seaborne attack. It is generally accepted, furthermore, that in a one-to-one duel between a surface combatant and a submarine, the latter would probably either prevail or escape. For these reasons, and because surface combatants in a major conflict would be otherwise engaged, as for example in the protection of high-value ships, it is not expected that surface ships (other than possibly vessels towing acoustic arrays) would be involved in trying to find and destroy SSBNs.

Where and when they can operate, aircraft may be the most flexible and versatile of mobile platforms. At transit speeds in excess of 100 knots for helicopters and exceeding 300 knots for fixed-wing aircraft, they can be sent quickly on demand to monitor a barrier or to track, localise, and attack a target. What they generally cannot do as well as submarines and in some cases as surface ships is to trail. One reason is endurance – 12 hours being the general maximum which a maritime patrol aircraft could stay aloft. Aircraft working in series can, however, overcome this problem, but must always contend with the fact that they operate in a different medium than submarines. They also operate at much higher speeds which, while it can be a problem, is also a blessing should they lose contact. This is because speed allows them to search the immediate area quickly before the submarine gets away.

The ability of aircraft to conduct wide-area search partly depends on the coverage of on-board sensors, sensing speeds, and the number of aircraft working together. Roger Speed points out, for example, that thirty aircraft, flying 300 knots and each sweeping a band 14 NM wide, can cover 1 000 000 NM in eight hours.[1] Only ten aircraft would be necessary if their sensors swept a band of 40 NM. Nonetheless, it is instructive that neither superpower generally uses aircraft to search wide areas. One explanation is that the on-board sensors for detecting non-communicating, non-radiating submerged submarines directly have generally been very short-ranged. A second may well be costs: continuous search operations would certainly be very expensive, especially since an inventory of at least three and closer to six aircraft are needed to keep one in the air at all times. Unless search operations are to be disrupted, additional aircraft would be needed to localise and attack targets. Two other factors may be a lack of appropriate bases and the effects of weather on air operations. Commercial aircraft regularly fly above or around heavy weather, but ASW aircraft cannot do so if they are not to leave gaps in their coverage.

When weather is not a problem, large-area search could also be feasibly conducted by flight vehicles not generally in use today.[2] These are airships, lighter-than-air craft, and wing-in-ground (WIG) effect planes. A strength of these platforms is their endurance. WIGs are particularly interesting because they can fly at normal aircraft speeds (that is not using ground effect) to reach a search area quickly and then switch to the WIG mode of flying very low (within one wing chord of the surface) and slowly. In that configuration, a WIG might stay up for 24 hours if crew fatigue problems could be resolved. The Soviet Union has experimented with WIG craft, but there is no indication that it will soon put them in operational service.[3] There is also no indication that either superpower is experimenting seriously with any of the other craft mentioned.

What about space vehicles? Much interest surrounds their use in ocean surveillance and other military roles. Spacecraft in high geosynchronous orbit (around 40 000km) move at the same speed as the earth. This means that they are constantly over the same point on the globe. They thus provide continuous coverage of whatever is in the field of view of their sensors, but they do not, of course, provide global coverage since their position relative to the earth is fixed. These spacecraft are also too high for the effective use of most ocean surveillance sensors, which are usually found on satellites whose orbits do not exceed 1000km. Low-orbit satellites have a remarkable speed over ground of about 25 000km per hour and a period – the time it takes to circumnavigate the globe – of roughly 90–100 minutes. While developing anti-satellite (ASAT) technologies may put them in hazard, they constantly overfly regions where no manned aircraft would be risked except in special cases.

Spacecraft in very low orbits (such as 300km) stay up for only a few days before air-drag effects on the fringes of the atmosphere cause them to fall towards earth and burn up. A higher orbit makes for longer endurance – 500km can result in a lifetime of several years, but, as noted earlier, too high an altitude restricts the effective use of on-board sensors. Specifically, a sensor's spatial resolution – that is, its ability to discriminate objects of minimum size or area – generally decreases with height.

Fitting a satellite with a drag-compensation propulsion system enhances its endurance; the system regularly boosts the satellite upwards to compensate for loss of altitude. Such evolutions can consume much fuel, however, and the system takes up space and weight which could otherwise be devoted to sensors and sensor support systems.

A drag-compensation system can also serve to manœuvre a satellite from one orbit to another. This can be important since the orbit determines where a spacecraft overflies the world, when it does so, and how often. As Jasani tells us, 'it often takes a long time before a satellite is positioned over an area of interest'.[4] Consider, for example, a satellite sensor which circles the earth fifteen times daily in a near-polar orbit between 500 and 700km and has an extremely broad (2700km) swath width. It would take one day both to provide fully-global coverage and to revisit the same spot. It could take eighteen days to do so for a satellite sensor sweeping a narrower swath only 148km across. By manœuvring a satellite from one orbit to another, the propulsion system reduces the time otherwise required for a satellite to overfly a desired area, but as with drag-compensation, these manœuvres can themselves be propellant-intensive and therefore also limited in number and extent. A space shuttle offers the possibility of refuelling and servicing satellites, but it remains to be seen if and when refuelling will occur regularly and what this will imply for manœuvring beyond simple drag-compensation.[5]

Rather than refuel other military reconnaissance vehicles, a space shuttle might be used to conduct its own reconnaissance. Again, it remains to be seen whether shuttles will be assigned any type of surveillance role (of submarines or otherwise) as a regular mission. Speaking of the US space shuttle, Abdel-Hady and Sadek conclude that 'for purposes of military reconnaissance . . . [it] could be of limited value because of its short flight duration, its high orbital inclination and difficulty of repetitive coverage of exact locations'.[6]

A study by the US Congress's Office of Technology Assessment (OTA) usefully illustrates some strengths and limitations of space vehicles as sensor platforms.[7] The study posits a low-orbit radar satellite which completes a revolution of the earth every ninety minutes and whose ground track moves westerly 22.5° per orbit. (See Figure 3.1.) The OTA analysis simply focuses on how long the satellite overflies a proposed ballistic missile submarine deployment area. The latter comprises approximately 2–3 million square nautical miles flanking both continental US coasts (including Alaska) out to a distance of 1000–1500 NM (the darker areas in Figure 3.1). The satellite cuts across the area six or seven times per day, and each overflight is four or five minutes

FIGURE 3.1 *Ground track of radar search satellite*

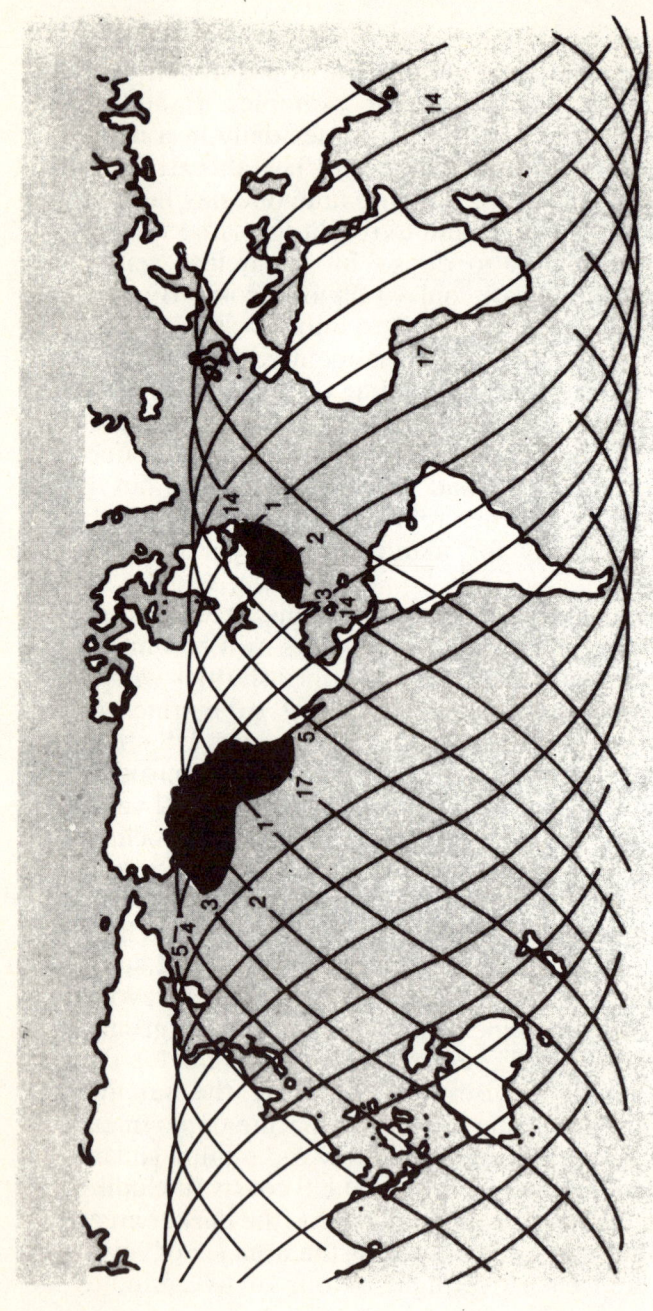

60° inclination
160–170 nmi altitude
1.5–1.6 hr period

SOURCE US Congress Office of Technology Assessment, M-X Missile Basing (Washington: GPO, 1981) p. 188.

long for a daily total of 24–35 minutes. In other words, with only one satellite there are approximately 23.5 hours of no coverage, with the maximum periods without coverage being 15 hours on the Atlantic and 16.5 hours on the Pacific side of the deployment area. Satellites working in phase, while potentially demanding from an information processing perspective, do reduce the temporal gaps in coverage: eight such satellites would spend 8 of every 90 minutes or slightly over two hours per day over the area; twelve such satellites, 16 of every 90 minutes or 4.5 hours; and twenty-four such satellites, 32 of every 90 minutes or about one-third of each day.

It should be clear, then, that it is only as spacecraft numbers increase and work in phase that wide- or small-area recurring search and, at best, loose intermittent tracking become practical possibilities. Localisation would not seem practical since space vehicles have only limited ability to change orbits and must keep moving forward inexorably and leave the target behind them. Localisation, trailing and continuous tracking would be left instead to more flexible air- and water-borne platforms which would rely on sensors in space or elsewhere to cue them as to where to begin their activities.

SENSORS

There are too many potential ASW sensors to describe each in detail. This section outlines some sensor characteristics and the factors conditioning sensor use and evaluates the relative suitability of the sensors for various ASW tasks. Many evaluations, especially of non-acoustic systems, should be viewed only as hypotheses. One reason is that the practical utility of some sensors must be established and continually reassessed in the light of new knowledge, new techniques, and new calculations of opportunity costs.[8] A second reason is that governments do the testing and reassessment and, for proper security reasons, they often choose not to disseminate their findings internally or publicly.

Acoustic sensors

The breakdown of acoustic indicators into reflected and submarine-radiated signals parallels the twofold breakdown of acoustic sensors into active and passive systems. The former detect reflected and the latter submarine-generated signals. Active sensors such as sonars can be used in a passive listen-only mode, but when used actively they can provide not only bearing but also range to a target, the latter being calculated by measuring the time a signal takes to travel to the target and return. A passive hydrophone also provides a bearing of the source, but a range estimate necessitates two or more hydrophones picking up the same signal. Plotting or 'triangulating' where the lines of bearing cross yields the approximate location and hence distance of the sound source from the hydrophones.

There are many different sensor and deployment possibilities. Ships and submarines carry sonars fixed to their hulls or they can tow listening-arrays. The latter – chains of hydrophones up to hundreds of metres long – are free of their own ship-noise interference and can cut across temperature and density layers where sound may be ducted or trapped. Lowered by cable from a ship or helicopter, variable depth (VD) or dipping sonars can also cut through the surface isothermal layer to the thermocline below. Sonobuoys are expendable sensors carried by helicopters and fixed-winged aircraft to areas of interest and dropped into the water. Small buoys operate for a few hours and can lower a hydrophone to shallow or moderately deep depth. If a signal is acquired, a radio transmits it to a monitoring airborne platform for processing. There are also very large long-life (weeks or more) sonobuoys sown by aircraft, surface ships, or submarines. They too release strings of hydrophones into the depths and transmit acquired signals to ships, aircraft and possibly satellites. Finally, contrasting with the transportable or mobile sensors are large sonars or chains of hydrophones anchored to the ocean floor and usually cable-connected to shore for power and signal processing.

The ship- and submarine-fixed sensors, the variable depth

and dipping sonars, and the small sonobuoys have poor capability for open-ocean search and are essentially limited to localisation, barrier, tracking or trailing operations. Because of problems of sensor size, shape, power and space available for processing, these systems are inherently short-ranged covering distances which vary from a few tens of kilometres for a small sonobuoy to a few hundred kilometres under highly favourable convergence zone conditions for the ship and submarine passive sensors.[9] Of the last two, the submarine sensors have a consistently better overall capability because a submarine usually operates more quietly and can place itself in the same ocean layer as the target.

Though ships and submarines are capable of 30 knots or more, they must restrict themselves to quite low speeds when relying upon hull-mounted or cable-lowered systems; otherwise they themselves generate so much hydrodynamic noise across the sensor as to drown incoming signals. Helicopters and aircraft are capable of much better speeds, allowing them to cover great distances in short time but when sensing they are of course restricted to the area covered by the devices they put into the water. Some ASW aircraft carry as many as 100 or so small sonobuoys, far too few to search a large area, and the sonobuoy operations can be adversely affected by high sea states. The latter can also cause the buoys to drift farther than desired and can also interrupt buoy transmissions to aircraft by washing water over the transmitter antenna.[10] Helicopter dipping-sonar coverage is also small, not only because such sensors are themselves short-ranged but also because they are operational only when the helicopter is stationary. A dipping sonar has little utility when dragged through the water.

Towed arrays, very large sonobuoys and systems tethered to the ocean floor provide the best possibility for limited to extensive wide-area coverage. The length or size of these systems, the power provided to them, and the means made available for processing their input data can allow them to capture both faint and low-frequency (hence, long-range) sounds embedded in the ambient noise. The detection of such sounds is also markedly enhanced by relying on chains of receivers, since proper processing can allow the signal picked up by one receiver to be added to that picked up by the others. The net effect is an augmentation of the signal relative to its background noise. Moreover, if the hydrophones are positioned at the right depth, they can intercept signals which enter the SOFAR channel, that generally deep-ocean layer wherein sound propagates for great distances.

If deployed and dispensed in very great numbers, very large sonobuoys, towed arrays and fixed passive systems could obviously search extensive areas. For example, 1000 to 1500 very large sonobuoys could monitor 1 million square miles if the detection radius of each were 15–20 NM at the surface. 100 towed-array vessels, each with a 200 NM detection range, could cover 12 million sq. NM at a time.

Searching large areas could also be done with active systems. Some claim that fixed sonars connected to shore could generate so much acoustic energy as to fill whole oceans with sound, but the extent to which they might be useful is critically dependent on solving a reverberation problem.[11] The greater the power of such sonars, the more they produce multiple echoes which drown the return of desired signals. The solution lies with devising very complex signal-processing, and there is no indication that such a solution is near or that large fixed sonars will be deployed.[12] One factor which may influence research and development decisions is that, as noted earlier, a large fixed active sonar is especially susceptible to destruction. Its emissions readily give away its location.

While self-generated reverberations characterise the use of large active sensors, a 'time-late' problem affects acoustic systems in general, with active systems naturally being doubly affected. As it applies specifically to acoustic sensors, the time-late problem refers to the time it takes for sound to travel through water and be received and processed by a sensor. The problem is negligible for short-range sensors but is obviously more serious for longer-range ones. The sound of a submarine 90km away is only 1 minute or so old when received, but it is already 50 minutes old if the target is 4500km distant. Because active sonar signals must make a two-way journey, the times would be doubled. A 6-knot submarine advances 1 NM in 10 minutes and 5 NM in 50 minutes. In short, the longer the range of an acoustic system, the more the system indicates where the submarine was but not where it may be at the time the signal is received. Processing time must then be added.

Compounding the time-late problem is the fact that – all other things being equal – the farther a submarine is from a sensor, the greater the uncertainty as to its exact location. Focusing and beam-forming techniques can lower the uncertainty; so too can triangulation techniques where the signals picked up by different sensors are overlapped together, but the point remains that any one listening beam or window must widen with distance from the sensors. Thus, Garwin writes 'The detection of a submarine by several . . . listening devices . . . could . . . localize the submarine to an accuracy which *under the best of circumstances* might be in the range of some tens of km' (emphasis added).[13]

To whatever accuracy, localising a submarine requires that it first be detected, and for the foreseeable future there seems to be no prospect for a practical acoustic system which will guarantee acquiring all submarines entering its nominal area of search – which will vary with changing environmental conditions.[14] Quiet submarines moving slowly in a noisy ocean and taking advantage of the ocean's thermal/density structure – for example, staying shallow so as to avoid detection by a sensor in a deeper layer – might well avoid passive acoustic detection 'no matter how one improves the quality of detectors and signal processing'.[15] Staying shallow, seeking out areas of poor acoustic propagation, designing submarines to lessen acoustic cross-section, and coating them with sound-absorbent materials can all severely hamper active sonar detection whether or not the sensor-generated reverberation problem were solved.

Should the improbable occur and should a system be devised which guaranteed finding all submarines which entered its nominal area of search, there would still be the problem of false alarms. As Kosta Tsipis put it 'In a real world situation, a false alarm with the resulting commitment of forces to counter its presence can be as costly tactically as the failure to detect the presence of a submarine. These large, sensitive [acoustic] processors may often have a high false alarm rate . . .'[16] This problem is not easily resolvable and requires ASW forces to adjust a sensor in terms of its probability of detection (PD) and probability of false alarms (PFA). The problem is that to adjust a sensor so as to increase the threshold of acceptability of a signal, and thus eliminate false alarms, also risks losing true signals. Any lowering of the threshold to capture those signals can in turn increase the possibility of false alarms. Improved signal-processing increases the probability of correctly sorting through incoming sounds, but ASW forces must always decide between PD and PFA and accept the consequences in terms of lost signals or unwanted ones. Adjusting PD and PFA, furthermore, may do little to screen out signals deliberately generated by a wily adversary who realises that decoys can indeed be a cost-effective way to help to protect strategically critical and highly expensive SSBNs.

Non-acoustic sensors

Many different sensors are potentially suitable for detection of non-acoustic ASW phenomena, and they can be distinguished by their operational location. Some must be in the water or close to it; others function high above it, even in space; and others often operate on land.

Sensors in the water

Unlike acoustic systems, the sensors with the smallest coverage are, with one exception, those which operate within the water. These include some electric field, magnetic field and contaminant sensors as well as instruments for measuring pressure, temperature, salinity, or bioluminescence. These devices may be stationary (for example, dipoles on the ocean floor for sensing galvanic currents), free-floating or affixed to or towed from ships or submarines. Their use would seem to be restricted mainly to narrow barrier tasks and, for mobile sensors, localisation, trailing, and possibly tracking tasks. This is because the observables they seek remain restricted to the submarine's track with little lateral propagation and because the sensors themselves simply do not detect signals at long ranges.[17]

The one exception to the above conclusion is a non-acoustic sensor which detects acoustic signals. Davis and Einzig tell us that a '10 metre long strand of plastic coated optical fiber, approximately one millimeter in diameter and configured in a small receiving coil, provides the acoustic receiving sensitivity equivalent to the best conventional hydrophones today'.[18] The basic operating features of such an 'optical sonar system' are simple. Light (as from a laser) is transmitted through an optical fibre which is surrounded by an acoustically transparent material. An acoustic signal striking it causes an observable variation in the phase or intensity of the light signal. Such a system has the 'potential of being smaller, lighter weight, more reliable, and cheaper ... than conventional [acoustic hydrophone] systems' at present in use. It would also be capable of extremely high data rates since data within the system would travel at the speed of light if optical-fibre cables are used throughout.

Short-range out-of-water sensors

Operating out of water on a mobile platform gives greater opportunity for more extensive coverage. Some systems, however – such as magnetic anomaly detectors at present in ASW use and some contaminant sensors – have inherently short-range detection capabilities. Magnetic anomaly systems, for instance, must be within 1000–2000 feet of a submarine to find a detectable signal.[19] Because magnetic or contaminant sensors must remain close to the water to be effective, they can operate only from ships and low-flying aircraft and thus are limited to barrier-keeping, localisation, or, when shipborne, to trailing and possibly tracking should contaminants persist for long periods.

The most significant development among these sensors concerns magnetic detection systems, for recent improvements may result in a seven-to-ten-fold increase in their detection ranges.[20] One is improved sensor technology with

SQUID magnetometers being 300 times more sensitive than the magnetometers at the previous state-of-the-art level and 1000 times more sensitive than the level before that. These improvements, however, allow only a seven-to-ten-fold increase in detection range because, as noted, magnetic anomalies decrease roughly as the inverse third power of the range. A second development is better signal-processing derived from the application of advanced computer technology and more sophisticated analytical models. With regard to the latter, 'effort appears to be concentrated on creating mathematical models of the noise which permit substraction of the noise contribution from the total measurement'. Because of these developments, detection ranges could potentially reach 20 000 feet. This would still be too little to allow for economical wide-area search by a group of aircraft, but it would certainly facilitate the performance of the other ASW tasks.

Chilton *et al.* were cited earlier to the effect that SQUID magnetometers might allow high-sweep-rate aircraft-mapping of the surface and internal wave conditions of entire ocean basins. Unfortunately they provide no information as to the number of aircraft such an operation would entail, but the aircraft would probably fly at a very low altitude, minimising the amount of coverage per aircraft. The Podney and Sager experiment, for instance – which showed that magnetic gradients originating from oceanic internal waves are minute – was done with a SQUID placed merely 7m above water which was only 18m deep.[21] Both wave amplitude and heading, furthermore, affected their measurements, and presumably would complicate the planned utilisation of groups of aircraft searching wide areas.

General characteristics of sensors operating high above the water

Providing better prospects for wide-area search are remote electromagnetic (EM) sensors. These operate high above the water from air and space platforms and rely on the detection or generation of energy mainly from the ultraviolet through to the microwave portion of the electromagnetic spectrum. Oceanographers, meteorologists, and Earth-resource specialists have written extensively about remote EM sensing of the ocean environment, and they have identified characteristic features of EM sensors used in this way.

One is that no remote EM sensor 'is sensitive to only one oceanographic variable; rather, each instrument responds to a combination of atmospheric and oceanographic phenomena'.[22] For example, to an infra-red radiometer designed to measure sea-surface temperature, low clouds are indistinguishable from slightly cool sea-water. As a result, the interpretation of data can be complicated and 'usually requires that a number of observations, each sensitive to somewhat different phenomena, be combined to provide unambiguous information'.[23] With infra-red radiometers one partial solution is to photograph the area observed and combine the photographic information on the presence of clouds with the IR data.[24]

A second characteristic is that remote EM sensors 'generally do not measure oceanic phenomena directly'.[25] A radar satellite, for instance, does not see internal waves directly.[26] Rather it receives backscatter from capillary waves (specifically, 30cm Bragg resonant waves) superimposed on the ocean swell (termed 'gravity waves'). If internal waves are modulating the capillary waves, then the modulation would be detectable, and not the internal waves *per se*. Similarly, both infra-red and passive microwave radiometers measure emitted thermal radiation, and their outputs are temperature values. What is actually being measured, however, is the amount of energy received in a designated spectral region by an instrument located hundreds to thousands of metres above the water. The level of energy received (which also includes stray radiation from the intervening atmosphere) does not equate to the amount of radiation directly at the ocean surface. An estimate of the stray radiation must be made and subtracted from the value of the overall radiation which entered the sensor. An additional complicating factor is that the temperature assigned to the energy sensed is not its true temperature but rather the postulated equivalent temperature of an idealised radiator (termed 'black body') which would produce the same amount of radiation.

A third characteristic flows directly from the second; it is the need for calibration to help to ensure that what is measured and the value assigned to it correspond accurately. The need for calibration requires 'ground' or 'ocean-truth' data. This means, for example, establishing water's actual surface temperature and comparing it with remote sensor values. Such a process also requires establishing why errors may exist, a problem which can be highly complicated because of the first two characteristics that have here been identified.[27]

Fourth, EM signals vary with the extent to which they are limited by weather and atmospheric conditions on the one hand and with the extent to which they can be readily sensed on the other. The shorter wavelengths – from ultraviolet through thermal infra-red portions of the spectrum – are weather-limited. They do not easily penetrate clouds, rain and atmospheric water vapour. Their utility for any ocean surveillance is thereby sharply circumscribed since it is estimated that 'on average, any given area of the earth is completely free from clouds for only 10–14 per cent of the time'.[28] Honhart nicely illustrates some implications of these facts. He refers to the experience of the Naval Eastern Oceanography Center at Norfolk, Virginia, which utilises satellites to monitor sea-surface temperatures in the Atlantic. 'The only satellite sensor' he states 'which provides fine detail of sea surface temperature is an infra-red system . . . **unblocked by clouds. As a consequence, the oceanography center often goes days or weeks without receiving fine detail data in an important operational area.**'[29] The longer wavelengths – microwave and higher – are generally free of such problems, but they have a lower energy content. This fact has implications for remote sensing since such radiation is more difficult to sense than that of shorter wavelengths. One is that the resolution of longer wavelength systems tends to be coarser, less capable of providing the 'fine detail' which Honhart credits to thermal IR. A second implication is that a moving sensor relying on naturally-emitted long-wavelength radiation may have to 'view' large areas of earth before obtaining a detectable signal. The ultimate significance for ASW is that if the area which must be viewed is much larger than the observable that one is trying to sense, then that observable may not be distinguishable as a discrete entity separable from the larger area. This point will be better appreciated after a fifth feature of remote EM sensors is presented: namely, the capability of any sensor is a function of its spatial resolution, contrast resolution/accuracy, coverage, and the trade-offs made among them.

Spatial resolution, as stated earlier, is the minimum-size object or area reliably distinguishable by the sensor. Contrast resolution (also termed sensitivity or precision) refers to the smallest contrast between resolvable objects or areas reliably detected. It can be conceived of as an ability to distinguish shades of grey. Accuracy is a measure of the range of values within which a variable measured to some precision may lie. For instance, an infra-red radiometer may resolve sea-surface temperature to increments of 0.1°C and the reading may be accurate within a range of ±0.5°C. Coverage is the area which can be sensed at one time or over a period of time. Swath width is the width of the area viewed by a sensor on an æroplane or satellite.

The above variables are interdependent and subject to trade-offs. For instance, greater precision and accuracy can be achieved by increasing the amount of data over which to average incoming signals. This can be done by dwelling over an area so as to collect as much data as necessary, but this procedure obviously limits coverage. Another solution, applicable to a sensor which must inexorably move forward, is to increase the area over which information is drawn. The problem with this procedure is that it can limit spatial resolution if the signals being sought are too small or weak relative to the average of the area's total inputs. A variation of this problem can arise whenever attempts are made to increase coverage since, for any given angle of view, greater coverage generally means less spatial resolution. Human experience provides a simple analogy. If one were to stand 1″ from a wall in order to read a tiny sign, one would not be able to see the wall's outer edge. As one moved away to see more of the wall, the sign would become less readable (or resolvable) to the point that it might no longer be distinguishable.

The ideal remote sensor would clearly be a system which simultaneously had broad and constant coverage as well as high spatial resolution, sensitivity and accuracy. In practice, however, coverage may be sacrificed for increased spatial resolution and – if longer dwell-times are accepted – for increased sensitivity and accuracy as well. Spatial resolution, in turn, may be sacrificed and coverage can benefit if larger areas are viewed for the sake of greater sensitivity and accuracy. The capabilities of any system will reflect the trade-offs made among these variables, and the trade-offs must, in turn, reflect the realities of the phenomenon to be sensed. Since most postulated surface-effect observables remain in the general vicinity of the submarines's track with little lateral propagation, a sensor would require high spatial resolution. In addition since most effects are highly subject to masking (that is, low contrast) or mimicking (that is, high false alarm rates) or both, a sensor would require high precision and accuracy derived either from a long viewing period over an area or the viewing of a large area by a moving sensor.

Features of specific air and space EM sensors

To this point the discussion has focused on characteristics of remote EM sensors in general and only incidentally on characteristics of specific sensors. When considering the latter, it is useful to group sensors in terms of their positions on the electromagnetic spectrum. One can identify four groups: optical wavelength, thermal IR, microwave and multi-spectral sensors.

The optical wavelength sensors include photographic systems, low-light-level image intensifiers (LLLII) and lasers. Even at satellite altitudes, high-resolution narrow-swath photographic systems could distinguish surfaced submarines, but the use of such systems would seem to be restricted to daytime cloud-free monitoring of ports and harbours.[30]

Aircraft-based LLLII and lasers could perform barrier and localisation tasks. During periods of darkness, intensifiers might detect bioluminescent disturbances subject, of course, to interference from any other sources of light, including moonlight, as well as from clouds and rain. If used in a scanning mode or with proper lenses, intensifiers might have some capability for limited wide-area search if enough are used together. It may be, however, that intensifiers, especially those mounted on satellites, may not be able to achieve the necessary balance between coverage and spatial resolution to allow for such a search. Blue-green lasers are highly versatile in that they might directly sense a submerged hull or towed body, turbulent wakes, associated underwater thermal anomalies, possibly some contaminants, and, with laser range-finders (or lidars), any detectable submarine-generated surface hump.[31] In contrast to this versatility are a number of factors, some already mentioned, militating against the adoption of blue-green lasers for wide-area search and restricting their use to less demanding barrier, localisation, and possibly tracking roles. These are the generally narrow and directional nature of laser beams, their inability to penetrate and return from all depths where submarines could be, and their sensitivity to atmospheric conditions and to water turbidity. It seems generally agreed, furthermore, that any blue-green laser utilised in the foreseeable future for ASW detection will have to operate from an aircraft. Before a satellite-based blue-green laser ASW system becomes a practical possibility, scientists and engineers will have to solve 'a host of technical problems, including the development of high-power laser sources'.[32]

Thermal infra-red sensors might find a surfaced submarine or towed body by the temperature difference between the object sensed and the surrounding water. Presumably this could be done from satellite heights, but there are no indication that either Superpower relies at present on such satellite-based systems to search for surface ships, much less submarines. Forward-looking infra-red (FLIR) systems are often used from airborne platforms (in search and rescue as well as military missions, for instance) to find surface ships in very small areas, but these systems are very adversely affected by clouds, rain, whitecaps, and medium-to-high sea states.[33]

Thermal IR systems on satellites in geosynchronous orbit can easily observe whole ocean basins. They can detect the hot plume from a launched missile, and, with proper signal-processing, could indicate quite accurately the area from which the missile was launched. A localisation or attack platform could then be sent after the submarine if it could reach the area quickly enough. Of course, if the submarine had fired all its missiles, there might be less incentive to attack it.

Infra-red radiometers (IRRs) and passive microwave radiometers (PMRs) might be able to sense thermal scars on the surface. While clouds and the presence of water vapour severely degrade the performance of any IR sensor, the best prospects for an operational system would seem to lie with an airborne IRR in view of the desired contrast and spatial resolutions. Hodara and Wells claim that an airborne IRR could detect temperature changes in the order of millikelvins, a sensitivity consistent with Rodionov's assertion, cited earlier, that thermal scars would differ from ambient on the surface only by about 0.005°K. To achieve the postulated sensitivity, Hodara's and Wells's radiometer would operate at altitudes as low as 100m, which would allow for high spatial resolution but would probably also cause coverage to be so small as to preclude wide-area search.[34]

An airborne PMR could have greater coverage and overcome the problems of clouds and water vapour, but, being less sensitive than an IRR, it would have greater difficulty detecting a signal. Nevertheless, Windsor and Mooney postulate the possibility of an airborne PMR with a 1km 'footprint'. It might be capable, they say, of 'detecting local "hot spots" generated by submerged submarines'.[35] Their postulated system, however, has a sensitivity of only 0.1°K, not nearly enough if thermal scars differ from ambient on the surface by only thousandths of a degree.

It remains to be seen whether any space-based IRR or PMR will be able to obtain the desired precision, accuracy and spatial resolution because of satellite speeds and altitudes. Present satellite-based IR systems come closest to the mark with contrast resolutions of tenths of a degree Kelvin averaged over 1km. They can do this with swath widths of 2700 km which, independent of other factors, clearly allows wide area search. Huh *et al.*, however, argue 'that true all-weather day–night sea-surface temperature data [from satellites] must await development of high-resolution multi-spectral passive microwave radiometers'.[36] These now achieve sensitivities in tenths of a degree (0.2°K on the Tiros–N satellite, for example) but require tens of kilometres to do so.[37] By itself such spatial resolution should negate the utility of satellite PMRs for the detection of any observable remaining in the vicinity of a submarine's track with little lateral propagation.

PMRs could detect observables other than thermal scars. Aircraft-based systems have detected surface ships, aircraft, ship wakes and surface manifestations of internal waves, but they are not suitable for doing so from space.[38] Rather, it is active microwave sensors, that is, radars, which offer most promise in this respect.

As noted earlier, microwave radars do not penetrate the water; they sense what is on the surface. They are sensitive to size of the observable (bigger is better) and to sea state (calmer is generally better). Radar being an active system, a quarry could ascertain that it is in use and take measures to counter it. Indeed, since it is anticipated that a ballistic missile submarine would be careful not to expose its hull, sail or masts to radar detection, the potential for radars (other than detecting missiles in flight, discussed later) lies in attempting to find potential ocean surface dynamics.

Radar altimeters even on satellites could conceivably sense detectable hump phenomenon and Kelvin wakes since altimeter 'accuracies . . . will ultimately allow . . . obtaining sea topography to a few cm'.[39] A problem is that altimeters have swath widths on the order of 10km or less – too narrow for wide-area search.[40] They may prove useful for localisation, but only from aircraft since satellites are generally unsuited to the task.

Rather than an altimeter, a forward- or side-looking radar would be more appropriate to seek out Kelvin wakes or surface manifestations of internal waves should either prove useful indicators. Such radars can easily sweep bands 80–100km.

One type of side-looking-radar – the 'synthetic aperture' (or SAR) variety[41] – is exceptional in its ability to achieve both good coverage and outstanding spatial resolution. The SEASAT satellite in 1978, for instance, had typical spatial resolutions of 25–40m in range and azimuth. With its 100km swath width and the speed of the satellite, it covered 720sq. km per second. The maximum length of a SEASAT SAR image track, 4000km, was determined by the satellite's need to be in the vicinity of a ground receiver station since the SAR could not store or process its own data.

The presence of a companion data relay satellite could lessen this limitation on SAR, but would not lessen the load on signal-processing facilities on the ground. SEASAT SAR was an extremely prodigious data producer (110 megabits or 10^7 numbers per second) and 'approximately a billion operations were needed to generate a high-resolution image from the information recorded in one second'.[42] In addition, the fastest available digital processor for space-borne imaging radars 'has a "throughput ratio" of 1:500, that is, the data collected in one second require 500 seconds of processing'.[43] Ratios of that magnitude help to explain why 'four hours is considered to be in principle . . . a timely basis' for SAR images to become available.[44] That time could well be cut back since a processor with a 1:1 ratio is under development and 'scheduled for completion in 1985'.[45] From an ASW standpoint, any processor is welcomed which lessens the 'time-late' problem, that is, the delay between when a target submarine generates a signal and when ASW forces can be commanded to react to it.

If the data-processing problems are resolved, then SARs would seem to be among the most promising of potential non-acoustic sensors, not only because of their spatial resolution and coverage potential (if enough SARs are mobilised) but also because of their proven sensitivity for detecting internal wave surface effects – albeit so far only of large natural waves in shallow water. This sensitivity is important in contributing to SAR's promise because of the long persistence of natural internal waves and, by implication, the possibly long persistence of submarine-generated waves.

It is still early to say how well SAR will realise its potential against submarine-produced surface manifestations. Obvious considerations are whether submarines produce long-persisting internal waves, whether those waves produce in turn observable surface manifestations, and whether environmental conditions strongly affect either process. A less obvious consideration concerns SAR's ability to image all types of internal waves under varying conditions. Natural scientists agree that much research remains to be done in order to understand better 'the mechanisms for the visibility of internal waves in SAR images'.[46] They do know, however, that wind and rain do condition SAR imaging by having 'great influence' and 'strong effect' on the roughness of those particular waves (30cm Bragg resonant waves) on which SAR focuses.[47] They also know that the angle at which and the direction from which radar signals strike the surface also influence the strength of the return which is achieved.[48] The question of direction is particularly interesting since, it may be recalled, the generation of surface manifestations is itself a function of the direction both of the surface waves and the internal waves. In short, it seems that three directional variables may come into play and need to interact in particular ways if SAR is to image the surface manifestations of internal waves.

A lingering question is whether SARs might be able to sweep widths much larger than 100km, thereby further enhancing coverage. (A follow-on to the SEASAT SAR, the Shuttle Imaging Radar–A, had a swath width of only 50km). The answer at the moment would seem to be no. A SAR is designed to try to maintain a constant sensitivity to the return it receives across the range against which its signals are directed. It is also designed to ensure the proper synchronisation of its signals as the radar approaches, passes over and looks behind to some spot on the ground. Both these and other factors impose geometric constraints on a SAR which would seem to limit its ability to go to significantly larger swath widths without major design changes.[49]

Finally, the remote EM sensors mentioned thus far each

occupy a specific portion of the EM spectrum – that is the optical, thermal IR, and microwave wavelengths. The final type worth mentioning – the multi-spectral scanners – differ in that they collect data from a very wide range of frequencies, generally from the optical through the IR regions. Hence, while they could search for some of the same indicators as the optical and thermal IR systems, they would also, like those systems, be hindered by clouds and moisture. Some satellite scanners have coverages in the order of 1000–1500km and spatial resolutions of 0.8km which means that, if precision could ever be sufficiently increased, these scanners might have some potential to search wide areas if a number of satellites work in phase.[50] Yet another scanner – that on the most recent of the LANDSAT series (LANDSAT 4) – has an even more remarkable spatial resolution (less than 100ft) but its coverage (115 miles square) would require a great many satellites to work in phase.[51]

Land-based sensors

Paradoxically, land-based sensors are among the systems with the longest ranges, yet they are also probably the least useful. Two sensors often based on land as well as on mobile platforms are signal intelligence (SIGINT) collectors and over-the-horizon backscatter (OTH-B) radars. Both can search over thousands of kilometres, but with both the specificity of location estimates decreases as distance to the target increases. In addition, if SIGINT systems are to provide a location estimate, the target must emit a detectable radio or radar signal, and the signal must be acquired by at least two separate interlinked receivers for location to be identified by cross-bearings.

OTH-B radars could certainly sense missiles after launch and might provide a basis for estimating where the submarine was when it fired. From an anti-SSBN perspective, the utility of this information ranks with that from IR satellites which detect thermal plumes. Specifically, the value of the information may depend on whether an ASW attack platform can reach the area before the submarine gets away.

OTH-B radars could conceivably detect ocean-surface effects produced by a submerged submarine, but there are very severe environmental and signal-processing limitations to doing so practically.[52] Some of these have already been identified in connection with SAR. Suffice it to say that OTH-B radars can detect targets as small as an aircraft or missile because the target's speed makes it distinguishable from background clutter. As the speed of a sensed phenomenon decreases, especially below a lower limit, it is generally the case that the phenomenon must increase in size if it is to be distinguished. The rate of movement of submarine-generated ocean-surface dynamics and their spatial area may not be adequate to allow the design in the foreseeable future of an OTH-B radar to detect them in a practical way.

Concluding observations on non-acoustic sensors

Many non-acoustic systems free ASW forces from keeping a sensor in the water and, except for optical sonars, the systems which operate farthest from the ocean surface have the greatest potential for wide-area search. To some extent, wide-area potential is also linked to the possible persistence of a signal in the submarine's wake, and, as noted earlier, picking up such a signal means knowing generally where the submarine was when it generated the signal as opposed to where it is when the signal is acquired. If non-acoustic ASW forces know in which direction the submarine is travelling, then the decision as to which way they ought to follow the track is basically easy. Without such information, they would be uncertain (at least for some time) as to which of two opposite directions they should take. Splitting up forces to go in both directions is one (costly) solution.

The most critical problem for the bulk of non-acoustic sensors is whether the phenomena which they might detect do indeed constitute reliable submarine indicators. This is the reason why numerous individuals have over many years argued that *only* acoustic systems provide a realistic basis for large-area search. Richard Garwin recently expressed that view in this way: 'Long-range detection mechanisms of strategic significance are limited to acoustic detection and readily countered'.[53] Yet it is precisely because acoustic systems can be 'readily countered' that others such as Michael MccGwire argue that 'there appears to be no intrinsic reason why, in the longer term, [satellite-based ocean-surface-phenomena detection systems] should have a lower detection rate' than fixed passive acoustic systems.[54] Nevertheless, if Garwin is correct, then there may be a reason: acoustics may provide the only reliable indicators. Time alone will tell.

Specifically on the question of countermeasures, there are already enough data available to argue that non-acoustic systems are not significantly less vulnerable than their acoustic counterparts. Simply operating the submarine deeply and slowly, for example, would probably negate most ocean-surface-effect signals. Non-acoustic systems could also be destroyed or jammed and their communications links disrupted. The earlier discussion of potential non-acoustic indicators suggests also that possible non-acoustic sensors might be just as subject to natural and enemy-produced false alarms (and to the PD/PFA problem) as are acoustic sensors. In other words, improving the technical sophistication of non-acoustic sensors could conceivably result in finding all submarines only to have to sort out the desired signals from similar ones generated by nature and a wily adversary.

ACTUAL AND POTENTIAL SENSORS: SUMMARY REMARKS

The discussions of sensors and of platforms contained expressed and sometimes implied judgements of the potential uses of various sensor and platform combinations. Table 3.1 draws these judgements together.

Not surprisingly, most sensors except those which are space-based are generally well suited to barrier-monitoring and localisation. These are the least demanding of ASW tasks. The former essentially involves waiting for the sub-

TABLE 3.1 *Estimated potential uses of actual or potential sensors**

Sensor	BAR	LOC	TRL	TRK	WAS	Remarks
Acoustic						WAS by passive systems depends on number of hydrophones deployed. Fixed passive sensors could localise to 'some tens of km' only 'under the best of circumstances' Extended trailing with small sonobuoys requires aircraft working in series.
Ship and sub-fixed sensors	X	X	X	X		
Variable depth (VD) and dipping sonars	X	X				
Small sonobuoys	X	X				
Towed array	X	X	X	X	X	
Very large sonobuoys	X	?		X	X	
Fixed passive sensors	X			X	X	
Large active sonars	X	X		X	X	
Non-acoustic						
Sensors in water						
Fixed systems (other than optical sonars)	X					
Optical sonars	X	?		X	X	
Mobile/dual-mode systems	X	X	X			TRK potential depends on persistence of observables
Short range out-of-water sensors	X	X	X	?		TRK potential based on detecting contaminants should they persist for long periods. Uncertainty as to whether contaminant sensor is sensitive enough to acquire any submarine-generated observables

continued on page 86

TABLE 3.1 continued

Sensor	BAR	LOC	TRL	TRK	WAS	Remarks
Mobile EM Sensors					⟩	Utilities specified below based on assumption that submarine is not deep
Photo (air- and space-based)					⟩	Useful for daytime cloud-free monitoring of ports and harbours only
LLLII					⟩	Night-time only. Obstructed by clouds, moisture, and any intervening light. Uncertain whether necessary balance can be achieved between coverage and spatial resolution to allow for WAS or TRK; such tasks would clearly require large number of platforms
Ship-based	X	X				
Air-based	X	X	X	X	?	
Space-based				?	?	
Blue-green lasers					⟩	Satellite system does not seem feasible for foreseeable future. Obstructed by clouds and moisture. TRK possibility related to detecting turbulent wakes, underwater thermal anomalies and contaminants and depends on persistence of those phenomena
Ship-based	X	X	X			
Air-based	X	X		X		
Forward-looking IR (FLIR) sensor on aircraft					⟩	Obstructed by clouds, moisture, and high sea state and requires part of submarine to be on surface
IRR (space-based for missile plume detection)					X	Obstructed by clouds and moisture until missile is high enough

Sensor / Platform				Comments
IRR (against thermal scar)				Obstructed by clouds and moisture. TRK by satellite and WAS possibilities depend on persistence of signals and number of search platforms. Uncertain whether space sensor can achieve required sensitivities
Ship-based	X	X		
Air-based	X	X	X	
Space-based	?	?	?	
PMR (air-based)	?	?	?	TRK possibilities depend on persistence of observables. WAS possibility also depends on numbers of sensors. Uncertain whether PMR can achieve required sensitivities. Contrast and spatial resolution problems would seem to rule out satellite-based system
Microwave radars				Radars cannot detect submerged submarines and require part of submarine to be on surface. Satellite-based altimeters are not well-suited to barrier or localisation tasks. SAR potential requires solution of data-processing and other problems (including better understanding of mechanisms by which SAR images ocean-surface phenomena)
Altimeters (air-based)	X	X		
Radar (for detecting hull or appendages) (2)				
SAR (for detecting ocean surface effects)				
Ship-based	?	?		
Air-based	?	?	?	
Space-based	?	?	?	
Multi-spectral sensor				
Space-based	?	?	?	Obstructed by clouds and rain

continued on page 88

TABLE 3.1 continued

Sensor	BAR	LOC	TRL	TRK	WAS	Remarks
Land-based sensors						
OTH-B radar					X ····>	WAS possibility relates to sensor detecting launched missile
SIGINT collectors		X			········>	Require submarine to radiate electromagnetically before signal can be acquired

*The reader should keep in mind:
(1) Any judgements on use-potential are not intended to imply that sensors are now or actually will be used in the designated way by US or Soviet ASW forces.
(2) It is assumed that the target submarine is fully submerged, and neither communicating nor radiating in any way.
(3) It is also assumed that all signals on which sensors might key are viable regardless of whether or not they have yet proven to be so.

BAR   Barrier
LOC   Localisation
TRL   Trail
TRK   Track
WAS   Wide-area search

marine to come within the sensor's field of view; the latter involves searching a relatively small area usually on cue from a wide-area sensor. Space-based devices are tied to orbits and must inexorably move forward (except in the too-distant geosynchronous orbit) and thus cannot stay over an area long enough to perform either task well. Far fewer sensors and platform combinations have been judged suitable for trailing because this task is, for the most part, restricted to instruments carried on surface ships and submarines of which there are both acoustic and non-acoustic candidates. Tracking being less demanding than trailing, it is potentially open to air- and water-borne acoustic and non-acoustic systems. To judge that satellite sensors may have a tracking potential may have been generous; any satellite system could at best probably achieve only intermittent detection and holding if a large number of platforms were massed for the purpose. As for wide-area search, the picture is one of undisputed potential for acoustic sensors but of questionable potential for their non-acoustic counterparts except for optical sonars (which rely on acoustic signals) and two sensors which can only help to find a ballistic-missile submarine rather (too) late in the game – after it has already launched some or all of its missiles.

NOTES

1. Speed, *Strategic Deterrence*, p. 158, footnote 65.
2. See for example, M. Ranken, 'Airships for Maritime Operations', *Naval Forces* no. 1 (1983) p. 86, and F. D. Buckley, 'MATASS: A Moored Airship Towed Array Sonar System', *US Naval Institute Proceedings* (March 1980) pp. 124–6.
3. Moore (ed.) *Jane's Fighting Ships 1983–84*, p. 549.
4. B. Jasani, *Outer Space – Battlefield of the Future?* (London: Taylor & Francis, 1978) p. 18.
5. See M. Settle and J. V. Taranik, 'Use of the Space Shuttle for Remote Sensing Research: Recent Results and Future Prospects', *Science* (3 December 1982) p. 995.

6. M. Abdel-Hady and A. Sadek, 'Verification Using Satellites: Feasibility of an International or Multilateral Agency', in B. Jasani (ed.) *Outer Space – A New Dimension of the Arms Race* (London: Taylor & Francis, 1982) p. 284.
7. OTA, *M-X Missile Basing*, pp. 188–9.
8. Wohl, 'Ocean Transparency' p. 28.
9. See Starkey, 'Anti-submarine Warfare Oceanography: Part II', *Military Electronics/Countermeasures* (June 1981) pp. 70–1.
10. Anderson 'Ocean Technology' p. 203.
11. Speed, *Strategic Deterrence*, p. 59.
12. See OTA, *M-X Missile Basing*, pp. 184–6 and Perry, 'Technological Prospects', p. 137.
13. Garwin 'Will Strategic Submarines be Vulnerable?' p. 57.
14. Garwin has outlined what it would take to have a foolproof system: the sowing of SSBN operating areas with short-range, direct path hydrophones in interlocked 10km grids. Blanketing an area with sensors placed so closely together ensures that submarine sounds could not escape detection because of the bending of the sound waves or their being trapped in layers or the like. The system seems impractical, however, not only because, as Garwin states, hundreds of thousands of hydrophones would be needed per area, but also because there are possible SSBN operating areas (for example, the Barents Sea or under ice) where it seems highly improbable such a system could be implanted or maintained. In addition, 'such a dispersed array of short-range sensors might be countered by the use of jammers and decoys, or by attack on the sensors or their communication nets'. Ibid, p. 66.
15. OTA, *M-X Missile Basing*, p. 186.
16. Tsipis and Forsberg, *Tactical and Strategic ASW*, p. 20.
17. See, *inter alia*, W. J. Broad, 'Strategic Lessons from an Elusive Sub', *Science* (29 October 1982) p. 450; B. E. Tossman *et al.*, 'An Underwater Towed Electromagnetic Source for Geophysical Exploration', *IEEE Journal of Oceanic Engineering* (July 1979) pp. 84–9; D. L. Thayer *et al.*, 'A Triaxial Coil Receiver System for the Study of Subsurface Electromagnetic Propagation', *IEEE Journal of Oceanic Engineering* (April 1982) pp. 75–82.
18. C. M. Davis, Jr, and R. E. Einzig, 'ASW: What Role Will Fiber Optics Play?' *Sea Technology* (November 1979) pp. 20–3.
19. See, for example, Garwin, 'Will Strategic Submarines be

Vulnerable?' p. 60, footnote 8; *RUSI and Brassey's Defence Yearbook – 1981* (Oxford: Brassey, 1980) p. 169.
20. Polvani, 'Current and Future Underwater Magnetic Sensing', pp. 442–6. Information in this paragraph is drawn from this source.
21. Podney and Sager, 'Measurement of Fluctuating Magnetic Gradients', pp. 1381–2.
22. R. H. Stewart, 'Satellite Oceanography: The Instruments', *Oceanus* (Fall 1981) p. 66.
23. Ibid.
24. See H. Hodara and W. H. Wells, 'Infra-red Radiometry and Visible Spectrometry', in AGARD, *Applications of Remote Sensing*, p. 6–2.
25. Stewart, 'Satellite Oceanography', p. 66.
26. F. P. Bretherton, 'The Climate, the Oceans, and Ocean Sensing', *Oceanus* (Fall 1981) p. 54.
27. Stewart, 'Satellite Oceanography', p. 67.
28. E. C. Barrett and L. F. Curtis, *Introduction to Environmental Remote Sensing* (London: Chapman & Hall, 1976) p. 63.
29. Honhart, 'Navy Requirements', p. 482.
30. Allen and Polmar, *The Silent Chase*, p. 17, and G. Kaplan, 'International Approaches to Peacekeeping', *Technology in War and Peace: An IEEE Spectrum Compendium* (October 1982) pp. 102–3.
31. See, *inter alia*, Wilkes, in SIPRI, *Yearbook, 1979* pp. 440–1; Speed, *Strategic Deterrence*, pp. 60–1; Barrett and Curtis, *Introduction to Environmental Remote Sensing*, p. 73; O. K. Huh and V. E. Noble, 'Remote Sensing of the Environment: Achievements and Prospects', in E. I. Salkowitz (ed.) *Science, Technology and the Modern Navy* (Arlington, Virginia: Office of Naval Research, 1976) p. 314.
32. W. Perry, Statement in *The Role of Technology in Meeting the Defense Challenge of the 1980s*, Report of a Conference Sponsored by the Arms Control and Disarmament Program, Stanford University, 6–8 August 1981, pp. 41–2.
33. G. L. Hover *et al.*, 'Evaluation of Forward-Looking Infra-red Radar (FLIR) as a Coast Guard SAR Sensor', in IEEE, *Oceans 82 Conference Record*, pp. 491–4.
34. Hodara and Wells, *Infra-Red Radiometry*, p. 6–1.
35. E. P. L. Windsor and H. McD. Mooney, 'Microwave Scanning Radiometry (Applications)', in AGARD, *Applications of Remote Sensing*, p. 5–25.
36. O. K. Huh *et al.*, 'Outbreaks of Polar Continental Air:

Windows on the Mesocale Structure of the Upper Ocean', *Naval Research Reviews*, no. 1 (1982) p. 36.
37. Kritikos and Shiue, 'Microwave Sensing from Orbit', p. 37.
38. Windsor and Mooney, 'Microwave Scanning Radiometry', p. 5–1.
39. J. R. Apel, 'Some Recent Scientific Results from the Seasat Altimeter', *Sea Technology* (October 1982) p. 24.
40. Stewart, 'Satellite Oceanography', p. 72 and W. S. Wilson, 'Oceanography from Satellites', *Oceanus* (Fall 1981) p. 13.
41. There is no simple way to describe a synthetic aperture radar (SAR). Suffice it to say that a SAR is an exception to the proposition that, all other things being equal, an increase in coverage means a decrease in spatial resolution. It overcomes the coverage/resolution trade-off by 'synthesising' or simulating a very long antenna. A real aperture radar (or RAR) is limited by the true size of its antenna (up to ten or more metres long) in the amount of attention it can direct to any spot on the earth before the satellite or aircraft moves it on to another spot. In contrast, a SAR takes advantage of the forward movement of its platform and of discernible shifts which occur to its signals (termed Doppler shifts) as it approaches, goes over, and leaves behind some Earth location. It takes multiple looks of the same spot, and by exploiting the shifts, it integrates them together to produce what is analogous to a composite picture or hologram much richer in detail than a RAR picture. From the perspective of an object on the ground imaged by a satellite SAR, the latter equates to a RAR whose antenna is several kilometres long.
42. Stewart, 'Satellite Oceanography', pp. 72–3 and Elachi, 'Radar Images', pp. 57–8.
43. Elachi, 'Radar Images', p. 59.
44. Vesecky and Stewart, 'Observation of Ocean Surface Phenomena', p. 3415.
45. Elachi, 'Radar Images', p. 59.
46. Vesecky and Stewart, 'Observation of Ocean Surface Phenomena', p. 3424–5. See also Fu and Holt, *SEASAT Views*, p. 14 and R. Goody, 'Satellites for Oceanography: The Promises and the Realities', *Oceanus* (Fall 1981) p. 5.
47. Fu and Holt, *SEASAT Views*, p. 99.
48. See C. Elachi *et al.*, 'Shuttle Imaging Radar Experiment', *Science* (December 1982) p. 1003.
49. See Beal, 'Introduction', in Beal *et al.*, *Spaceborne Synthetic Aperture Radar*, pp. 15–16 and R. L. Jordan, 'The SEASAT–A

Synthetic Aperture Radar System', *IEEE Journal of Oceanic Engineering* (April 1980) p. 161.
50. S. Tanner, *Handbook of Sensor Technical Characteristics* (US National Æronautics and Space Administration: July 1982) pp. 38–42.
51. C. Covault, 'Landsat 4 Boosts Remote Sensing Uses', *Aviation Week and Space Technology* (7 February 1983) pp. 77–8 and F. Golden, 'The Earth in Living Color', *Time* (21 February 1983) p. 60.
52. See Wilkes in **SIPRI**, *Yearbook 1979*, p. 33.
53. Garwin, 'Will Strategic Submarines be Vulnerable?' p. 66.
54. MccGwire, 'Technological and Operational Trends', p. 24.

Part II
US ASW and Soviet SSBNs

4 Soviet SSBN Forces and Operations

TRENDS IN THE NUMBER AND COMPOSITION OF THE SOVIET SSBN FLEET

The Soviet Navy or VMF (*Voyenno-Morskoy Flot*) had 62 first-line SSBNs in 1984 consisting of 24 *Yankee* (or *Y*) I and II units, 36 *Delta* (or *D*) I, II and III units, and 2 *Typhoons*, the first boats of a new series.[1] The lead ships of each class appeared in 1967, 1972, and 1980 respectively. It is unclear whether *Typhoon* is yet fully operational since the development programme of its on-board missile has been uncharacteristically slow.[2] Production of the D-III continues, but it is expected to cease soon.[3] Production of the *Typhoon* should continue at least through the decade, with 10–12 being the only estimate found of eventual class size.[4]

Table 4.1 outlines some characteristics of the submarines and their missiles. As with SSBNs in general, the VMF units tend to be very big – *Typhoon* being the largest submersible ever built. The majority carry sixteen missiles but *Typhoon* carries twenty, and the SSBNs as a group have 40 per cent of the USSR's SALT-accountable strategic-missile-launchers, 20–25 per cent of the associated throw-weight, and 15–20 per cent of the warheads.[5] There is no indication that these percentages will change significantly in the foreseeable future, though the actual number of warheads will certainly increase since one *Typhoon* alone should carry from 120 to 200 or more.

The USSR attained the SALT-I limit of 62 first-line ballistic missile submarines in the late 1970s. SSBNs are extremely expensive, and the fact that the USSR has built 62 (and

TABLE 4.1 Characteristics of Soviet SSBNs and SLBMs

A. Characteristics of Soviet SSBNs

	Yankee		Delta			Typhoon
Variant	I	II	I	II	III	
No. of SSBNs	23	1	18	4	14	2
Displacement (submerged)	9300	9300	10000	11000	11000	25000
Number of missiles carried	16	12	12	16	16	20
Type of missile	SS-N-6	SS-N-17	SS-N-8	SS-N-8	SS-N-18	SS-N-20

B. Characteristics of Soviet SLBMs

	SS-N-6			SS-N-8		SS-N-17	SS-N-18			SS-N-20
Variant (termed 'mod')	1	2	3	1	2	1	1	2	3	
Re-entry vehicles (RVs)	1	1	2	1	1	3	1	1	7	6–12
Range (NM)[1]	1300	1600	1600	4200	4900	2100	3500	4300	3500	4500
Independently-targetable?	—	—	NO	—	—	Yes	—	—	Yes	Yes
Throw-weight (lbs)	1500	—	—	1500	8000	2500	5000	—	—	—
Yield	IMT	—	200KT	IMT	800KT	MT(?)	KT(?)	450KT	200KT	—
Guidance	Inertial			Steller-Inertial				Stellar-Inertial		

[1] It should be noted that US estimates of range on Soviet missiles are somewhat 'nebulous because we are not sure how many RVs [are on the missiles] or their weight', testimony of Admiral Carter in US House Armed Services Committee, *Hearings on Military Posture*, 97th Congress, 1st Session (1981) Pt. 3, p. 149.

SOURCES IISS *Military Balance 1983–84* (London: IISS, 1983) pp. 14 and 119; US Department of Defense, *Soviet Military Power* (Washington: GPO, 1983) pp. 22–3; U. J. Schulz-Torge, 'Soviet SLBMs', *Naval Forces*, no. 3 (1983) p. 29; R. Berman and J. Baker, *Soviet Strategic Forces* (Washington: Brookings, 1982) pp. 106–7; N. Polmar, *Strategic Weapons: An Introduction* (New York: Crane Russak, 1982) pp. 118–19.

maintains that figure) suggests a strong desire for security in numbers. Moreover, in order to remain within the SALT limit, the USSR has taken older *Yankee*-class SSBNs out of ballistic missile service as newer *Delta* and *Typhoon* boats enter the inventory. Nine *Yankee*-class boats have been withdrawn from strategic service to date (and are believed to be being converted to attack or cruise-missile boats), even though each probably had at least some years of life remaining as a strategic platform. The willingness to sacrifice these (and possibly other *Yankees* in the future) may have been influenced by a desire to maximise the invulnerability of the USSR's overall sea-based missile force. Carrying only 1600 NM range missiles, *Yankees* must hazard Western ASW barriers and go out into the open oceans in order to be capable of striking targets in North America. As will be discussed further later, *Deltas* and *Typhoons* need not run the same risks. With missiles having from two-to-three times the range of those on *Yankee* boats, they are within striking distance of the same targets while remaining in protected waters near the Soviet homeland. Possibly within the next decade, no Soviet SSBN will have to venture outside home waters.

Beyond providing their submarines with longer-range missiles, the VMF may also be making them more difficult to detect acoustically. It certainly had incentive to do so from frequent American statements that Soviet submarine noise benefits US detection systems. Without singling out SSBNs, some statements have also recently emphasised, however, that Soviet submarines are generally becoming quieter.[6] Nevertheless, from a submarine versus submarine perspective, 'the rate at which we are quieting ours', says an American admiral, 'is about the same so we are keeping the same relative [submarine-*versus*-submarine acoustic] balance'.[7]

If VMF SSBNs are not as quiet as their US counterparts, it could be because the Soviet Union has not fully mastered the necessary technologies to make them so, but there are some who would dispute this contention. For instance, Polmar argued in 1981 that the Soviet Union 'could make their boats quieter' if it wished.[8] If technological sophistication is not the reason, it could be that the relevant decision-makers did not believe extensive silencing was worth the heavy costs in money and time involved. It took only a decade to build a fleet of sixty-two modern SSBNs. It would almost certainly have taken much longer had the boats been extensively silenced. It also would have cost more; the SSBNs built during those years may have taken up to one-half of the Navy's construction budget as it was.[9] In short, while making submarines quieter is paramount to the Americans – who are willing to pay the costs in time and money of doing so and settle for smaller numbers – it may be only one of several important considerations to the Soviet Union. A higher noise level than is found on US boats could seem acceptable, furthermore, if the Soviet Navy intends to: operate its SSBNs where the US has no long-range acoustic detection systems; spoof, jam, destroy or otherwise negate acoustic systems in areas where the submarines must operate; assign general-purpose forces to protect SSBNs against attack; and compensate for the loss of some SSBNs by maintaining a large inventory of them. Building to sixty-two is probably relevant to this last consideration, and, as we shall see later, Soviet determination to act against enemy ASW forces and to keep its SSBNs in defended bastions close to home are relevant to the first three.

Before turning to these issues, two other submarine-design factors should be mentioned. One is that, according to numerous sources, Soviet submarines are coated with a rubber-like 'anechoic' material which absorbs the signals generated by enemy ship or torpedo-guidance sonars.[10] A 'covering of this sort' said one Soviet writer 'reduced a submarine's detection range by sonar substantially . . . .'[11] A second factor concerns the Soviet practice, as described in their writings, of building double-hulled submarines. 'The two submarine hulls – pressure and outer – are designed' says a Russian author 'to withstand high external water pressures at great depths and ensure high sea-going qualities.'[12] According to the editor of *Jane's Fighting Ships*, the water cushion between the inner and outer hulls on *Typhoon* is so 'very wide' that it 'presents a major ASW problem: resistance to torpedo hits'.[13] As a result, these submarines will 'probably [be] less vulnerable than most and . . . require very sophisticated weapons to deal with them, weapons that . . . seek out weak spots such as propellors, hydroplanes, and keels'.

THE PRIMACY OF SSBN AND SSBN-SUPPORT MISSIONS

Former Defence Minister, Marshal A. A. Grechko, declared in 1975 that 'during the last few years a greater importance has been placed on the submarine missile fleet'.[14] He gave as the primary reason the fleet's 'greater survivability' when compared with land-based nuclear delivery systems and aircraft. His emphasis on survivability is consistent with the view of nearly all Western analysts that, while some Soviet SLBMs may be used in initial (retaliatory) strikes, a large proportion and probably the bulk would be held back as an 'important component of the national strategic reserve'.[15] There is uncertainty in the West as to when and against what targets SLBMs would be used,[16] but, as MccGwire advises, it seems valid to 'assume that [Soviet] operational plans provide for the greatest flexibility in the use or withholding of these systems, as best to influence the progress and outcome of the conflict'.[17]

It is precisely because SSBNs can influence the progress and the outcome of a war that the Soviet leaders view them as the capital ships of their Navy, and consider their tasks and those of related support forces as of 'paramount importance . . . governing the technical policy of building a fleet and the development of naval art'.[18] In other words, the Navy's primary mission is to ensure that SSBNs are available and ready to do the bidding of the strategic leadership. Thus, SSBN survivability is also paramount and too important to be left to the SSBNs alone. General-purpose forces are very heavily committed to supporting the Soviet SSBNs, and the newest and best of those forces will be 'extensive[ly] use[d]' in that task.[19] According to the US Director of Naval Intelligence, these will include the *Kiev* aircraft carriers, the *Kirov* battle cruisers, the most modern destroyers, and the

Alfa and *Victor* III submarines.[20] The Director also stated that a major task for *Victor* submarines in general (Types I and II as well as III) is 'operating in conjunction with [SSBNs], trying to assure that we are not trailing'.[21] Secretary Weinberger has described the Soviet concept of operations as calling 'for Soviet anti-submarine forces to be concentrated in home waters in support of newer classes of Soviet ballistic missile submarines'.[22] He contrasted the Soviet concept with that of the US, which calls for 'our anti-submarine forces to be spread worldwide, protecting vital sea lanes and naval surface ships'.

Soviet writings clearly state that active measures are to be undertaken in war to counter enemy ASW systems and forces. Germany's failure to do so in the Second World War, writes Admiral Gorshkov, is the reason that 70 per cent of its submarines were lost on the way to areas of combat operations.[23] Even with the 'constant improvement' of ASW means since that time, he says, 'much research' shows that submarines can achieve 'strategic goals' during a war 'when rightly used and given proper combat backing'.[24]

SSBN AND SSBN-SUPPORT OPERATIONS

VMF SSBNs operate from bases in the Kola Peninsula/ White Sea area in north-west Russia and from Vladivostok and Petropavlosk-Kamchatkiy in the Far East. It seems to be generally accepted that only about 15 to 25 per cent or ten-to-fifteen submarines of the first-line fleet deploy beyond immediate home port waters in peace-time.[25] This is roughly consistent with the percentage of Soviet general-purpose forces on forward deployment and with the strong Soviet bent for husbanding military resources.[26] In addition, 60 per cent of the first-line units can strike most US targets without having to leave port and are effectively on patrol as soon as they are underway. The Soviet policy of deploying only a small portion of the SSBNs at sea in peace-time suggests confidence in being able to move the remaining deployable units to sea prior to any attack on them in their bases.[27]

According to the US Director of Naval Intelligence, SSBNs have 'surged', that is, moved rapidly from their bases, during exercises.[28]

Yankee units still patrol in the north-west Atlantic and the north-east Pacific Oceans so as to be ready to launch strikes against the continental USA. The combined two-ocean patrol area equates to roughly 3 million sq. NM of water if the submarines are to remain within missile range of their targets.[29] The area for *Delta* and *Typhoon* would be 30 million sq. NM, or more, and would include all waters of the northern hemisphere as well as parts of the South Atlantic and South Pacific Oceans.[30] It does not seem, however, to be Soviet intent regularly to send their modern long-range missile submarines out to such distances. Rather, the policy is generally to keep them in sanctuary behind a defended maritime perimeter encompassing all or parts of the Greenland and Norwegian Seas on one side of the USSR, the Seas of Japan and Okhotsk and parts of the north-west Pacific on the other, and the various Arctic seas to the North.[31] *Yankee* submarines retained for use against the Eurasian land-mass would also find sanctuary in those waters.

The bulk of Soviet naval forces – including the most modern – would operate in these areas supported by elements from other services.[32] Their use would be consistent with the recently increased attention given to the concept 'sea control' (or 'command of the sea') in Soviet literature. The concept has been specifically linked to a need to provide support to strategic submarines. Admiral Gorshkov has written:

> It is particularly important to note that submarines have become the main branch of the forces of fleets. A major role is also played by the new strategic orientation of the fleets for struggle against the shore. All this is making more necessary the all-around backing of the actions of the forces solving strategic tasks. Therefore the struggle to create in a particular area of a theatre and in a particular time, favourable conditions for successfully solving by a large grouping of forces of the fleet, the main tasks facing it and at the same time creating conditions such as would

make it more difficult for the enemy to fulfil his task and prevent him from frustrating the actions of the opposing side will apparently be widely adopted.[33]

As noted earlier, it is generally accepted that the Soviet Navy's primary general-purpose mission is ensuring that SSBNs are available and ready to do the bidding of the Soviet leadership.

In short, if American forces sought out the SSBNs in sanctuary, they would enter an area where Soviet naval forces would be most concentrated. It is also an area whose marine geography favours the defender rather than the attacker. Western observers have traditionally viewed geography as constraining the development and long-distance use of the Czarist and Soviet navies.[34] They have noted, among other things, that much of Russia's home waters are ice-laden and that choke points restrict free maritime access to the open seas. Yet these same factors can be put to advantage to keep enemy forces away from SSBNs in their sanctuaries.

A barrier-line intersecting Greenland, Iceland and the United Kingdom (termed the G–I–UK Gap) and running on through the North Sea could restrict Western access into the Norwegian and Greenland Seas just as much as it would constrain Soviet egress. Entry into Arctic seas from the north-west is across a curved line taking in North Greenland, Spitzbergen, Bear Island and North Cape. In the east there is the Bering Strait, and over the North Pole on the North American side of the Arctic are various straits and channels separating Greenland, Ellesmere Island and the Queen Elizabeth Islands. In the Far East open-water passage to the enclosed seas of Japan and Okhotsk is via straits flanking the Japanese home islands (Tsushima, Korea, Tsugaru and Soya) or the narrows linking the Russian-controlled Kurile Island chain. Particularly because of proximity to the Soviet homeland, the USSR should be able to control or mine all these choke points except possibly the G–I–UK–North Sea line and the Arctic entries on the North American side. As for the former, the VMF may settle for a more northerly barrier, somewhat closer to homeland air cover although the evidence of recent naval exercises suggests that they are pushing southwards. It is difficult to say how well the straits above Canada could be controlled. Ice would make passage through them hazardous, suitable only for submarines and then only in areas deep enough for their operations.[35] Soviet attack submarines or mines might attempt to intercept incoming enemy submarines.

Seizing Spitzbergen (Svalbard) would greatly facilitate the maintenance of a barrier-line running from North Greenland down to North Cape. The island is under Norwegian sovereignty but, in accordance with the Treaty of Sèvres, it is demilitarised and the Soviet Union has formal commercial access rights. It has exercised them to establish a larger presence on the island than that maintained by Norway (2500 as against 1200 people).[36]

In wartime the USSR might also attempt to seize parts of Norway itself and parts of other countries too, most noticeably Japan, which sit athwart or inside the waters encompassed by the maritime perimeter. The costs of such activity would probably be high, so the USSR would undoubtedly prefer that both states leave the Western alliance structure 'voluntarily' after appropriate urging. Specifically, should the USSR see war to be (nearly) inevitable, the incentive to exert strong leverage against them during a pre-war crisis might become irresistible. The past need not be prologue, but prior to the Great Patriotic War, both Finland and the Baltic states fell victim to Soviet determination to improve its military position *vis-à-vis* Germany. Simply to have Norway or Japan become neutral would greatly improve the USSR's ability to defend the maritime perimeter, for Western intelligence-gathering and ASW force deployment would be severely hampered if neither state were available either to add their own assets or provide bases for the Western Allies. The USSR's position would be better yet if it were also able to use either country's bases or intelligence resources.

Beyond contending with Soviet naval forces concentrated within the maritime defence zone, US ASW units will also have to deal with ice. It is another factor serving Russian naval interests today after being traditionally regarded as detrimental to them in the past. Significant portions of waters close to the Soviet Union are ice-covered for much of the year and the central Arctic is so covered all the year round. In the words of the US Chief of Naval Operations (CNO), the Soviet Union exhibits a 'strong interest' in hiding their ballistic missile submarines under ice.[37] This interest is long-standing. For example, in 1961, Defence Minister Marshal Malinovsky made a point of saying: 'our rocket-carrying submarines have learned to operate well under the ice of the Arctic and accurately to take up positions for launching rockets, which is important for reliably hitting targets'.[38] Submarines operated in this way either would not be used against time-urgent targets (which they need not be if their tasks were deterrence and counter-value retaliation) or would have to remain either near leads and *polynyas* (holes in the ice which can be found even in winter) or near skylights (ice thin enough for a submarine to break through). There have been suggestions that the *Typhoon*-class boats are strengthened to enable them to do this. The distribution of holes and thin ice is random, but 'they seem to appear with sufficient frequency to satisfy the operational needs of nuclear submarines'.[39] A submarine might also choose to remain on the edge of the pack ice, termed the marginal sea-ice zone, from where it could move out to open water to fire.

A submarine under ice must navigate with great caution, but for an SSBN with no time-urgent targets, it can be an excellent patrol area.[40] A Soviet author, Admiral Rodionov, summarised some of the advantages of operating there very well:

> It is considered that nuclear-powered missile submarines can constitute a constant threat of a nuclear missile strike . . . from the regions of the Arctic while being covered by the ice against the anti-submarine forces of an enemy. While remaining in the assigned region, the missile-armed submarine can maneuver freely in the deep,

which enables it to receive radio transmissions from the command and to take up the initial position at the right moment, to make the necessary calculations, and to carry out missile launchings at the assigned targets.[41]

Very-low-frequency radio does indeed provide 'good possibilities for reaching submarines . . . beneath the polar ice pack, not only with ordinary messages but with navigational signals as well'.[42] Possibly most important of all, however, is Rodionov's point about ice providing cover against the anti-submarine forces of an enemy. When under ice a submarine is protected from missile barrage and probably from any overhead sensor except aircraft with magnetic detectors, but even the latter may have difficulty because of the vagaries caused by the North Magnetic Pole.[43] The only mobile ASW platform useful for operating in ice-covered waters would be another submarine, but the capability for large-area search by any one submarine (even with a towed array) would seem to be limited.

Acoustic conditions in the Arctic are very unlike those of large open seas such as the Atlantic, Pacific or Mediterranean. On the one hand ambient noise is lower under the permanent ice during periods of rising temperature but higher during periods of falling temperature and in areas of non-continuous ice-coverage.[44] The latter areas, especially the marginal sea-ice zone, can be extremely noisy as a result of waves slapping up against the ice, and sections of ice breaking off and rubbing against one another. The noises can have very long-range effects. This is because the ice canopy and a nearly isothermal temperature gradient cause the formation of a 'surface-bounded waveguide' akin to the SOFAR Sound Channel of the open ocean except that its 'axis is not "deep"; it is at the surface'.[45] As a result, some sounds travel great distances because the temperature gradient forces them up to the ice canopy, against which they are repeatedly reflected.

Most of the sounds produced by a submarine, however, might not generally travel great distances, since most submarine-generated noise occurs at frequencies where the intensity of sound degrades rapidly in Arctic waters. Tsipis notes that 'the entire composite spectrum' of submarine-generated noise is 'confined to a frequency range between 10 and 1000 Hertz or so'.[46] The frequency range he identifies is significant because:

> the transmission [of sound] in the Arctic degrades rapidly with increasing frequency above 20Hz. It is better than it would be in the [ice] free field (i.e. with spreading) out to some range, and is poorer beyond. This peculiarity is the result of opposing influences on the propagation. At short and moderate ranges, ducting [because of the ice cover] improves the transmission; at long ranges the repeated encounters with the under-ice surface degrade it.[47]

In short, nearly the entire spectrum of submarine-generated sound is in the frequency range where intensity falls off rapidly under northern ice.[48]

Accounting for most of the degradation of under-ice sound is the presence of numerous ice ridges with keels – some quite deep – extending downward from the ice canopy. Their orientation and spacing is 'generally random' with 100m being a 'representative spacing'.[49] They are important not only because they absorb sound and lessen its energy, but also because, if a ridge is large enough, it provides a submarine with a nearly perfect place to hide. A submarine could remain 'well hidden' by lying quietly against an undersea keel since noise generated by the submarine would tend to be refracted upward and not downward where an enemy SSN would be.[50] Also should an enemy SSN utilise sonar to search actively, the echo would reverberate against the surface and any coherent return would probably not distinguish the submarine from the ice keel.

It may also be relevant that the Russians have operated in and explored the Arctic and related areas for centuries. More than any other navy, theirs is experienced in polar operations. In addition there is a very extensive national programme (including the use of satellites) for monitoring ice conditions in waters close to the USSR. The programme supports not only naval forces, but also fishing and merchant ships, including those using the Northern Sea Route in the summer months.[51]

If *Yankee* SSBNs are to be used against North American targets in war (as opposed to being employed only against theatre targets in Eurasia) they will have to deploy to far Atlantic and Pacific waters. Those not deploying to those waters in a pre-war period might well wait to do so until after Western ASW assets had been reduced by Soviet action.

Attrition of Western ASW forces would benefit Soviet submarines on both sides of the maritime perimeter, and Soviet literature makes clear that 'disorganising [US] ASW surveillance' includes 'destroying surveillance facilities'.[52] A variety of conventional and unconventional means could be employed to that end, including bottom-crawlers and mini-submarines of the kind already used in Swedish territorial waters.[53] The Soviet Navy controls significant numbers of *spetsnaz* (special forces) whose missions are presumed to include sabotage once ashore. The targets would undoubtedly include fixed detection devices, any cables interlinking them to each other and to shore processing stations, mobile surveillance platforms such as vessels towing acoustic arrays, and associated processing and communications sites on land.[54] The Soviet intent is to spoof or jam any detection and related communication systems which do survive. Spoofing of detection systems will include 'setting out dummy targets and submarine simulators' and utilisation of 'sophisticated electronic countermeasures . . . to divert search forces in false directions'.[55] Jamming could include putting great volumes of noise into the water (including under-water explosions if necessary) to swamp or cripple acoustic receivers.

It is also expected that individual SSBNs will operate so as to minimise their signatures. In 1982 the US Navy's Assistant Secretary for Research, Engineering and Systems credited Soviet submarines with 'improvements in operational quieting'.[56] Such noise reduction is very much a function of crew proficiency, and one year later the Commander, US Atlantic Fleet, gave a possible reason for the improvements when he stated that 'noisy Soviet submarines with inexperienced crews are a thing of the past'.[57] Furthermore, Soviet literature notes how increased SLBM ranges allow SSBNs 'to manœuvre strategically and to select their operating areas so as to take advantage of the location of enemy forces, weather conditions and the level of biological noises and other phenomena which make their detection difficult'.[58] Among 'other phenomena' are the 'hydrological peculiarities of the oceans and seas, as well as their seasonal changes'. Referring to 'information in the American press', a Soviet writer states that these peculiarities can cause 'the probability of detection . . . by hydro-acoustic means to vary from 20 to 80 per cent'.[59] One of the major functions of the USSR's oceanographic establishment (collectively the world's largest) is to provide the Navy with hydrological data by which decisions on operating areas could be made.[60] It is said that it and the fishing fleet also play 'an inestimable, central role in efforts to monitor and penetrate [US fixed acoustic detection] systems'.[61] The linking of oceanographic data to information about possible locations of US systems could be invaluable for selecting where and how an SSBN should operate so as to avoid detection.

NOTES

1. See US Defense Department, *Soviet Military Power 1984* (Washington: GPO, 1984) pp. 24–6; J. L. Couhat and A. B. Baker, III (eds.) *Combat Fleets of the World 1984/85* (Annapolis, Maryland: Naval Institute Press, 1984) p. 671; and Moore, *Jane's Fighting Ships 1983–84*, pp. 486–9. In addition to the 62 first-line submarines, the USSR has 19 other older and far less capable ballistic missile submarines of the Golf (G) and Hotel (H) classes. All carry only three missiles each in contrast to the 12–20 carried on first-line boats. The Golfs are diesel-powered, and Hotels nuclear.
2. Contrast Couhat and Baker, *Combat Fleets*, p. 695, with J. Lehman, 'Statement by the Secretary of the Navy', in US House Appropriations Committee, *Department of Defense Appropriations for 1984*, 98th Congress, 1st Session (1983) Pt 2, p. 386.
3. US Defense Department, *Soviet Military Power* (Washington: GPO, 1984) p. 22.

4. Testimony of Rear Admiral A. E. Burkhalter, Jr, in US Senate Armed Services Committee, *Strategic Force Modernization Programs*, 97th Congress, 1st Session (1981) p. 18.
5. See, *inter alia*, J. Luns, 'Political–Military Implications of Soviet Naval Expansion', *NATO Review* (February 1982) p. 2; *Fiscal Year 1982 Arms Control Impact Statements*, 97th Congress, 1st Session, Joint Committee Print (1981) p. 109; and Brown, *Department of Defense Annual Report, 1981*, p. 89.
6. See, *inter alia*, Testimony of Admiral H. Train in US House Armed Services Committee, *Hearings on Military Posture and HR 6495*, 96th Congress, 2nd Session (1981) Pt 4, p. 775–6 and Testimony of Navy Secretary J. Lehman, in US House Appropriations Committee, *Department of Defense Appropriations for 1982*, 97th Congress, 1st Session (1981) Pt 1, p. 753. Cf. Captain 2nd rank A. Proshin and Captain 3rd rank G. Shatayev, 'Basic Trends in the Struggle to Reduce the Noise Level of Submarines', *Morskoy Sbornik*, no. 7 (1977) pp. 78–9.
7. Testimony of Vice Admiral S. R. Foley, in US Senate Armed Service Committee, *Department of Defense Authorization for FY 1982*, 97th Congress, 1st Session (1981) Pt 4, p. 1673.
8. N. Polmar, 'Soviet Nuclear Submarines', *US Naval Institute Proceedings* (July 1981) p. 37. See also P. Nitze *et al.*, *Securing the Seas* (Boulder, Colorado: Westview, 1979) p. 393, and A. Horelick, *The Strategic Mind-Set of the Soviet Military: An Essay-Review* (Santa Monica, California: Rand, 1977) p. 8.
9. The estimate was derived as follows: according to the CIA, 'Between 1967 and 1977, approximately two-thirds of naval ship procurement spending was for ballistic missile and attack submarines'. During that time, approximately half of the submarines produced were ballistic missile units. If one assumed that all submarines, regardless of type, cost the same, then the SSBNs alone would account for about 38 per cent of the construction budget. SSBNs however, are much larger than attack submarines (with about 80 per cent greater displacement *vis-à-vis* nuclear attack submarines and 200 per cent *vis-à-vis* diesel–electric boats). In view of the size consideration, it seems possible that the budget percentage might have been as much as one-half. See CIA, *Estimated Soviet Defense Spending: Trends and Prospects*, SR 78-10121 (June 1978) p. 6.
10. See, *inter alia*, Polmar, 'Soviet Nuclear Submarines', p. 120.
11. Captain 1st rank M. Mikhed'ko, 'Electronic Warfare and the Submarine', *Morskoy Sbornik*, no. 1 (1976) p. 91.

12. Captain 1st rank B. Makayev, 'Design and Equipment of Submarines', *Soviet Military Review* (July 1983) p. 37. See also Testimony of Admiral T. Hayward, in US House Appropriations Committee, *Department of Defense Appropriations for FY 82*, 97th Congress, 1st Session (1981) Pt 1, pp. 749 and 770.
13. J. Moore (ed.) *Jane's Fighting Ships, 1981–82* (London: Jane's Publishing Company, 1981) p. 131.
14. A. A. Grechko, *Armed Forces of the Soviet State* (translated and published under the auspices of the US Air Force; Washington: GPO, n.d.) p. 153.
15. M. MccGwire, 'Naval Power and Soviet Global Strategy', *International Security* (Spring 1979) p. 166.
16. See, for example, J. M. McConnell, *Possible Counterforce Role for the Typhoon* (Arlington, Virginia: Center for Naval Analyses, 1982); R. T. Ackley, 'The Wartime Role of Soviet SSBNs', *US Naval Institute Proceedings* (June 1978) pp. 34–42; and C. H. Clawson, 'The Wartime Role of Soviet SSBNs – Part Two', *US Naval Institute Proceedings* (March 1980) pp. 64–71.
17. MccGwire, 'Naval Power and Soviet Global Strategy', p. 166.
18. Admiral S. Gorshkov *The Sea Power of the State* (Oxford: Pergamon 1979) p. 221.
19. Rear Admiral S. Shapiro, US Navy, Director of Naval Intelligence, Statement before the Subcommittee in Seapower and Force Projection of the Senate Armed Services Committee (4 March 1981) pp. 14–15.
20. Ibid.
21. Testimony of Rear Admiral S. Shapiro, in US Senate Armed Services Committee, *Department of Defense Authorization for Appropriations for FY 1979*, 95th Congress, 2nd Session (1978) Pt 9, pp. 6664–5.
22. C. Weinberger, *FY 83 Annual Report of Secretary of Defense Caspar Weinberger* (Washington: GPO, 1982) pp. II-13–14.
23. Gorshkov, *The Sea Power of the State*, p. 121.
24. Ibid, p. 190.
25. See, *inter alia*, I. Bellany, 'Sea Power and the Soviet Submarine Forces', *Survival* (January/February 1982) p. 5; The American Broadcasting Corporation, Nightline: The Crisis Game (TV programme on 24 November 1983); General G. S. Brown, Chairman, US Joint Chiefs of Staff, 'Posture Statement', in US Senate Appropriations Committee, *Department of Defense Appropriations for FY 1979*, 95th Congress, 2nd

Session (1978), Pt 1, pp. 314–344; and H. Brown, *Department of Defense Annual Report Fiscal Year 1980* (Washington: GPO, 1979) p. 73.
26. See for example, Moore, *Jane's Fighting Ships 1983–84*, p. 486.
27. See, *inter alia*, M. MccGwire, 'Maritime Strategy and the Superpowers', in IISS, *Power at Sea–Part II: Superpowers and Navies*, Adelphi Paper no. 123 (London: IISS, 1976) p. 23 and R. Berman and J. Baker, *Soviet Strategic Forces* (Washington: Brookings, 1982) pp. 36–7.
28. Testimony of Rear Admiral D. Harvey, in US Senate Armed Services Committee, *FY 78 Authorization for Military Procurement*, 95th Congress, 1st Session (1977) Pt 10, p. 6665. See also, Bellany, 'Sea Power and Soviet Submarine Forces', p. 5.
29. The area estimate reflects the fact that the on-board missiles have a range of about 1600 NM (See Table 4.1). According to the US Congress's Office of Technology Assessment, a submarine patrolling roughly 1500 NM from either US coast would have a patrol area of about 3 million sq. NM. See OTA, *M-X Missile Basing*, p. 180.
30. This writer plotted on a globe the areas encompassed by 5000 NM arcs around Washington, DC, and San Francisco, California, and calculated that the areas encompassed 52 million sq. NM of open water. According to Besnault, about 20 per cent of the world oceans are too shallow for SSBN operations. If one accepted that another 20 per cent are unsuitable because of basing, shipping lanes or other reasons, then the total area available for *Delta* and *Typhoon* to strike at both cities would be about 30 million square NM. Besnault, *Genèse, Vie et Survie*, p. 124.
31. See, *inter alia*, the statements of the US CNO in E. Ulsamer, 'Bobbing, Weaving, and Fighting Smart', *Air Force Magazine* (August 1983) pp. 88–94; Statement of Rear Admiral J. L. Butts, USN, Director of Naval Intelligence, before the Senate Armed Services Committee (14 March 1983) p. 16; and Weinberger, *FY 83 Annual Report*, pp. II-13 to -14.
32. See citations in notes 19, 20, 21 and 22 above.
33. Gorshkov, *The Sea Power of the State*, p. 233.
34. See for example, C. Smith, 'Constraints of Naval Geography on Soviet Naval Forces', *US Naval War College Review* (September/October 1974).
35. See G. Synhorst, 'Soviet Strategic Interest in the Maritime Arctic', *US Naval Institute Proceedings* (May 1973) pp. 90–111.

36. See P. Wall, 'The Svalbard Challenge', *Sea Power* (September 1982) pp. 20–30.
37. As quoted in 'Admiral Urges US to Counter Under-Ice Subs', *International Herald Tribune* (20 May 1983) p. 3.
38. Marshal R. Malinovsky, Report to the 22nd Party Congress, 1961, as found in *Survival* (January/February 1962) p. 31. See also *Survival* (March/April 1962) p. 89.
39. W. Ostreng, 'The Strategic Balance and the Arctic Ocean', *Co-operation & Conflict* no. 1 (1977) p. 44. See his data, pp. 44–6. See also E. P. Stafford, *The Far and Deep* (New York: GP Putnam's Sons, 1966) p. 323.
40. Stafford, *The Far and Deep*, Chapter 8, and Captain A. S. McLaren, 'Under Ice in Submarines', *US Naval Institute Proceedings* (July 1981) pp. 105–9.
41. As quoted in R. Herrick *et al.*, *Soviet Perceptions of US Antisubmarine Warfare Capabilities* (Unpublished study: 1980) p. III-261.
42. R. Thoren, *Picture Atlas of the Arctic* (Amsterdam: Elsevier, 1969) p. 5.
43. L. Griswold, 'The Cold Front: USSR Has Strategic Advantage Above the Arctic Circle', *Sea Power* (December 1972) p. 19.
44. R. J. Urick, *Sound Propagation in the Sea* (Washington: DARPA, 1979) pp. 6–19.
45. N. Untersteiner *et al.*, 'Arctic Science: Current Knowledge and Future Thrusts', in Salkowitz, *Science, Technology and the Modern Navy*, p. 289. See also O. Diachok, 'Arctic Hydroacoustics', *Cold Regions Science and Technology*, no. 2 (1980) p. 186.
46. Tsipis, 'Underwater Acoustic Detection', p. 182.
47. Urick, *Principles of Underwater Sound* (New York: McGraw-Hill, 1975) p. 158.
48. See also McLaren, 'Under Ice in Submarines', p. 109, where he speaks of 'significantly reduced under-ice sonar ranges'.
49. O. I. Diachok, 'Effects of Sea Ice Ridges on Sound Propagation in the Arctic Ocean', in SACLANT ASW Research Center, *Oceanic Acoustic Modelling*, Proceedings of a Conference held at SACLANTCEN, La Spezia, Italy, 8–11 September 1975, p. 9-3.
50. Allen and Polmar, 'The Silent Chase', p. 13.
51. K. Gatland, 'Satellites Guide Soviet Ships', *Christian Science Monitor* (27 July 1978) p. 6.
52. Mikhed'ko, 'Electronic Warfare', p. 94.

53. See C. Bildt, 'Sweden and the Soviet Submarines', *Survival* (July/August 1983) pp. 169–70.
54. See Mikhed'ko, 'Electronic Warfare'; Rodionov. *Anti-submarine Forces* section 3.3. See also references to statement by former US CNO, Admiral J. Holloway, in G. C. Wilson, 'Navy Seeks $191 million to Fix Warning System', *Washington Post* (16 June 1978) p. A26 and 'Trawlers are Ripping up Navy's Secret Undersea Spy System', *San Francisco Chronicle* (16 June 1978) p. 21.
55. Mikhed'ko, 'Electronic Warfare', pp. 90 and 94.
56. Statement of M. R. Paisley, Assistant Secretary of the Navy (Research, Engineering, and Systems) before the House Armed Services Committee, Sub-committee on Research and Development on FY 83 Research, Development, Test, and Evaluation, Navy (17 March 1982) p. 15.
57. Statement of Admiral W. S. McDonald, USN, Commander in Chief, Atlantic, before the House Armed Services Committee on the Status of the Atlantic Command (10 March 1983) p. 19.
58. I. Kuz'min, 'Reconnaissance of Nuclear Ballistic Missile Submarines', *Morskoy Sbornik*, no. 5 (1979) p. 66.
59. Ibid p. 67.
60. C. Jacobsen, 'The "Civilian" Fleets: Notes on Military–Civilian Integration in the USSR', in J. Hardt (ed.) *Soviet Oceans Development* (Washington: GPO, 1976) pp. 276–9.
61. Ibid, p. 276.

5 US ASW Developments

BACKGROUND

Anti-submarine warfare (ASW) has had a high priority in the United States since the Second World War. The onset of the Cold War and the USSR's ambitious post-war submarine building programme – which gave it about 450–550 submarines in the mid-1950s – reinforced Western fears of another Battle of the Atlantic. The appearance of Soviet ballistic and cruise missile submarines in the late 1950s only reinforced the conviction in the West that ASW was important. When the Kennedy Administration, including Secretary of Defense Robert MacNamara, emphasised a new nuclear strategy based on counterforce, damage-limitation, and civil defence, it listed anti-SSBN warfare alongside BMEWS (Ballistic Missile Early Warning System) and anti-ballistic missiles (ABM) as important initiatives for protecting the US against ballistic missile attack.

With the subsequent MacNamara-led shift to a countervalue, assured second strike deterrent posture, references to anti-SSBN warfare generally were dropped, and since the mid-1960s policy-makers have usually referred to ASW in the context of traditional sea control and power projection missions.[1] The implication of their formulations was that the United States did not have an anti-SSBN policy *per se*, and unofficial spokesmen have stated, sometimes in a critical vein, that this was indeed so.[2]

Department of Defense (DoD) and Navy spokesmen, however, have for over two decades included enemy ballistic missile submarines as part of the threat justifying ASW research, development, and acquisition. Moreover, the American Chief of Naval Operations (CNO), Admiral James

Watkins, announced to the press in 1983 that US ASW submarines had begun training to hunt out any Soviet SSBNs seeking wartime sanctuary under the Arctic ice, but he refused to discuss what priority might be assigned to the anti-SSBN task: 'All I'm saying' he said, 'is that if there are forces up in that area of the world, we'd better know how to fight them'.[3]

Watkins' position is consistent with that of his immediate predecessor, Admiral Thomas Hayward, when the latter declared, without reference to SSBNs *per se*, that there would be 'no sanctuaries' accorded to any Soviet naval forces in a war.[4] It is also consistent with the long-held US naval view that the best way to protect Western maritime assets and sea-lanes is to put the Soviet Navy on the defensive: in other words, to seek out its forces not only on the high seas or as they pass through choke-points, but also at the source, that is, in Soviet home waters. The Commander-in-Chief, US Atlantic Fleet, put it this way in 1983:

> The majority of Soviet forces must be contained. This can be accomplished by offensive actions that keep the Soviet Navy focussed on the threats to their own forces in the Norwegian and Barents Seas. If offensive operations are allowed to shift into the North Atlantic, many more [US] forces may be required to defeat the threat – or the time to accomplish our tasks will be excessive.[5]

In short, it is unclear whether the United States officially has a specific anti-SSBN policy, but there is no ambiguity in official naval statements about putting the VMF on the defensive in war or preparing the US Navy to engage enemy SSBNs under ice if so ordered.

THE US EFFORT IN LONG-RANGE PASSIVE ACOUSTIC DETECTION

The former Principal Deputy Assistant Secretary of the Navy for Research, Engineering, and Systems, Mr Gerald Cann, stated in 1981 that America's path in ASW 'was set in

1967–8 and we've followed it since'.[6] He and other officials make it clear that 'acoustics has and will continue to be the nucleus of our ASW capability' with passive acoustics being primary.[7] US efforts have concentrated on advancing the technology incorporated in passive hydrophone arrays, signal-processing, acoustic modelling, overall integration of data, and on developing and deploying an area-search passive acoustic system.

Advancing the technology

Recent array technology improvements have included development of large aperture arrays with narrow reception beams or windows so as to isolate better the sources and direction of sounds. Line arrays are now also thinner, lighter, stronger and less expensive than before, thereby allowing them to be readily towed from moving platforms. Arrays can also now apply switching techniques, as in phased array radars, so as to eliminate the need to shift physically the directional orientation of an array.[8] US research and development (R&D) officials gave much prominence in 1980 to the Defense Research Projects Agency's (DARPA) success in demonstrating that 'continuous tracking of a simulated quiet submarine' could be done by a suspended line array of proper length, shape and electronic configuration.[9]

Stated to be more significant than array improvements are developments in signal-processing which apply advances in computer hardware (such as high-speed integrated circuits) and software. These advances allow the finding and amplification of submarine signals. One US Navy admiral has noted:

> If you have a speck of light, you can integrate that piece of light over and over again, compared to the background and make it blossom out . . . We are doing the same thing acoustically, that is, locating some discrete bit of noise at a certain frequency, integrating that compared to the background noise, and then suddenly it becomes a very discernible piece of noise.[10]

Signal-processing advances also allow large quantities of data to be dealt with in short periods, and this factor is important to ocean acoustic modelling efforts, which aim to increase understanding and prediction of ocean acoustic conditions. The keys to that goal are the acquisition and processing of large amounts of data and the development and application of numerical models of ocean acoustics. According to the Oceanographer of the US Navy:

> A massive processor of . . . enormous quantities of data would be able to predict . . . the weather and ocean acoustical conditions into the next hours, days, and weeks. In the absence of such ideals the Navy works with fewer observations and a powerful computer . . . to refine existing models of the atmosphere and the ocean and to use them daily in forecasting weather and acoustic conditions with increasing accuracy and service to the operating Fleet.[11]

DARPA has conducted experimental work at the Acoustic Research Center at Moffett Field, California, aimed at validating the simultaneous ('real time') integration of environmental and other data with the acoustic data drawn from wide-area search systems. DARPA's programme included a 'real-time search demonstration' of a 750 000 square mile area in 1980 and an area of 1 million square miles in 1981.[12] Sixty-four interconnected computers – termed ILIAC 4 and viewed as the world's largest computer system – assimilated the data, including information on the location of surface ships detected by electromagnetic as well as acoustic sensors. Uncertainties as to whether an acoustic signal comes from a surface ship or from a submarine were resolved, thereby allowing concentration on the possible submarine contacts.[13]

There are those who argue that the ILIAC system can then go on to localise and track all submarine contacts within the area of search. The basis for their claim – which is also a central feature of arguments that the United States will sooner or later make the oceans transparent – is that the ILIAC 4 used in conjunction with acoustic models can remove background noise and thus isolate hostile submarines.[14] Such arguments assume that an economically and operationally feasible system based on the ILIAC 4 model can be devised to search the tens of millions of square nautical miles in which Soviet submarines might operate. This is a questionable assumption even if Soviet submarines choose not to remain in relatively shallow waters, unsuited to long-range acoustic detection systems, or near home waters, such as the Arctic or the Seas of Okhotsk or Japan, not readily accessible for implanting, maintaining, or monitoring long-range detection devices.[15] Such arguments also assume that all submarines generate signals which are acquired – another questionable assumption in view of the information already presented about acoustic countermeasures.[16] The underwater acoustic analyst, Robert Urick, said in 1983: 'Twenty years ago people were saying that with the right little box to process signals you'd be able to detect subs anywhere in the ocean. But you can only do so much. There's minimum detection threshold, a minimum signal-to-[background] noise ratio, and we're pretty close to it'.[17]

Furthermore, it may well be that the oceans appear to be 'becoming more opaque as we understand more about them'.[18] Tierney provided one basis for this claim when he stated that oceanographers in the 1970s modified the 'classic view of the ocean . . . used by acoustic engineers for listening to subs'.[19] In contrast to viewing the oceans as a 'relatively stable mass of water – turbulent at the surface . . . and criss-crossed by great currents like the Gulf Stream, but generally constant and predictable, especially in deep waters', oceanographers came to appreciate the ubiquity of eddies cutting vertically across the water column, disrupting the horizontal transmission of sound even in the deep SOFAR channel. It was not that oceanographers had been unaware of eddies, but rather that they had not known how widespread they really were. Rear Admiral R. K. Geiger, a former Chief of US Naval Research, provided another basis for the opacity claim when he wrote:

> The classic picture of the deep ocean has been one consisting of large sluggish gyres and slowly changing structures,

except for the Gulf Stream. Recent basic research has revealed that the ocean is quite complex, and in many respects it is analogous to the atmosphere: it contains the oceanic counterpart of atmospheric weather. The oceanic 'weather' consists of highs, lows, fronts, jets, which, relative to general ocean climatology, travel quite rapidly. The sharp temperature gradients associated with this weather are known to cause rapid changes in sonar conditions and provide acoustic shadows that obscure an object from detection.[20]

Geiger's point about 'acoustic shadows' is one echoed by those who claim that the chief product of the powerful American computer/acoustic modelling effort is an ability to predict 'not where submarines are, but where submarines could hide'.[21] Because the models are said to simulate a 'synoptic picture of the ocean features', that is a picture based on values averaged over fairly large areas,[22] they would be useful for identifying how fronts, eddies, storms and the like would limit array performance, but they would not seem useful for cancelling out highly variable (as opposed to average) background noise so as to isolate submarines.[23] Knowing the limits of array performance and where submarines could hide would, of course, allow for efficient placement and utilisation of mobile sensors, an admitted purpose of the US computer and modelling effort.[24]

It is within the context of gathering information to feed into computers and support models that the US Navy uses many of the potential non-acoustic sensors mentioned in Chapter 3, but it uses them not to sense submarines directly but rather to obtain information about ocean temperature, winds, fronts and so forth. This information buttresses US efforts to find Soviet submarines acoustically (as well as to find acoustic hiding places for US SSBNs, said to be the top priority customers of the environmental mapping programme).[25] At present the US Navy obtains much of the desired information from satellite-based systems, the design and use of which are controlled by organisations other than itself. According to a Navy spokesman, the Navy has not been able to obtain the necessary global ocean data to support its environmental mapping requirements. Hence, it is developing its own satellite, NROSS (Navy Remote Oceanographic Sensing System), which will employ a radar altimeter, a forward or side-looking radar, a passive microwave radiometer and an infra-red imager.[26]

The United States has indeed gone far to advance these areas of ASW technology – in passive hydrophone arrays, signal-processing, acoustic modelling, and integration of data to support models. The practical application of these advances is found in the Integrated Undersea Surveillance System or IUSS.

The Integrated Undersea Surveillance System

IUSS encompasses three elements, the first of which is the SOSUS or the Sound Surveillance System, described as the 'backbone' or 'primary method' of US ASW search.[27] It consists of hydrophones moored underwater but cable-connected to shore stations for signal-processing. The first hydrophone array was laid in 1954, and the system has since been greatly expanded.

There is much speculation in the public literature as to where the arrays are located, but it is generally accepted that they are placed in areas of the North Atlantic and North Pacific through which Soviet submarines may pass or in which they may operate.[28] It is of significance that even the Soviet press has published charts which, according to one American intelligence official, depict 'the generalized location of our SOSUS system arrays'.[29] Soviet tampering with array cabling provides practical confirmation that the VMF may indeed know or may have correctly guessed where some elements of the system can be found.[30]

Also of relevance is the impact of the Soviet deployment of their SSBNs in waters close to home since, by so doing, they may have outflanked all or parts of SOSUS altogether. This is a clear implication of many statements by American officials that the SSBNs which deploy this way are 'much less vulnerable to detection'.[31]

By contrast, the more vulnerable submarines are likely to be those which still must travel to the far reaches of the Atlantic or Pacific in order to perform their mission. This is because SOSUS has been credited with detecting and sometimes tracking a sizeable proportion of Soviet submarines (including SSBNs) which have entered its area of coverage.[32] It is not clear, however, what the actual trend is in this regard, and in 1981 the US Navy's Director of Naval Warfare testified in connection with SOSUS that, as Soviet submarine 'noise level gets quieter, our processing capability has to go up to compensate. We would like to overtake him, but in fact we aren't'.[33]

It is said that information gathered by SOSUS and other acoustic means is fed into computers so that an acoustic picture or 'signature' of submarines is developed.[34] Later detections are compared with the information in the computer so as to facilitate classification of submarine contacts. Such a process would obviously be dependent on the quantity and quality of the stored and newly-acquired data and would be subject to the same environmental and countermeasures problems affecting search and tracking.

Individual arrays are believed to be positioned to take advantage of the SOFAR channel where detectable sound can travel thousands of kilometres. Richard Garwin has already been quoted to the effect that listening devices, such as contained in the SOSUS, could triangulate and localise a submarine 'to an accuracy which under the best of circumstances might be in the range of some tens of kilometres'. Other writers have made unsubstantiated claims that SOSUS had indeed achieved such accuracies – 80km often being mentioned – but how often 'the best of circumstances' occur to allow such localisation is an open question.[35] From the lengthy discussion on acoustics in Chapter 2, it should be obvious why the 'detection range capabilities of SOSUS arrays vary according to a large number of factors'.[36] The Commander-in-Chief of the US Atlantic Fleet provided a specific example to Congress in March 1981. He stated that, for a fixed 'array out in the area north of Bermuda', 'the acoustic ASW problem is a very serious one at this time of year when the [isothermal] layer depth drops to 400ft.' since submarines in the layer are difficult to detect by a sensor below it.[37] The Admiral then spoke of the need to have a mobile sensor in the area.

Two mobile systems are being developed to supplement SOSUS when and where its coverage is poor or nonexistent. One is SURTASS, the Surveillance Towed Array Sensor System. Dedicated surface ships will tow sensors embedded in a cable hundreds of metres long and with 'capabilities similar to the SOSUS arrays'.[38] They will collect passive acoustic data which will be relayed to shore for processing. The ships, resembling large tugs, will be civilian-manned, unarmed and patrol at three knots or less. Twelve are on order and the first of these was due to begin operations in late 1984. The 1984–8 Five Year Defence Plan calls for the purchase of six more.

The second system for supplementing SOSUS is the Rapidly Deployable Surveillance System (or RDSS). It is an 'air deployed, bottom moored, long-life passive acoustic surveillance buoy' that will fill 'time-urgent' surveillance needs in shallow as well as deep water.[39] It will either transmit its data as they are acquired or store them for later transmission. The data recipient will be a maritime patrol aircraft, but a satellite link to shore is also being considered.[40] Initial RDSS deployment is planned for the late 1980s.

The United States thus possesses a geographically-dispersed wide-area search system in SOSUS, and it is supplementing that system with SURTASS and RDSS. Though SURTASS and RDSS are not yet operational, they and SOSUS are already referred to collectively as the Integrated Undersea Surveillance System or IUSS. That each relies on acoustic signals reflects America's strenuous efforts to maximise the possibilities of finding submarines by acoustic detection and from the perspective of a recent director of American military R & D, William Perry, the United States has achieved 'remarkable success in the development of passive acoustic systems able to detect submarines at very long ranges'.[41] Perry acknowledges, however, that these systems benefit from the tendency of Soviet submarines to be noisy. In contrast, he adds, '[a]s long as the United States continues to emphasize quiet submarines, it can probably avoid open ocean detection by [Soviet passive] acoustic means' even if the 'Soviets . . . eventually catch up with US detection technology'.[42] In other words, target noise is an independent variable. Should the Soviet Navy make great strides in reducing the propagation of submarine radiated sounds (through design changes or by changes in operational methods) they too could probably avoid – or at least significantly lessen – the possibility of open ocean detection by passive acoustic means.

Concern that Soviet submarine noise levels are likely to be reduced is probably the major factor encouraging the US to experiment with active acoustic and non-acoustic technologies for wide-area search. Another is the ocean's rising ambient noise level, which 'may cause our passive [acoustic] surveillance systems to become much less effective, even if they are capable of performing to the limits allowed by the medium'.[43]

US EFFORTS WITH ALTERNATIVE TECHNOLOGIES FOR WIDE-AREA SEARCH

In the late 1950s the US Office of Naval Research financed *Artemis*, a large active sonar used bistatically.[44] A transmitter installed on *Mission Capistrano* generated very strong low-frequency acoustic signals to be picked up by both stationary and mobile receivers. Probably because of technical difficulties, the programme lapsed. In 1977 the DARPA Director stated that long-range active acoustic surveillance had 'not received major emphasis in prior years' because 'the drawbacks were correctly perceived to outweigh the potential pay-off'.[45] Yet, in order to hedge against the possibility of a decrease in passive acoustic effectiveness, he stated that DARPA would undertake an active acoustic programme to concentrate on medium-range surveillance. The programme would address problems of reverberation and false targets. It aimed to be low-cost and exploratory only, taking advantage of relatively inexpensive technologies which had recently become available. An experiment was carried out in 1979 in the Pacific where simulated submarine echoes 'were received from moderately long ranges'.[46] As a result, design changes were to be made to an experimental array to render it 'more reliable at depths required'. There is no information as to whether further experimentation occurred, and it may be revealing that former Under Secretary Perry stated, shortly after leaving office in 1981, 'No existing sonar system is useful for the [wide area] detection of strategic submarines, nor is one likely to be useful in the foreseeable future'.[47]

The non-acoustic detection route may be the primary alternative to passive acoustics now being investigated. This is suggested in official statements applied to acoustic detection in general. It is said that, because the potential of acoustic detection 'has nearly been met and [because] any additional advances can be expected to be expensive and difficult to implement, non-acoustic approaches must be systematically studied'.[48] Though the approaches are viewed as 'high risk and innovative', the hope expressed is that research will yield 'low cost complementary methods' to acoustic detection.[49]

Information about US non-acoustic development is relatively sparse. It is known that the United States does have signal intelligence collection systems on the ground as well as on mobile platforms. It also has over-the-horizon radars and satellite-based infra-red sensors to detect missiles in flight.[50] For reasons given in Chapters 2 and 3, it should be clear why these systems are of very limited utility. None was devised to find submarines *per se*.

William Nierenberg states 'A great deal of time, effort, and resources were [also] expended on [thermal scar research], but no remote sensing resulted'.[51] Rather, says Nierenberg, experiments showed that if scar sensing had a role it would be localisation. There is no indication that any such sensor is in operational use. The US has fitted ASW aircraft with infra-red detectors, but these are 'to identify surface targets day or night. The capability is particularly important in the dense shipping regions such as the Mediterranean Sea, Sea of Japan, and South China Sea where submarines frequently operate on the surface at night'.[52] The submarines in question would not be ballistic missile submarines; they would probably be diesel boats which would take advantage of darkness to recharge batteries and replenish air.

There are two non-acoustic sensors in use specifically devised to deal with submerged submarines, but both are restricted to localisation and cannot undertake wide-area search. These are magnetic anomaly detectors carried on aircraft and wake detectors carried on submarines. A US Navy admiral described the latter as 'useful in determining the depth of a target's wake' but only 'after the submarine had been found acoustically'.[53]

Of more restricted utility are US photographic satellites able to reconnoitre port areas, but again, as with satellites for signal intelligence collection and for detecting missiles in flight, they were not designed specifically to find submarines.[54] Addressing that prospect in 1981, Deputy Under Secretary of Defense Seymour Zeiberg commented: 'there is no conceivable way of knowing how to do anything by satellite. Probably that will remain true, as far as I can see it, into the future for many decades'.[55] In the light of the lengthy (and sceptical) discussion in Chapter 3 of the possible uses of potential space-based ASW sensors, Zeiberg's view is understandable.

On a more general level, those Defense Department and Navy officials who express an opinion generally seem to agree that prospects are low (some would say zero) for a non-acoustic ASW breakthrough in the foreseeable future, whatever the platform.[56] Nevertheless, the US is hedging against the unexpected with their Non-acoustic ASW Development Programme. Though much enquiry had previously been conducted into non-acoustic ASW, it was not until 1979 that the Programme was formally constituted. It was initiated to bring together existing and planned research and to encourage industry to pursue active non-acoustic experimentation.[57] Consistent with the 1979 date for initiation is 1981 testimony by Dr Zeiberg where he noted that, *vis-à-vis* the Soviet Union, US investigation into possible air- and space-based detection systems had achieved 'comparable dedication in the last two years'.[58] The momentum and relative success of the acoustic programme until this time may have made it difficult to find anyone prepared to expend great sums on attempting to develop a non-acoustic wide-area sensor. In addition, investigations carried out to determine whether US SSBNs might be susceptible to non-acoustic detection may have contributed to scepticism in the 1960s and 1970s about the prospect of successfully developing such a sensor or sensors.

The stated aims of the Non-acoustic ASW Programme are to determine the extent to which signals of submarine presence can be distinguished from background and to find suitable sensors for trial purpose.[59] The only specific information about progress is found in yearly DARPA Reports. According to its Director, the Agency has 'transferred two highly promising sensor techniques to the Navy' for further research and development, and confirmed the detectability of submarine-generated waves.[60] The latter was done with a sensor unsuited for operational use, and follow-on work includes search for a practical method.[61] DARPA is also investigating 'airborne sensors to detect the submarine hull. A laser hull detection model was developed and efforts are . . . under way to expand the model to consider other observables'.[62] A planned scanning of 'ocean optical properties' will serve 'to characterize the background environment' within which laser must operate.

There is no information about the conditions surrounding the Agency's experiments. For example, do submarines utilised in the experiments stay shallow or deep? Are sensor operators told where to look, or do they search blind? Without answers to such questions, it is impossible to gauge the true significance of DARPA's efforts, but some insight may possibly be gathered from observations by William Perry because DARPA reported to him when he was Defense Under Secretary. After leaving office in 1981, Perry singled out two areas of non-acoustic ASW as having 'potential significance in submarine detection'.[63] The areas were the same two specified in the DARPA reports: submarine-generated waves and lasers. Perry predicted that no open-ocean search system would come to fruition in either of these areas for the foreseeable future.

To sum up, the US still hopes to complement its passive

acoustic wide-area search capability with an active acoustic sensor or a non-acoustic system which can find submerged electromagnetically 'quiet' submarines. What sensors it does have can either search only small areas, or require a submarine either to be on the surface or to radiate electromagnetically. US officials are not sanguine about the development of a practical and operationally-reliable area search system.

ASW ATTACK PLATFORMS

Collectively the US Navy's land-based ASW aircraft and its attack submarines significantly enhance America's anti-SSBN potential. While US surface combatants and ship-based anti-submarine aircraft are well-equipped for ASW *tactical* engagement, their commitment to convoy and carrier battle group (CBG) duties means that they would probably have little direct involvement in anti-SSBN operations. These would be the responsibility principally of P-3 *Orion* maritime patrol aircraft and various classes of nuclear-powered attack submarines (SSN), but hunting SSBNs would be only one of their tasks. They would also be heavily committed to countering the Soviet Navy's 300 or so torpedo-attack and cruise-missile submarines, with some of the latter being equipped now with conventional and nuclear land-attack missiles.

The P-3 *Orion* operates from land and, with an airborne endurance of about twelve hours, it can fly out 1200 NM, spend four hours on patrol chasing submarines and then fly back another 1200 NM to base. While it has a radar as well as equipment to detect a submarine's active electronic emissions, its primary submarine search and localisation sensors are its magnetic anomaly detector and its sonobuoys. The former, as noted earlier, has fairly restricted area coverage, and it is utilised only after the submarine has been found with sonobuoys. An *Orion* carries eighty-eight of the latter. They can be laid in patterns across a submarine's expected path and operate either passively or actively. Their signals are processed by sophisticated on-board computers. If a submarine is confirmed, the aircraft can then attack with nuclear or conventional depth charges or torpedoes.

P-3 *Orions* have been in operation for over twenty years, and the P-3C Update 3 (which began to enter service in May 1984) will be the seventh version of the aircraft since its inception. This latest update's major feature will be an advanced signal-processor termed *Proteus*. The US intends 'a balanced P-3C production and modernization program that will keep pace with the threat without the need for an expensive development program for a new follow-on aircraft'.[64] There are twenty-four active and thirteen reserve squadrons of nine aircraft each for a total of 333 aircraft. This number should not change significantly in the foreseeable future as older planes are retired and new ones enter service. It is intended that all active squadrons should have the C-type aircraft by the early 1990s.

Based in Europe, Asia and North America, the squadrons are within range of many possible SSBN as well as tactical submarine deployment areas. To quote Norman Polmar, 'According to Department of Defense statements, the P-3 *Orions* "in conjunction with our undersea surveillance systems, would make the largest contribution to our antisubmarine warfare efforts prior to and during a major conflict with the Soviets".'[65]

America's nuclear attack submarines (SSNs) may individually constitute the most effective ASW attack platform. It is generally accepted that, compared with Soviet nuclear boats, they are quieter and have superior acoustic sensing and processing capabilities. The result is that American boats have an acoustic advantage which, US officials say, allows them to detect Soviet nuclear submarines before the latter are aware of the American underwater presence.[66] What may be significant in considering the SSNs' role are statements by American officials that SSNs 'can go into the enemy's backyard', and can 'penetrate deeply into hostile seas to conduct sustained independent operations against enemy submarines and surface ships'.[67] In short, the burden is on the SSN to operate in 'waters . . . untenable for other forces'.[68]

The US has ninety-five SSNs and SSGNs at present.

Conversion of older SSBNs and continuing construction of the *Los Angeles* class should bring the number to 98 by 1988. It remains uncertain what the force level will be thereafter, but '600-ship' Navy projections call for a total inventory of 100. Navy spokesmen have stated that 130 or so is the number actually needed.[69]

Of all the Navy's attack platforms, the SSN may be the most overburdened. For example, when their use to support aircraft CBG was given a high priority in the 1970s, one result was the dropping of the mission of forward offensive mining – potentially very disruptive to Soviet SSBNs deploying from base – from a primary to a secondary role.[70] More recently, the emplacement of land-attack cruise missiles [TLAM-N] on the boats has added yet another mission to the SSN force.

Present SSN construction now centres exclusively on the *Los Angeles* class (SSN 688). There were twenty-nine in 1984 with another thirty-three either already authorised or planned for authorisation by the end of the FY 1985 to the 1988 Five Year Defense Programme. The production rate has fluctuated considerably but has generally averaged two to three per year. Defense Department officials are aiming for an annual average of three-to-four in order to reach and remain at the 100 level.

From the point of view of acoustic sensing, the *Los Angeles* class boats may be the finest submarines in the world. They have both hull-mounted and towed-line array sensors. In order to stay ahead of Soviet noise reduction measures, future boats will incorporate new sensor and processing capabilities, termed the 'submarine advanced combat system'. It will replace 'a combat system which was bought when computer hardware was expensive and software cheap. Now . . . precisely the opposite situation exists and we have saturated the central computer complex which we provided to the earlier ships'.[71]

It is also intended to improve the capability of the *Los Angeles* class for Arctic operations. Spokesmen for the US submarine community have stated that there are 'significant areas of concern in our ability to effectively and consistently conduct ASW' in the Arctic. As a result the Navy is 'investigating ways to improve the Arctic warfare capabilities of the SSN 688 class, its sensors and its weapons'.[72]

According to published sources, the number of weapons which the *Los Angeles* class can carry internal to the pressure hull ranges from the low to mid-twenties, which causes some to view the ships as 'underarmed'.[73] The low number does indeed make the weapon selection prior to deployment 'most difficult' since candidate systems are intended to perform very different tasks and the submarine will have to make do with what it has once it is at sea.[74] The weapons load could, for example, consist of Mark 48 heavyweight torpedoes, mines, SUBROCs (a rocket assisted depth charge with nuclear warhead), and anti-surface ship cruise missiles fired through the torpedo tubes. According to *Jane*'s, SSNs 688 through 720 carry twelve anti-surface ship cruise missiles 'as part of the torpedo load'.[75] In newer submarines, land-attack and anti-surface ship missiles will be placed in vertical launchers set in a ballast tank outside the pressure hull. This could allow a larger number of ASW weapons to be stored internally.

A follow-on submarine is now being considered since 'additional advancements to further improve 688 class performance will not be feasible due to design, weight, and space limitations'.[76] The new boat which will not be operational before the mid-1990s, is projected to displace 10 000 tons submerged. This is 3100 tons more than *Los Angeles*, considered by some to be already too large for an attack submarine. The size could restrict manœuvrability, especially under ice or in shallow waters. The US Navy, however, is also studying what characteristics should be designed into the submarine to make it better suited to the Arctic than its 688-class predecessors.

Greater size also means greater costs, and Navy officials acknowledged in 1983 that 'fiscal constraints have precluded an Administration request for more than two SSN 688 a year since FY 1977'.[77] It remains to be seen whether the minimum of three-to-four a year projected for future budgets will become reality. *Los Angeles* boats are now being budgeted at close to $ 800m each, and defence officials stress that a less costly submarine is not possible in view of the many missions assigned to attack submarines and the improvements in noise reduction, speed and diving depth being incorporated into new Soviet submarines.[78]

ASW WEAPONS

Much effort is going into improving America's ASW weapons in order to forestall potential problems. An Assistant Secretary of the Navy described the situation in 1981:

> [M]any of our existing weapons could become relatively ineffective against the newest Soviet . . . submarines – particularly under circumstances in which the Soviets made extensive use of decoys, intensive levels of jamming and other forms of countermeasures available to them. We must continue to increase the lethality and operating characteristics of our anti-submarine weapons if these weapons are to be effective against the latest double-hulled, high speed, deep-diving Soviet submarines.[79]

The Mk 48 torpedo is possibly the most effective weapon. It is a heavy, submarine-carried, torpedo with much space devoted to a powerful warhead and a sophisticated acoustic guidance system. It can operate independently after firing, or be wire-guided for part of its run. When wire-guided, its acoustic sensors transmit what they hear back to the firing submarine via a wire link and the submarine's computers direct the torpedo's actions.

The weapon is now undergoing a major electronics and acoustics modification. 'Service weapons tests of warshot torpedoes have borne out the soundness of the decision to undertake the upgrade program'.[80] Nearly half the inventory was modified by early 1983; additional modifications are planned and will include, as already noted, improvements in its under-ice performance.

The 'most universally used' weapon, however, is the Mk 46 lightweight torpedo, described as the 'primary kill mechanism employed by our surface ships, our aircraft, and the

Captor mine'.[81] It also is undergoing a major improvement programme which, among other things, aims to 'make certain its warhead can . . . penetrate' the inner hull of double-hulled Soviet submarines.[82] As will be seen, the design of the most recent Soviet SSBNs in particular does call into question the effectiveness of unmodified Mk 46 torpedoes.

In addition to torpedoes, submarines also carry SUBROCs. Fired from torpedo tubes, the weapon leaves the water, flies ærodynamically for some miles and then adopts an unguided ballistic profile. The warhead detonates after re-entering the water, and the force of the nuclear explosion can incapacitate submarines within a considerable area. The system is being phased out as too old and difficult to handle, and an ASW 'Stand Off Weapon' (or SOW) is being designed to replace it. SOW development has been accelerated in the hope that a weapon will be operational before all SUBROCs are retired at the end of the decade.

A 1981 report from the US General Accounting Office (GAO) concluded that the 'Navy would find it hard to conduct even the most limited type of mining or mine countermeasures operation'.[83] It is not that Navy officials see mining as ineffectual or unnecessary; rather, it is a question of other programmes having prior claim on resources. For example, when the Navy cancelled the development of an intermediate water depth mine in 1981, Assistant Secretary Mann gave this explanation:

We do need the mine, and I think this is well recognized and understood. Unfortunately, in the balancing of resources and priorities . . . by the time the process drew to a conclusion, there was simply not going to be enough money to sustain an adequately structured program, particularly when risk reduction was a paramount issue.[84]

The Navy's one type of deep water mine, *Captor* (or encapsulated torpedo), began development in the early 1960s but entered operational production only in the early 1980s. It was plagued with problems, and at one point Secretary Brown cancelled the programme, only to reverse himself after additional tests had 'demonstrated a successful modification to improve utility . . . under most operational conditions'.[85] Another factor affecting Brown's decision may have been that, if the Navy did not have it, this would 'seriously degrade' the Navy's ability to mine critical ocean areas such as the G–I–UK Gap, earmarked for *Captor* mining should war occur.[86] Since *Captor* relies on the Mk 46 torpedo to destroy submarines, the Mk 46 upgrade programme should directly affect *Captor*'s success against the most recent SSBNs.

Two other programmes help to fill gaps in the mine inventory. One is *Quickstrike*, designed to produce a 'family of shallow-water bottom mines based primarily on conversion of existing . . . bombs and torpedoes'.[87] The other is the Submarine Launched Mobile Mine (SLMM); it will give the attack submarine force a 'stand-off mining capability'.[88]

As for barrage attack, the United States has about 8000 warheads available if all its strategic missile launchers were primed for attack.[89] Of these, only about 500 are 1 MT or larger in yield. The remainder are 355KT or smaller with the overwhelming bulk of all warheads – that is, the 5500 on SLBMs – having yields of only 50KT or 100KT. As far as is known, none has ever been tested for under-water detonation.

THE US ASW EFFORT AS A UNIFIED SYSTEM

It should be apparent from what has been said that America's ASW effort encompasses a wide variety of fixed or mobile detection, localisation and attack systems as well as environmental support systems for reporting on ocean conditions. These are widely dispersed throughout Europe, Asia, North America, the high seas and, in the case of environmental monitoring systems, in space. The mounting of any major campaign against Soviet submarines would necessitate proper co-ordination of these systems to ensure that they are mutually supportive and synergistic. In addition, any ASW activities must also be co-ordinated with other forces and concerns. An effective system of command, control and communication (C^3) is the key to proper coordination and thus the key to American ASW effectiveness as a whole. It is unnecessary to go into the specifics of the US Navy's ASW C^3 system – indeed, there is little available reliable information of a specific nature but it is clear that it is an area where the Navy has exerted 'great effort', resulting in a system which is very complex and centralised at least to the theatre level.[90] According to one commentator who follows this question 'There is' he said in 1981, 'a continuing debate on the value of [greater] centralization with counter-arguments stating that area commanders should be focal points'.[91] Returning to the theme a year later, he indicated that the counter-argument won the day.[92]

Whatever the ultimate level of centralisation, the Navy's ASW C^3 system seems adequate to the task in the absence of active disruption and hence deserves to be regarded as a significant strength enhancing US potential for anti-SSBN warfare. A former US Secretary of the Navy, Graham Claytor, has pointed out 'our ability to orchestrate the many components in an effective anti-submarine hunter-killer force has enormously improved in recent years'.[93] The improvement seems to correlate with increased use of satellites for high speed communications and data transfer between ASW forces and processing facilities both at sea and ashore.[94]

NOTES

1. See for example, Weinberger, *FY 83 Annual Report of Secretary of Defense*, pp. II-13 to 14 and Statement of Vice Admiral C. A. H. Trost, Director, Navy Program Planning before the Seapower and Force Projection Subcommittee of the Senate Armed Services Committee (8 March 1982) p. 2.
2. See, *inter alia*, Lt. D. T. Easter, 'ASW: Issues for the 1980s', *US Naval Institute Proceedings* (March 1980) pp. 35–41; Lt. E. Mihalak, 'Where is Kedalion?', *US Naval Institute Proceedings* (March 1978) p. 110; Rear Admiral G. R. Larocque in 'Superpowers at Sea: A Debate', *International Security* (Summer 1976) pp. 61–6.
3. As quoted in G. C. Wilson, 'Navy is Preparing for Submarine

Warfare Beneath Coastal Ice', *Washington Post* (19 May 1983) p. 5. See also R. Halloran, 'Navy Trains to Battle Soviet Submarines in Arctic', *The New York Times* (19 May 1983) p. 17.
4. Testimony in US Senate Armed Services Committee, *Department of Defense Authorization for Appropriations for FY 1980*, 96th Congress, 1st Session (1979) Pt 3, p. 1255.
5. Vice Admiral McDonald, Statement on Status of Atlantic Command (10 March 1983) pp. 11–12.
6. Cann in US Senate Armed Services Committee, *Department of Defense Authorization for Appropriations for FY 1982*, 97th Congress, 1st Session (1981) Pt 4, p. 2175.
7. Testimony of Assistant Navy Secretary D. Mann, in US Senate Armed Services Committee, *Department of Defense Authorization for Appropriations for FY 1980*, 96th Congress, 1st Session (1979) Pt 6, p. 2970.
8. Heilmeier, *Department of Defense Appropriations FY 1978*, Pt 5, p. 54.
9. Statement of W. Perry in US House Appropriations Committee, *Department of Defense Appropriations for 1981*, 96th Congress, 2nd Session (1980) Pt 3, p. 139.
10. Testimony of Rear Admiral A. L. Kelln, in US Senate Armed Services Committee, *Department of Defense Authorization for Appropriation for FY 1980*, 96th Congress, 1st Session (1979) Pt 10, p. 6646.
11. Rear Admiral J. B. Mooney, Jr., 'Recognizing the Contribution of Oceanography', in *Oceans 82 Conference Record*, p. 371.
12. R. Fossum, *Defense Advanced Research Projects Agency Fiscal Year 1982 Research and Development Program: Summary Statement* (12 March 1981) pp. II-1 and II-2.
13. Statement of Dr R. Fossum in US House Armed Services Committee, *Hearings on Military Posture and HR 6495*, 96th Congress, 2nd Session (1980) Pt 4, Bk. 1, p. 595.
14. See for example, F. Hussain, 'No Place to Hide', *New Scientist* (15 August 1974) pp. 377–9; Aldridge, *The Counterforce Syndrome*, pp. 46–8; Silverstein, 'Caesar, SOSUS and Submarines', p. 408; and Wilkes, in SIPRI, *Yearbook, 1979*, pp. 431–432.
15. *FY 82 Arms Control Impact Statement*, p. 355.
16. Richard Garwin emphasised this point to the author.
17. As quoted in Tierney, 'The Invisible Force', p. 75.
18. Admiral Griffiths as quoted in Garwin, 'Will Strategic Submarines be Vulnerable?', p. 63.

19. Tierney, 'The Invisible Force', p. 74.
20. Rear Admiral R. K. Geiger, 'Remote Sensing in Ocean Surveillance – Promises, Problems, and Perspectives', in AGARD, *Applications of Remote Sensing*, p. 1–1.
21. K. Tsipis, 'New Technologies and New Weapons Systems', in D. Carlton and C. Schaerf, *Arms Control and Technological Innovation* (New York: Wiley, 1976), p. 50.
22. Heilmeier, *Department of Defense Appropriations FY 1978*, Pt 5, p. 482.
23. I am indebted to Richard Garwin for this point.
24. See for example, Mooney, 'Recognizing the Contribution of Oceanography', and Honhart, 'Navy Requirements'.
25. Mooney, 'Recognizing the Contribution of Oceanography', p. 374.
26. Honhart, 'Navy Requirements', p. 484.
27. Testimony of Rear Admiral J. Metzel, in US Senate Armed Services Committee, *Department of Defense Authorization for Appropriations for FY 1980*, 96th Congress, 1st Session (1979) Pt 6, p. 2925 and Mann, *Department of Defense Authorization, FY 1980*, Pt 6, p. 2946.
28. See, *inter alia*, charts which purport to show location of SOSUS arrays in Tierney, 'The Invisible Force', pp. 76–7; Wilkes, in SIPRI, *Yearbook 1979*, p. 429; Mather, 'The Most Secret Service', pp. 32–3; Wit, 'Advances in Anti-submarine Warfare', pp. 32–3. For charts in Soviet literature, see, *inter alia*, Captain 2nd rank S. Shapovalov, 'View of US and NATO Command on Anti-submarine Warfare', *Morskoy Sbornik*, no. 11 (1976) p. 88 and B. Chizhov, 'SOSUS Detects a Submarine', *Morskoy Sbornik*, no. 10 (1975) pp. 95–6.
29. Testimony of Rear Admiral D. P. Harvey, in US Senate Armed Services Committee, *Fiscal Year 1978 Authorization for Military Procurement, Research and Development and Active Selected Reserve, and Civilian Personnel Strengths*, 95th Congress, 1st Session (1977) Pt 10, p. 6620.
30. See references to statements by former US CNO, Admiral J. Holloway, in G. C. Wilson, 'Navy Seeks $191 Million to Fix Warning System', *Washington Post* (16 June 1978) p. A26 and 'Trawlers Are Ripping Up Navy's Secret Undersea Spy System', *San Francisco Chronicle* (16 June 1978) p. 21.
31. Statement of Vice Admiral J. G. Williams, Deputy Chief of Naval Operations for Submarine Warfare before the Seapower Subcommittee of the House Armed Service Committee (5 March 1981) p. 19. See also, *inter alia*, Testimony of Harold Brown, in US House Appropriations Committee,

Department of Defense Appropriations for 1980, 96th Congress, 1st Session (1979) Pt 4, p. 704.
32. See for example, *FY 1980 Arms Control Impact Statements*, 96th Congress, 1st Session, Joint Committee Print (1979) p. 109 and *FY 1981 Arms Control Impact Statements*, 96th Congress, 2nd Session, Joint Committee Print, (1980) p. 348.
33. McKee, *Hearings on Military Posture FY 1982, Pt 4*, p. 822. See also McKee's testimony in US House Armed Services Committee, *Hearings on Military Posture and HR 2970*, 97th Congress, 1st Session (1981) Pt 2, p. 497 and Foley, *Department of Defense Authorization for FY 1982*, Pt 4, p. 1673.
34. See, *inter alia*, Allen and Polmar, 'The Silent Chase', p. 15.
35. Ibid, p. 15 and Tierney, 'The Invisible Force', p. 75.
36. *FY 81 Arms Control Impact Statement*, p. 340.
37. Testimony of Admiral H. Train, in US House Armed Services Committee, *Hearings On Military Posture and HR 2970*, 97th Congress, 1st Session (1981) Pt 4, p. 776.
38. Statement of Vice Admiral R. L. Walters, Deputy Chief of Naval Operations for Surface Warfare, before the Seapower and Force Projection Subcommittee of the Senate Armed Services Committee (22 March 1982) p. 2.
39. Ibid, pp. 2–3.
40. Cann, in US Senate Appropriations Committee, *Department of Defense Appropriations for FY82*, 97th Congress, 1st Session (1981) Pt 4, p. 546.
41. W. Perry, *The FY 1982 Department of Defense Program for Research, Development, and Acquisition* (20 January 1981) p. I-19.
42. Perry, 'Technological Prospects', p. 137.
43. Heilmeier, *Department of Defense Appropriations FY 1978*, Pt 5, p. 89.
44. *SIPRI Yearbook 1969–70*, p. 151.
45. Heilmeier, *Department of Defense Appropriations FY 1978*, 1st Session (1977) Pt 5, p. 89.
46. Fossum, *Hearings on Military Posture* and *HR 6495*, Pt 4, Bk 1, p. 596.
47. Perry, 'Technological Prospects', p. 137.
48. Fossum, *Defense Advanced Research Projects* (12 March 1981), p. II-2.
49. R. Fossum, *Defense Advanced Research Projects Agency Fiscal Year 1983 Research and Development Program* (Arlington, Virginia: DARPA, 1982) p. III-29.
50. See, *inter alia* 'Looking and Listening in the Heavens', *Time*

(22 November 1982) pp. 92–5 and Jasani, *Outer Space–A New Dimension*, Chaps. 4 and 6.
51. Nierenberg, 'US Navy and Satellite Oceanography', pp. 12–13.
52. Statement of Vice Admiral W. L. McDonald, Deputy Chief of Naval Operations (Air Warfare) before the Subcommittee on Seapower and Force Projection of the Senate Armed Services Comitee (22 March 1982) p. 8.
53. McKee, *Hearings on Military Posture FY 1982*, 1st Session (1981), Pt 4, p. 827.
54. See, *inter alia*, Jasani, *Outer Space – A New Dimension* pp. 43–58.
55. Testimony of Zeiberg in US Senate Armed Services Committee, *Department of Defense Authorization for Appropriations for FY 1982*, 97th Congress, 1st Session (1981) Pt 7, p. 4052.
56. See for example, *ibid.*; Perry, 'Technological Prospects' pp. 137–8; McKee, *Hearings on Military Posture FY 1982*, 1st Session (1981) Pt 4, p. 825; Cann, *Department of Defense Authorization FY 1982*, Pt 4, p. 581; and Rear Admiral P. Carter in US House Armed Services Committee, *Hearings on Military Posture and HR 2970*, 97th Congress, 1st Session (1981) Pt 3, p. 144.
57. See Mann, *Department of Defense Authorization FY 1980*, Pt 6, p. 2969 and 'Navy Seeks Industry Aid in Non-acoustic ASW Effort', *Aerospace Daily* (22 August 1969) p. 273.
58. Zeiberg, *Department of Defense Authorization FY 1982*, Pt 7, p. 4052.
59. Fossum, *Defense Advanced Research Projects FY 1983*, pp. III-29 and 30.
60. Fossum, *Defense Advanced Research Projects FY 1982* (12 March 1981) p. II-3.
61. Fossum, *Hearings on Military Posture* and *HR 6495*, Pt 4, Bk 1, p. 601.
62. Fossum, *Defense Advanced Research Projects FY 1982* (12 March 1981) p. II-3.
63. Perry, 'Technological Prospects', pp. 137–138.
64. C. Weinberger, *Annual Report to the Congress Fiscal Year 1984* (Washington: GPO, 1983) p. 150.
65. N. Polmar, 'The US Navy: Naval Aircraft, Part 3', *US Naval Institute Proceedings* (December 1980) p. 113.
66. See for example, Perry, *FY 1982 Department of Defense Program* (20 January 1981) p. I-19.
67. Metzel, *Department of Defense Authorization FY 1980*, Session (1979) p. 2933 and Statement by Vice Admiral N.

Thunman, USN, Deputy Chief of Naval Operations for Submarine Warfare before House Armed Services Committee Seapower Subcommittee (2 March 1983) p. 3.
68. Statement of Vice Admiral W. H. Rowden, Deputy Chief of Naval Operations for Surface Warfare before the Seapower and Force Projection Subcommittee of the House Armed Services Committee (11 March 1981) p. 5.
69. Testimony of Rear Admiral D. M. Smith in US House Armed Services Committee, *Hearings on Military Posture and HR 2970*, 97th Congress, 1st Session (1981) Pt 4, p. 555.
70. Testimony of Admiral Thomas Hayward, in US Senate Armed Services Committee, *Department of Defense Authorization for Appropriations for FY 1981*, 96th Congress, 2nd Session (1980) Pt 2, p. 867.
71. Thunman, Statement before Seapower Subcommittee (2 March 1983) pp. 8–9.
72. Ibid, p. 12.
73. Commander A. Von Saun, 'Attack Submarine: The Hidden Persuader', *US Naval Institute Proceedings* (June 1982) p. 101. See also N. Polmar, 'The US Navy: Attack Submarines', *US Naval Institute Proceedings* (January 1980) p. 113.
74. Polmar, ibid, p. 113.
75. J. Moore (ed.) *Jane's Fighting Ships 1982–83* (London: Jane's Publishing Co., 1982) p. 600.
76. Thunman, statement before Seapower Subcommittee (2 March 1983) p. 9.
77. Statement of Vice Admiral R. L. Walters, Deputy Chief of Naval Operations for Surface Warfare before the House Armed Services Committee Subcommittee on Seapower and Strategic Materials (1 March 1983) p. 16.
78. See Thunman, statement before Seapower Subcommittee (2 March 1983) pp. 3–4.
79. Cann, *Department of Defense Authorization FY 1982*, Pt 4, p. 533.
80. Thunman, statement before Seapower Subcommittee (2 March 1983) p. 10.
81. Metzel, *Department of Defense Authorizations FY 1980*, Pt 6, p. 2922.
82. Hayward, *Department of Defense Appropriations FY 82*, Pt 1, p. 746.
83. 'Navy's Abilities in Mine Warfare Called Lacking', *The New York Times* (18 June 1981) p. 22.
84. As quoted in 'Budget Priorities Forced IWD Action', *Aerospace Daily* (23 January 1981) p. 106.

85. Statement of Rear Admiral J. W. Nyquist, Director, Surface Combat Systems, before the Seapower and Strategic and Critical Materials Subcommittee of the House Armed Services Committee (17 March 1983) pp. 8–9.
86. 'Navy's Captor Mine Cleared for Full Production', *Aerospace Daily* (17 December 1980) p. 233.
87. Perry, *The FY 1982 Department of Defense Program* (20 January 1981), p. VII-58.
88. Nyquist, statement before Seapower Subcommittee (17 March 1983) p. 10.
89. See *Soviet Military Power*, pp. 19 and 23.
90. L. Booda, 'Russia Ocean Surveillance Improved', *Sea Technology* (November 1979) p. 28.
91. Booda, 'Anti-submarine Warfare Reacts to Strategic Indicators', *Sea Technology* (November 1981) p. 18.
92. Booda, 'Consolidation, Integration Mark ASW Effort in US Navy', *Sea Technology* (November 1982) p. 7.
93. As quoted in Wit, 'Advances in ASW', p. 35.
94. See Assistant Navy Secretary M. Paisley, 'US Navy Strategic and Tactical C^3I for the 80s', *Signal* (September 1982) pp. 18–20.

6 US ASW and Soviet SSBNs: Conclusions

This section looks at the intersection of US 'strategic' anti-submarine warfare capabilities and Soviet SSBN developments in order to assess America's potential to conduct a strategically destabilising anti-SSBN campaign.

FACTORS ENHANCING US ANTI-SSBN POTENTIAL

1. The United States has been developing a formidable ASW capability for over forty years. It has devoted considerable resources to the endeavour and can draw on extensive operational and developmental experience.
2. Critically important is America's possession of SOSUS, a large area-search passive acoustic system. There are numerous claims that the system has detected submarines at great distances and localised some to fairly narrow areas.
3. Two companion systems will soon enter service to help to fill some gaps in SOSUS coverage. These are SURTASS and RDSS, both also passive acoustic systems. Together with SOSUS they constitute what is already referred to as the Integrated Undersea Surveillance System (IUSS).
4. The signal-processing and computing systems which support US acoustic sensors are excellent. They allow the enhancement of sought-for signals, the incorporation of vast amounts of environmental data supporting

complex acoustic propagation models, and the integration of data from other search systems in order to filter out surface-ship sources of acoustic signals.
5. In order to ensure that it obtains the environmental data it specifically needs, the US Navy is developing its own dedicated satellite, the NROSS or Navy Remote Oceanographic Sensing System.
6. US acoustic systems in the past have benefited from a tendency of Soviet submarines to be noisy and from the practice of some SSBNs (notably the Y-class) to pass through SOSUS waters in order to reach patrol areas off US coasts.
7. The United States is striving to broaden its capability to search large areas for submerged, electromagnetically 'quiet' submarines by investigating both active acoustic and non-acoustic alternatives. Non-acoustic development efforts seemed to have been given some momentum in 1979, and DARPA has since claimed some success in its non-acoustic research.
8. There are numerous P-3 *Orion* ASW aircraft well dispersed around Europe and the Far East and in North America. The aircraft has been continually improved over the course of twenty years, and the latest '-3c Update' constitutes a major augmentation of its airborne processing capability.
9. US ASW submarines are impressive in their ability to detect acoustically Soviet nuclear submarines before the latter can detect the US SSNs. The sensors on the most recent class, the *Los Angeles* (SSN-688) submarines, are being upgraded to stay ahead of any Soviet quietening measures and will be modified to improve their Arctic warfare capabilities. A follow-on submarine is scheduled to begin construction in 1989.
10. The US has a variety of the ASW weapons consisting of light- and heavy-weight torpedoes, SUBROC, and mines. It is working to fill inventory gaps and to correct perceived deficiencies in existing systems.
11. The US ASW effort seems, on the whole, to be well co-ordinated in peacetime as information from individual search sensors and support systems is brought

together at central nodes, processed, and quickly disseminated to attacking forces. Recent improvements correlate with increased reliance on satellites for high-speed communication and data transfer.

FACTORS DEGRADING US ANTI-SSBN POTENTIAL

1. The USSR views its SSBN force as a strategic reserve and attaches very high priority to its protection and survival. This priority underlies the more specific factors mentioned below.
2. By building and maintaining a force of sixty-two first-line strategic ballistic-missile submarines, the Soviet Navy ensures that any wholly disarming SSBN campaign must be an endeavour of considerable proportions. The USSR could lose a high percentage of SSBNs and still have enough SLBMs for devastating retaliation. This is particularly true if only one or two SSBNs are enough to deter and eight to eighteen enough to forestall succumbing to 'use or lose' arguments.
3. The performance of any long-range acoustic detection system depends upon many environmental variables. The United States has gone to great lengths to account for the variables and their fluctuations, but doing so requires continual readjustment which may not necessarily allow for all factors all the time. Under the best of circumstances, SOSUS-type arrays might indeed be able to find and place an SSBN within a very narrow circle, but to strike at all SSBNs simultaneously would require finding, localising, and holding each until the time to attack, filtering out excessive false alarms, and doing all that across widely-separated ocean areas, each with its own peculiar environmental context. From this perspective, the possibility of a simultaneous strike based on large area-search detections would seem poor even before one considers Soviet countermeasures.

4. Numerous countermeasures are available. One of the most effective is keeping SSBNs outside the search areas of US large area-detection systems. As far as this writer can determine, no one has ever claimed that the United States can, does or could monitor all Soviet home or under-ice waters where *Delta* or *Typhoon* submarines can patrol. When all the *Yankee* submarines retire in the 1990s, no Soviet SSBN will have to venture outside such waters to strike at targets in the United States. A second measure is lessening submarine noise propagation. This can be done by building submarines to be quiet or by operating them skilfully (for example, taking advantage of the environment and any intelligence information on the location of US area-search systems). As noted in Congressional testimony, the Soviet submarines have become more quiet and SOSUS does not seem to have kept up. Finally, Soviet writings make clear a wartime intent to destroy, spoof or otherwise disrupt Western search, prosecution, and related support systems.
5. The obstacles to a non-acoustic breakthrough are extremely formidable, and US officials are highly sceptical that one will occur in the foreseeable future. Any breakthrough will undoubtedly remain subject to changing environmental conditions and countermeasures. Operating under ice, for example, seems an elegant way to neutralise large overhead area-search systems and the prospect of barrage.
6. The Soviet Navy's general purpose forces are committed to establishing a maritime defence perimeter around the homeland to protect SSBNs. US SSNs will be the only platforms able to operate for any extended period within the defended areas and under the ice. Yet their supply of weapons and their size leads some to consider them underarmed and unwieldy for operating in shallow waters or under ice. Into the foreseeable future, furthermore, their numbers seem likely to remain too small for searching out and destroying all or even a high proportion of Soviet SSBNs kept in the bastions. This seems especially true if war lasts only a

few months or less, if SSBNs are distributed throughout the Sea of Okhotsk, the Sea of Japan, and various Arctic Seas, and if they are directly supported by Soviet attack submarines.

7. It seems reasonable to assume, in view of the importance that the Soviet leadership attaches to SSBNs, that the Soviet Navy acts to ensure that they are not trailed. As argued earlier, a determined nation should be able to keep most of its deployed SSBNs free of this threat most of the time.

8. American officials have acknowledged a need to improve ASW weapons. This need reflects specific problems identified with the mines, SUBROC, and the Mk 46 torpedo. It also reflects a general concern that US weapons should remain effective in the face of the Soviet building of double-hulled submarines, operating them in the special environment of the Arctic, and, should war come, countering US weapons with decoys, jamming and other measures. Assistant Navy Secretary Cann offered a sobering thought in 1982 when he stated 'Every torpedo I have associated with . . . we oversimplified the reliability problems'.[1] No less sobering is that it took nearly two decades to bring the *Captor* mine to its present level of efficiency and even then its primary kill mechanism is still the Mk 46 torpedo.

9. Barrage as an option would seem ruled out for the USA even if there are only thirteen-to-fifteen SSBNs normally deployed in peacetime. Extrapolating from William Perry's calculations presented here in Chapter 1, it would take 100 (probably 1 MT each) warheads to destroy a submarine whose radius of uncertainty was no more than 25 NM. It would take 400 if the radius were 50 NM. In the latter case 5200 warheads (assuming no faulty launchers or weapons) would sink thirteen boats, but this is clearly too great a proportion of the US warhead numbers (about 8000 for a one-time strike from all missile-launchers). Superficially, barrage would seem feasible in the 25 NM case since only 1300 warheads would be expended, but the US does not have 1300 one-megaton warheads. Only about 500 are

one megaton or larger in yield, and the most powerful of these, about forty-three remaining on *Titan* missiles, are being dismantled because they are too difficult to maintain. Most US warheads are between 50 and 335 KT, and the highest yield on planned warheads is to be 500KT on the M-X. US warheads, furthermore, are not of the plunging variety and would have little or no utility against SSBNs under ice and not much even in open waters. As argued earlier, it is also highly doubtful whether the US could simultaneously localise all thirteen-to-fifteen SSBNs to a small enough area while filtering out excessive false alarms.

10. US ASW forces in war will be heavily engaged protecting aircraft carriers, amphibious ships, critical naval resupply ships, and convoys. There will thus be a limit on the extent to which the US could concentrate ASW assets against SSBNs. It will be impossible to ignore the 300 or so Soviet torpedo-attack and cruise-missile submarines, with some of the latter equipped with land-attack weapons.

11. Finally, because much of the US anti-SSBN potential consists of inter-linked search, attack and related support systems, and because many of those systems are vulnerable to military attack, jamming, or sabotage, the Soviet Union could seriously degrade the overall potential simply by concentrating against selected parts of the system. No matter how good SOSUS or SURTASS may be, for example, their effectiveness could be of little consequence if their processing facilities were destroyed or communications links with attack forces were broken. Similarly, it may not mean much that the P-3 *Orion* is the world's best ASW aircraft if it cannot be directed where to look or if its airfields and fuel dumps are destroyed.

NET ASSESSMENT AND CONCLUSIONS

Conventional war scenario

As summarised in Table 6.1, there are numerous factors which enhance and numerous factors which degrade America's capacity to eliminate Soviet SSBNs. A weighing of both makes it seem implausible the US could so reduce the numbers of Soviet SSBNs that the USSR might be pushed into using the remainder. The uninterrupted operation and synergistic meshing of qualitatively impressive acoustic area-search, attack and support systems against relatively noisy submarines found in areas monitored by US devices might encourage the belief that the US could go some way to sink Soviet SSBNs. On the other side of the ledger, we have to note that no non-acoustic back-up is foreseen for the acoustic area-search systems, that area-search, attack and support components are vulnerable to disruption or destruction, that even in peace-time environmental factors are problematic and recent Soviet efforts to lessen sound propagation make detection harder, and that war will also bring the USSR's unhindered application of countermeasures. The cumulative effect of all of these developments is that the USSR may reduce America's anti-SSBN capacity faster than the Americans can sink Soviet SSBNs. In addition, the USSR has a very large number of SSBNs, and, if this writer's calculations in the Introduction have any validity, the Soviet Union could afford to lose the bulk of them and still remain quite confident that it could deter the US. Also, by keeping the bulk of its SSBNs in defended waters or under ice, the USSR will sharply limit what can be done against them. The burden will fall mainly on US SSNs but, like all US ASW forces, they will also be busily engaged against the Soviet Union's many general-purpose submarines, some of which will directly support Soviet SSBNs, as well as against Soviet land-attack cruise-missile submarines and naval surface-ships.

In short, it is very difficult to see where the US would find, after a war began, the residual capability to sink all or even a destabilising proportion of the USSR's SSBNs. This is not

TABLE 6.1 *Summary of factors enhancing and degrading the US's anti-SSBN potential*

Factors enhancing	Factors degrading
1. The United States has been developing a formidable ASW capability for over forty years	1. Moscow attaches high priority to protecting its SSBNs
2. SOSUS provides the US a large area-search capability	2. It maintains a very large SSBN fleet
3. The US is supplementing SOSUS with SURTASS and RDSS	3. US area search systems must continually contend with environmental factors limiting their performance, and only under 'the best of circumstances' can they be expected to pinpoint a target within a narrow circle
4. US passive acoustic capabilities in general are excellent	
5. The US Navy is developing its own dedicated satellite to collect environmental data	4. Soviet countermeasures will compound the effect of environmental factors
6. Soviet submarines have tended to be noisy, and some SSBNs have passed through SOSUS areas	5. A non-acoustic breakthrough is difficult to achieve and is not expected in the foreseeable future Should one occur, it should remain subject to environmental conditioning and countermeasures
7. The US is seeking to develop active acoustic and non-acoustic alternatives to its passive acoustic area-search systems	
8. The US has a qualitatively and quantitatively impressive inventory of P-3 aircraft	6. Only SSNs should be able to penetrate the defended bastions and operate under ice, but their numbers seem too small to have a destabilising effect
9. US ASW submarines are extremely quiet and have impressive acoustic-sensing capabilities	7. Trailing is very difficult against an opponent determined not to be trailed. One must assume the USSR is such an opponent
10. The US has a variety of ASW weapons. It is striving to correct problems in some areas and generally to improve the effectiveness of all systems	8. American officials have acknowledged a need for improvements in ASW weaponry
11. US ASW capabilities consist of a series of systems which seem well co-ordinated in peacetime	9. Barrage would seem ruled out for numerous reasons
	10. US ASW forces in war will

be busily engaged against torpedo attack and cruise-missile submarines

11. Because America's anti-SSBN potential resides in interlinked systems, many of which are highly vulnerable, the Soviets can degrade the overall potential simply by acting against selected parts

---

to say that the US will not be able to protect CBGs or convoys against general-purpose submarines which must usually pass through choke points and approach US forces to carry out their attacks. It is also not to say that all Soviet SSBNs will survive. Some will undoubtedly be lost, and, the ones most at hazard may be the older *Yankee* SSBNs operating far from the homeland, but, as US Navy officials and others have pointed out, a submarine dedicated to staying as far as possible from enemy ASW forces will be very difficult to destroy.[2] Avoiding detection will be the main task of the strategic reserve SSBNs kept in the maritime bastions close to the USSR. Enough of them should survive to give the Soviet leadership confidence that it could still confront the United States with unacceptable retaliation.

This conclusion assumes, of course, that any attack in a campaign to sink SSBNs will not automatically trigger a nuclear response. One author has argued that:

> A deliberate conventional campaign against Soviet SSBNs could be understood by the Soviets as the beginning of a damage-limiting first strike. Given the importance of nuclear weapons and nuclear war in Soviet doctrine, even the appearance of such a campaign could trigger dire consequences. American leaders may be surprised by the Soviet response . . . [A] Soviet nuclear response cannot be ruled out.[3]

While a nuclear response cannot be ruled out, it *would certainly be surprising* in any situation except the one alluded to at the beginning of the citation, namely one where the Soviet Union was sure that the US would strike pre-emptively at all Soviet land-based intercontinental systems *after* the sea-based missiles had been (nearly) eliminated. Otherwise it seems not only sensible but imperative for the Soviet Union to accept, albeit grudgingly, the loss of some SSBNs. One reason is that Soviet adoption of a 'use-if-attacked' posture would be almost certain to trigger a response (by surviving US SSBNs if by no other systems) which Soviet leaders would certainly wish to avoid. A second reason, as will be seen, is that Soviet writings have consistently declared American strategic submarines to be legitimate targets of Soviet ASW, and it thus seems likely that the Soviet leadership would accept their own submarines to be no less legitimate targets of US ASW. A third reason is that the bulk of (some 70 per cent) of Soviet nuclear warheads by number and yield are still on land-based systems. The Soviet Union could afford to lose sea-based missiles in a conventional war and still remain extremely powerful at the nuclear level. In short, the most rational choice for the USSR would seem to be to wait for unambiguous indication that the Americans intended to launch a wholly disarming first strike before initiating a Soviet strike after losing some SSBNs.[4]

If, furthermore, the US did not have the residual capability after war began to destroy a destabilising proportion of Soviet SSBNs, then this would seem to render moot any question of Soviet pre-emption on the grounds that it might believe that the Americans would surely strike all other Soviet missiles after (nearly) eliminating the sea-based ones. The Soviet leaders do not themselves seem to believe that the prerequisite for pre-emption – namely, elimination of (nearly) all SSBNs – will occur, and they credit their measures to protect SSBNs as the cause. Admiral Gorshkov addressed the issue as follows:

> Can submarines, despite constant improvements in the means of anti-submarine defence, achieve strategic goals in a war at sea? The answer to this question demanded much research. All of it invariably confirmed the high

effectiveness of submarines when rightly used and given proper combat backing. This conclusion proved particularly convincing in relation to atomic-powered submarines.[5]

The surprise strike scenario

This scenario initially seems to offer somewhat more potential for a destabilising strike than that of a period of conventional war since, unlike the latter, it posits full use of unreduced US ASW systems against only thirteen-to-fifteen or so Soviet SSBNs said to be on patrol in peacetime. Nevertheless, if one accepts the argument in the introductory chapter that only one or two surviving submarines would be enough to deter, then such an attack would effectively have to be perfect. It seems impossible that the United States could achieve the confidence to stage such a disarming attack in the foreseeable future. The possibility of continuous trailing (as a prelude to [near] simultaneous torpedo or SOW attacks) would also seem low because of presumed Soviet anti-trail precautionary measures. A combination of some trailing (to keep track of actual and suspected SSBNs outside IUSS coverage) and IUSS vectored P-3 *Orion* attacks (against false alarms as well as true SSBNs in the area covered) might seem just possible under highly favourable environmental circumstances, but the time for holding and closing with all the real and suspected contacts would seem so small as to rule out this option also. In addition, the co-ordination of the attack would be very complex, possibly too much so in view of the difficulties which will always tend to hinder smooth two-way communications between submerged submarines and command authorities.

Possibly the most important factor, however, militating against a US surprise attack on Soviet SSBNs is one not mentioned until now because it does not deal with ASW *per se*. It concerns the context within which *any* anti-SSBN surprise strike might be presumed to take place. For instance, barrage nuclear attack against deployed SSBNs could rationally occur only in the context of an overall disarming attack against all Soviet intercontinental systems.[6] Yet, because of timing and uncertainties such as the effect of the earth's gravitational field on missiles as they go over the Pole, it is generally accepted that such a strike could not be carried out with any reasonable assurance of rendering Soviet retaliation acceptable. Moreover the US does not (yet) possess the kind of hard-target kill capability to contemplate simultaneous strikes on all Soviet silos.

At a more general level, any surprise move to eliminate deployed SSBNs (by nuclear barrage or by simultaneous torpedo or SOW attacks from SSNs and P-3s) cannot occur *in vacuo*. The United States would have to prepare itself and call on its allies in Europe and Asia to be ready for major war. It is inconceivable that any American leadership bent on such a course (an improbability in itself) could ever convince all key US military commanders, much less allies, to agree. It is also inconceivable that preparing for war on a worldwide level, even under the guise of an unusually large exercise, could be carried out without alerting Soviet suspicions and the triggering of precautionary countermeasures and possibly a pre-emptive attack, for it is clearly stated Soviet policy to pre-empt should the Soviet leadership judge that an attack is imminent. Hence, it seems reasonable to conclude that even if the US could put the entire Soviet SSBN force in peril in a surprise strike, it would not do so because of the context of such an attack and the associated uncertainties and risks.

Soviet practice suggests that they may share the same view for, if they really thought that their SSBNs were susceptible to an 'out-of-the-blue' surprise strike, then logically they would maintain more than thirteen-to-fifteen on patrol. After all, they have sixty-two first-line boats, and deploying a larger proportion would vastly complicate further any plans to attack them simultaneously. The Soviet Union could simply push up the number of SSBNs (and decoys) to be trailed or barraged to such an extent as to leave absolutely no doubt of the impossibility of a surprise disarming attack against them. If a country as security-conscious as the USSR does not do so, then that may be the strongest indicator possible that such a strike is absolutely implausible.

NOTES

1. Testimony of Assistant Secretary Cann in US House Armed Services Committee, *Hearings on Military Posture and HR 5968*, 97th Congress, 2nd Session (1982) Pt 5, p. 699.
2. McKee, Testimony in *Hearings on Military Posture FY 1982*, Pt 4, p. 823.
3. B. R. Posen, 'Inadvertent Nuclear War? Escalation and NATO's Northern Flank', *International Security* (Fall 1982) pp. 43–4.
4. Paradoxically, if the USSR believed the US would surely attempt such an attack, then the SSBNs which had survived to that point might be seen as important elements of strategic reserve (for possible intimidation of the PRC and other states as well as the USA) and thus as systems which should definitely not be used 'now', but rather defended with even more vigour.
5. Gorshkov, *The Sea Power of the State*, p. 190.
6. The reasoning is simple. A barrage strike would require the equivalent of 1300 warheads (probably one megaton each) to thirteen SSBNs if one accepts, for purpose of argument, that each could be localised to 25 NM radius of uncertainty. In order to carry out such a strike, the US would probably employ its 450 *Minuteman* II single warhead missiles because their warheads have one to two megaton yield. Additional missiles would be needed to carry out the strike. Whatever their number, a launch of more than 450 missiles would certainly be detected by the USSR shortly after it occurred, and, because of its surprise nature, it would constitute a very strong incentive for the USSR to respond immediately with whatever systems it had available. If the US wanted to limit damage from the Soviet response, it would have to attack all Soviet systems.

   At this point the reader may rightfully ask if the tail is not wagging the dog, for it seems absurd that the US would decide to destroy all Soviet systems because of some original (and, to this writer's mind, bizarre) urge to strike at only the deployed SSBNs. Such are the consequences, however, of spinning out the logic of strategic alternatives. Why the US would originally want to eliminate *only* the deployed SSBNs is incomprehensible, yet barrage is often discussed in a vacuum, that is, as if deployed SSBNs were the only targets of a US or Soviet war initiating surprise nuclear strike.

Part III
Soviet ASW and US SSBNs

7 United States SSBN Forces and Operations

TRENDS IN THE NUMBER AND COMPOSITION OF THE US SSBN FLEET

The United States had thirty-five operational SSBNs in 1984: thirty-one of the *Lafayette* class[1] and four of the *Ohio* class. The former became operational between 1963 and 1967 and the first of the latter in 1982. Table 7.1 outlines some characteristics of both classes and their missiles. SSBNs are the largest submarines built by the US, and *Ohio* boats are exceeded in submerged displacement only by the USSR's *Typhoon*-class ballistic missile submarines. Carrying the 2500 NM *Poseidon* C-3 missile, nineteen *Lafayettes* can patrol approximately 3 million sq. NM of ocean and remain effective against targets in the Soviet Union.[2] That total area includes part of the North Atlantic, North Pacific, and Indian Oceans as well as the Mediterranean Sea.[3] The *Trident* 1 or C-4 missile is currently on the remaining twelve *Lafayette* and on the *Ohio* boats. Its 4200 NM range widens the patrol area to between 30 and 40 million sq. NM.[4] When the ninth *Ohio* submarine appears in 1989, it will be armed with the *Trident* 2 or D-5 missile with a nominal range of 6000 NM. Thus it will theoretically be able to patrol over 50 million sq. NM, though the actual total will be somewhat less because some ocean areas will be deemed unsuitable for very large submarines because of shallow depth or other reasons.[5] The area generally includes nearly all the North Atlantic and Pacific Oceans as well as much of the Indian Ocean.

TABLE 7.1 Characteristics of US SSBNs and SLBMs

	SSBNs	
	Lafayette	Ohio
Displacement tonnage (submerged)	8250	18700
Number of missiles carried	16	24
Type of missile	(*Poseidon* C-3 on 19 units) (*Trident* C-4 on 12 units)	(*Trident* C-4 on 8 units*) (*Trident* D-5 on remainder*)

	SLBMs		
	Poseidon C-3	Trident C-4	Trident D-5
Maximum range at normal re-entry vehicle (RV) load (NM)	2500	4230	6000
Throw-weight (lbs)	3300	2900	—
Re-entry vehicle (RV) yield	40–50kt	100kt	—
Guidance	Inertial	Stellar/inertial	Stellar/inertial
Independently targetable?	Yes	Yes	Yes
Maximum number RV	14	8	14(?)
Normal number RV carried	10	8(?)	—

* Projected
SOURCE J. J. Tritten, 'The Trident System: Submarines, Missiles, and Strategic Doctrine', *Naval War College Review* (January–February 1983) p. 65, Table 4 and 'The Missile Tables', *Defense and Foreign Affairs* (April 1983) p. 47.

The US strategic ballistic missile force consists of the SLBMs and the continental US land-based ballistic missiles (ICBMs). The SLBMs constitute about 35 per cent of all the missiles and 36 per cent of the megatonnage. More importantly, however, they also account for about 70 per cent of all the strategic ballistic missile warheads.[6] A *Poseidon* submarine might 'normally' carry 160 warheads and *Trident* I submarine either 124 or 192 depending on whether the carrying platform had sixteen missiles (on the older boats) or twenty-four (on *Ohio*).

Figure 7.1 is drawn from US Navy testimony and illustrates past and projected trends for SLBM launchers. It is consistent with the *Ohio*-class building programme as implemented to the end of 1984 and as projected in official statements (one submarine to begin construction each year) for 1985 through to the end of the century. The 656 launchers shown in 1978–9 were on forty-one *Lafayette* and pre-*Lafayette* (that is, *George Washington/Ethan Allen*) SSBNs. The retirement from strategic service of the ten pre-*Lafayettes* caused the launcher total to fall to a low of 484 in 1981. By 1992 it is projected to rise to 832 on forty-five boats (including fourteen *Ohios*). Beginning in 1993, block obsolescence will force out the *Lafayettes* over a six-year period, resulting in a new low of twenty-one ships and 504 launchers in 1999. Continued construction could mean 600 missile tubes on twenty-five *Ohio* boats in 2002, twenty years after the first of the class entered service.

What the actual number of *Ohio* boats will be is as yet undecided. If the FY 84–88 Five Year Defence Plan holds, there will be at least fifteen of them. Some Navy officials have utilised twenty as an interim planning figure while stressing that the actual total depends on hard-to-predict and sometimes hard-to-control variables.[7] These include decisions about the make-up of the land-based missile force and the outcome of START. Another factor is cost: an article in March 1983 on Pentagon expenditures pointed out, for example, that the 'expected cost of building all fifteen *Trident* boats [i.e. *Ohios*] has risen . . . to $31.1bn, an increase of 9.5 per cent in only three months'.[8] Part of the reason for the increase was the decision to go ahead with the *Trident* II missile, but the arguments justifying the missile's high research and development expense stressed that the additional cost over that of *Trident* I could be recovered by building fewer submarines. Because *Trident* II will be unique among US SLBMs in its presumed ability to strike at very hard targets, and because it may carry more warheads than *Trident* I (possibly fourteen as against eight), fewer missiles and thus 'fewer submarines will have to be procured to achieve desired mission capability'.[9]

Counterbalancing this potential argument for limiting

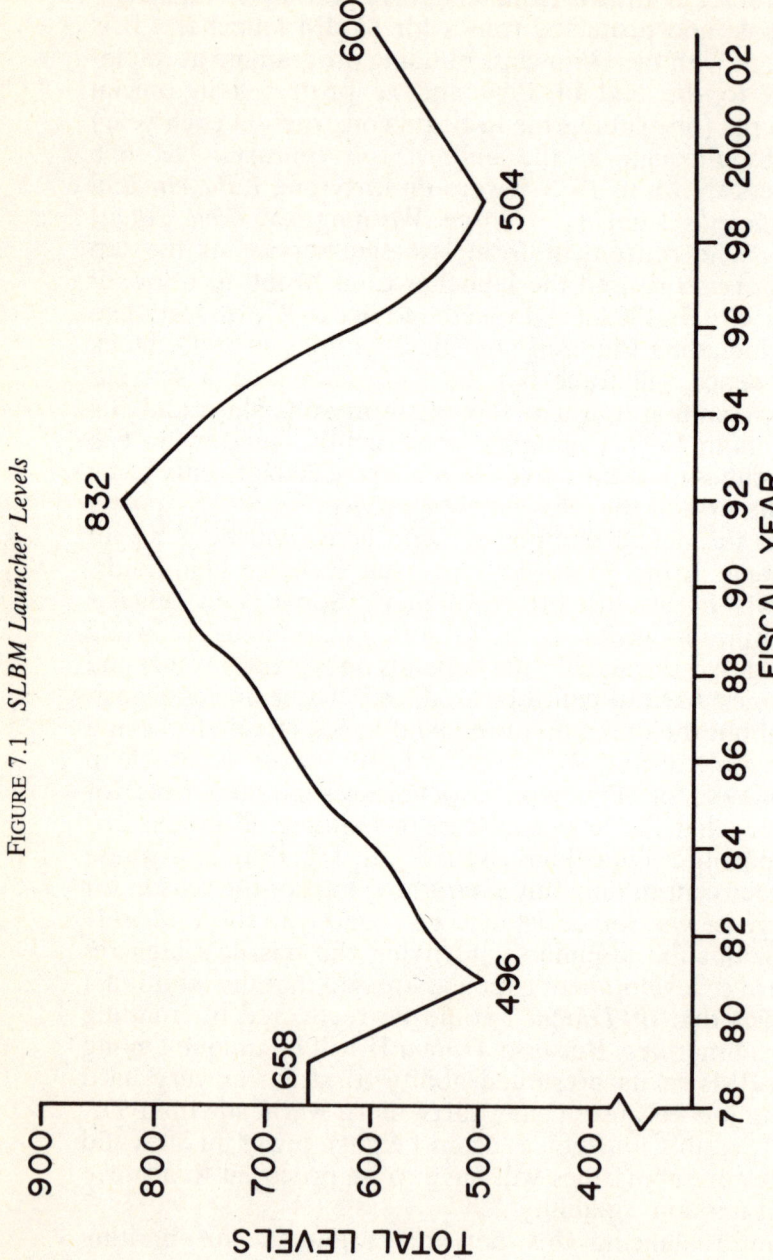

FIGURE 7.1 *SLBM Launcher Levels*

SOURCE Vice Admiral R. L. Walters, Statement before the Defense Subcommittee of the Senate Appropriations Committee (5 May 1982) p. VG–2.

Ohio procurement is the frequently expressed concern that, with an ultimate fleet of twenty or fewer *Ohios*, the US would be concentrating too many missiles and warheads (twenty-four missiles and possibly 192 warheads) on too few submarines.[10] (If *Trident* II is deployed with fourteen warheads, the latter figure goes to 336.) This situation contrasts with that prevailing in the 1970s when the American SSBN force was made up of forty-one boats each carrying sixteen missiles and possibly 160 warheads. It remains to be seen what the impact of this concern will mean, either for *Ohio* numbers or the building of a smaller ballistic missile submarine.

Ohios were designed to be as big as they are, partly to accommodate the installation of the very large S8G nuclear reactor and partly to achieve economies of scale in two senses. One is monetary. The bigger a submarine the more missiles it can carry, and the greater the number of missiles the less the monetary cost per warhead. A second sense is the manpower cost. By having two crews per submarine (one of which remains in port while the other patrols) the US has maintained a very high operational tempo for its SSBN fleet, but the two-crew policy and the difficulty of retaining officers to man nuclear-powered submarines (partly the result of the demanding two-crew policy) greatly strained the Navy's manpower resources. Building larger numbers of smaller submarines would only have worsened already severe manpower difficulties, for each ship (whatever the count of its on-board missiles) requires its own captain, executive officer, chief engineer, navigator and the rest.

SSBN AND SSBN SUPPORT OPERATIONS

Little can be said about the planned utilisation of SSBNs in war, but it is clear that they have a 'strategic reserve' role.[11] With the recent greater emphasis in US nuclear doctrine on selective counterforce options, however, and with the move to D-5 and its unique hard-target kill capability, it is not clear whether SSBNs carrying D-5s will be kept only in strategic reserve or could also be used in early retaliatory or selective strikes.

What is also not fully clear is the extent to which any SSBN is exclusively assigned to the NATO commander (SACEUR) for contingencies in the European theatre. A former Deputy Assistant Director of the US Arms Control and Disarmament Agency (ACDA) has stated that forty SLBMs are set aside for the Supreme Allied Commander, Europe;[12] others have suggested that SACEUR can call on 400 warheads on US submarines for his nuclear strike plans. However, a US Navy Admiral stated categorically in 1977 that 'no [ballistic missile] submarine was dedicated to a theatre mission as such'.[13] Rather, he added immediately, 'I think the question . . . is . . . could we take off some national targeting and use it in a theatre role on a contingency to prevent escalation? Our submarines . . . have that capability to retarget one or more missiles should the national command authority so deem'.

Once targets are selected, the time it takes to fire missiles may be an important consideration for SSBN survivability. Even though remaining submerged, the submarine is both exposed and in a situation of extremely limited manœuvrability when in the firing sequence. All US SSBNs can evidently launch at a rate of better than one missile per minute.[14] Firing all missiles would thus consume a quarter of an hour or less for *Lafayette* boats and twenty minutes or less for *Ohio* boats. These times seem short enough to ensure that, unless an enemy ASW platform were in the immediate vicinity (a situation which might cause the SSBN to withhold launching any missiles) a boat would seem assured of loosing its entire battery before being subjected to attack.

Other measures have been instituted to protect the SSBN fleet. One is fitting the boats with towed acoustic arrays for detecting submarines which attempt to trail or approach from behind. Another is a strong emphasis on reducing SSBN radiated noise. Outer hulls are streamlined and internal equipment is precision-machined and shock-mounted. US submarines in general are regarded as being very quiet indeed and the *Ohio*-class is termed 'virtually the quietest submarine in the world'.[15] It is stressed that *Ohio*'s low noise propagation allows faster patrol speeds, thereby making more difficult both acoustic trailing and barrage attacks.[16] Furthermore, the faster speed for any given level of noise is important in situations where SSBNs fire only a part of their battery (as might occur in theatre or selected counterforce strikes) and wish to get away quickly for fear that the firing has revealed their location.

US submarines also operate so as to lessen noise propagation, and the Oceanographer of the US Navy has stated that the SSBN fleet has first priority in the collection of environmental data used to find areas of the oceans where submarines could hide.[17]

As noted earlier, modern SSBNs tend to be very large and questions have been raised as to whether *Ohio*'s size – twice the tonnage of *Lafayette*-class boats – significantly increases its detectability by active acoustic as well as non-acoustic devices.[18] *Ohio* does present a much greater sonar echoing area but, because of the difficulties inherent in using active sonars for wide-area search, *Ohio*'s large size should not significantly affect its initial detectability in the open ocean. A more serious concern would be enemy efforts to localise any SSBN with sonar after detecting it by passive acoustic or non-acoustic means. To handle that contingency the US submarine community has put in hand measures 'to provide added protection against active sonar used by ASW warships and submarines and against active sonar torpedoes'.[19] One measure may be coating submarine hulls with an anechoic material, a rubber-like substance which can absorb incoming sound such as from a sonar. Funding for anechoic coating research and development was requested in the late 1970s.[20] Other measures would include decoying and the use of systems described later.

As for potential non-acoustic threats, Defense Department and Navy officials agree that, in the words of William Perry, 'the evidence is not compelling that size needs to be an important consideration'.[21] David Mann, Perry's counterpart as Assistant Navy Secretary for Research, Engineering and Systems, did, however, include some caveats when expressing his own view: 'The influence of and uncertainties about these [non-acoustic] phenomena permit only preliminary observations that are inconclusive about the potential detectability . . . induced by the larger *Trident* [that is, *Ohio*] submarine'.[22] Such questions, however, are said to be under continuous review by the US Navy in its SSBN Security Programme (discussed hereafter) and confidence is expressed that, should any threat develop, timely countermeasures would be taken. Indeed, Mann made reference to one obvious measure to frustrate some non-acoustic detection, namely to have submarines operating deeper.

Much emphasised as enhancing survivability are efforts to keep 'the maximum percentage of SSBNs at sea . . . submerged' and operating over large areas.[23] There were about eighteen SSBNs deployed at any one time in 1983. This number reflects the facts that *Lafayette* units patrol for periods of sixty days at a time and spend approximately 55 per cent of their life at sea, while *Ohio* patrols are seventy days long with these ships scheduled to spend 66 per cent of their time on deployment.[24] That the *Ohio* submarines will spend 11 per cent more time at sea results from planned shorter refit periods, longer intervals between major overhauls, and development of an 'integrated logistic support system' where entire pieces of equipment are easily replaced so that time-consuming upkeep and repair are done ashore while the boats are on patrol.[25]

US SSBNs evidently take advantage of the extent of the patrol areas allowed by the range of their missiles, which, with *Trident* I, could, as noted already, include nearly all Northern Hemisphere waters. In addition, not all SSBNs restrict their patrols to areas bounded by the missile range. According to a former US CNO, some 'patrols, designated "mod-alert", assign the SSBN a period of time to get within range of its assigned target'.[26] The longer-range *Trident* missile provides the further advantage that a boat can be on patrol, that is, target-effective, as soon as it leaves port. It need not take time to move to a patrol area.

US SSBNs deploy from Bangor, Washington, on the US Pacific coast; Charleston, South Carolina, and King's Bay, Georgia, on the Atlantic; and the Holy Loch in Scotland. They are obviously detectable when in port and when moving from port to the open sea. Elaborate measures are undertaken to ensure security in both circumstances.[27] These might include, for example, US SSNs acting to frustrate attempts by enemy submarines to trail an outbound SSBN. Soviet mining of US SSBN ports, however, could pose serious problems for submarines which had not left before the mines were laid or for boats which needed to return to port after the laying. As noted earlier, a 1981 US General Accounting Office (GAO) report concluded that the 'Navy would find it hard to conduct even the most limited . . . mine countermeasures operation'.[28] Description of the US capability in the FY84 DoD Posture Statement clearly suggests that no improvements have occurred since the GAO report.[29] Twenty-five mine countermeasures (MCM) ships and some MCM helicopters are planned for purchase, but it remains to be seen how many survive future attempts to constrain naval budgets. Mine countermeasures have never had a strong constituency in the US Navy.

Submarines can also be potentially vulnerable because of the need to communicate and the demands of navigation. SSBNs rarely if ever need to communicate with (i.e. send messages to) outside authorities, but they do need to be able to receive messages, most obviously firing orders from the National Command Authority (NCA). The difficulty associated with their receiving communications is that, other than at extremely low frequencies (ELF), communication signals cannot penetrate more than a few tens of feet of water. In order to permit submarines to operate at greater depths and still be in receipt of signals, a small communications buoy or a horizontal floating wire antenna (FWA) are towed behind the submarine. The buoy remains below but close to the surface while the wire floats on or immediately under it, and defence officials have expressed concern that, as 'near-surface observables', either might become detectable to a future technological breakthrough of a non-acoustic nature.[30] Cited as candidate systems for detection were aircraft-mounted optical, radar, infra-red and magnetic sensors. Because of this threat, the controversial extremely low frequency (ELF) communication system (also known as *Sanguine* or *Seafarer*) has been proposed. ELF signals can penetrate hundreds, as opposed to tens, of feet. Defence officials seem to agree, however, that there is no immediate detection threat to SSBNs from the use of either the shallow water buoy or a wire ærial and, to the surprise of many, the Chief of Naval Operations (CNO) indicated in 1981 that the Navy was willing to forego spending for ELF.[31] The White House and the Defense Secretary overruled that recommendation and authorised a modest operational ELF system which is now under development. Any such system involves a very long (tens or even hundreds of kilometres) buried antenna which is potentially vulnerable to attack. Moreover data rates with ELF transmissions are very low indeed so that even a brief (three-letter) message takes minutes to transmit.

Navigation is another important consideration for submariners, especially since SLBM accuracy is partly dependent upon feeding into the missile the submarine's precise position at the time of firing. An on-board submarine inertial navigation system (SINS) takes account of all course and speed changes to provide a continuous plot of the submarine's location, but such a system requires periodic update and correction. Navigational satellites can provide the data for this, but again the SSBN would have to raise an antenna mast toward the surface for a few minutes or less. It is said, however, that the intervals between updates have 'reached several weeks', and are complemented by stellar and radio-aided inertial navigation devices on the missiles themselves, by magnetic, gravitational, or topographical mapping of ocean basins, and by other methods.[32]

If a submarine commander believes that the vessel has been detected or may be attacked, he can release through its torpedo tubes a 'mobile submarine simulator' to confuse enemy acoustic sensors, and has available at least one (possibly two) other 'independent expendable subsystems to decoy enemy homing torpedoes and to jam enemy acoustic sensors'.[33] Still in research and development, furthermore, is a weapon for use against ASW aircraft: the 'self-initiating anti-air missile' (SIAM) is fitted with an infra-red sensor which seeks out the heat given off by aircraft engines.

Underlying the entire US effort to ensure SSBN survivability is the very high priority SSBN Security Programme. It 'continuously evaluate[s] real and postulated threats that could affect the future survivability of the US SSBN force and ... develop[s] countermeasures for potential ASW threats'.[34] Two main elements are the Tactical Development Programme and the SSBN Security Technology Programme. Speaking in 1979, the Navy's former R&D Director, Dr David Mann, stated that over sixty tactical development exercises had occurred in the previous ten years. They utilised 'our most modern submarines under a variety of environmental conditions in the Atlantic and Pacific Oceans'.[35] In addition, he said, over seventy scientific and technological exercises had also occurred, their objectives being to determine the signals which submarines do generate and the circumstances surrounding their detection.

The work of the Security Programme is supplemented on an *ad hoc* basis by special study groups which, for their own purposes, inquire into SSBN survivability. Organisations such as the CIA, the Air Force and Congress form or sponsor such groups, which are often inter-agency in nature. Decisions as to whether or not to go ahead with the *Ohio* class, build an ELF system, or scrap M-X in favour of *Trident* usually serve as the catalyst for the *ad hoc* studies.

NOTES

1. For convenience sake, the thirty-one are grouped together as the *Lafayette* class, but they actually consist of both the *Lafayette* (SSBN 616) and *Benjamin Franklin* (SSBN 640) classes. As *Jane's* points out, '*Benjamin Franklin* and later submarines are officially considered a separate class; however, differences are minimal (e.g., quieter machinery)'. J. Moore (ed.) *Jane's Fighting Ships 1983–84* (London: Jane's Publishing Company, 1983) p. 635.
2. Statement by Rear Admiral Charles Larson, Deputy Director, Strategic Submarine Division, Office of the Chief of Naval Operations, in US House Armed Services Committee, *Hearings on Military Posture and HR 1872 and HR 2575*, 96th Congress, 1st Session (1979) Pt 4, p. 595.
3. Ibid, includes a chart depicting the relevant ocean areas.

4. The present American CNO, Admiral Watkins, spoke in 1983 of SSBNs roaming 'some 30,000,000 square miles', as quoted in Ulsamer, 'Bobbing, Weaving and Fighting Smart', p. 88. In the same year, Secretary Lehman wrote of 'the 40 million miles encompassing our *Trident* patrol areas'. Lehman, letter to editors of *The Wall Street Journal* (30 September 1983).
5. This writer plotted on a globe the areas encompassed by a 5000 NM arc around Leningrad and Vladivostock and calculated that the area enclosed 50.8m sq. NM of open ocean.
6. Lehman, *Department of Defense Appropriations 1984*, Pt 2, p. 390.
7. See for example, statements by Secretary Lehman and high level US naval officers in US Senate Armed Services Committee, *Strategic Force Modernization Programs*, 97th Congress, 1st Session (1981) pp. 185–8.
8. G. Church, 'Who Says Numbers Never Lie', *Time* (4 April 1983) p. 23.
9. Statement by Dr S. L. Zeiberg Deputy Under Secretary of Defense for Research and Engineering before the Strategic Programs Subcommittee of the Senate Armed Services Committee (27 February 1981) pp. 2–3.
10. See for example, B. Scowcroft *et al.*, *Report of the President's Commission on Strategic Forces* (April 1983) p. 9.
11. Williams, statement to Seapower Subcommittee (5 March 1981) p. 12.
12. D. Linebaugh, 'Count the Sea-Based Missiles', *St Louis Post Dispatch* (17 April 1983) p. 2.
13. Kelln, Testimony in *Department of Defense Authorization FY 1980*, Pt 10, pp. 6666–7.
14. Commander J. J. Tritten, 'The Trident System: Submarines, Missiles, and Strategic Doctrines', *Naval War College Review* (January–February 1983) p. 33.
15. Testimony Vice Admiral N. Thunman, in US House Armed Services Committee, *Hearings on Military Posture and HR 5968*, 97th Congress, 2nd Session (1982) Pt 4, p. 233.
16. Williams, statement to Seapower Subcommittee (5 March 1981) p. 8.
17. Mooney, 'Recognizing the Contribution of Oceanography', p. 374.
18. See for example, Congressional Budget Office, *The US Sea-based Strategic Forces*, p. 51.
19. Testimony of Rear Admiral P. Carter in US Senate Armed Services Committee, *Department of Defense Authorization*

for Appropriations for FY 1982, 97th Congress, 1st Session (1981) Pt 7, p. 4107.
20. Kelln, *Department of Defense Authorization FY 1980*, Pt 10, p. 6649.
21. Perry, *Department of Defense Authorization FY 1981*, Pt 6, p. 3480.
22. Mann, *Department of Defense Authorization FY 1980*, Pt 6, p. 3002. It is unclear whether Mann intended his statement to apply to non-acoustic phenomena in general or a specific subset of them.
23. Williams, statement to Seapower Subcommittee (5 March 1981) p. 7.
24. Tritten, 'The Trident System', p. 63.
25. Williams, statement to Seapower Subcommittee (5 March 1981) p. 8.
26. Testimony of Admiral J. Holloway in US House Appropriations Committee, *Department of Defense Appropriations for 1977*, 94th Congress, 2nd Session (1976) Pt 2, p. 142.
27. See for example, Kelln, Testimony in *Department of Defense Authorization FY 1980*, Pt 10, pp. 6626–9.
28. See citation in Chap. 5, note 83.
29. Weinberger, *Annual Report to Congress FY 1984*, p. 156.
30. Citation is from Carter, *Department of Defense Authorization FY 1982*, Pt 7, p. 4107. See also, ibid, p. 4105; Reed, News Briefing, 4 March 1975, pp. 8–9; Williams, Statement to Seapower Subcommittee (5 March 1981), p. 13; Testimony of Vice Admiral R. Y. Kaufmann, in US Senate Armed Services Committee, *Fiscal Year 1978 Authorization for Military Procurement, Research and Development, Active Duty, Selected Reserve and Civilian Personnel Strengths*, 95th Congress, 1st Session (1977) Pt 10, pp. 6691–4; Testimony of Assistant Secretary of Defense G. Dineen, in US Senate Armed Service Committee, *Department of Defense Authorization for Appropriations for FY 1980*, 96th Congress, 1st Session (1979) Pt 1, p. 329; and Train, *Hearings on Military Posture* and *HR 2970*, 1st Session Pt 4, pp. 796–7.
31. See references listed in note 30 above and R. Halloran, 'Reagan Approves New Set-up to Radio Nuclear Subs', *The New York Times* (9 October 1981) p. 1.
32. J. Wit, 'American SLBM: Counterforce Options and Strategic Implications', *Survival* (July/August 1982) p. 172. See also OTA, *M-X Missile Basing*, pp. 174–6.
33. Citations are from listing of USN budget items in US Senate

Appropriations Committee, *Department of Defense Appropriations for 1981*, 96th Congress, 2nd Session (1980) Pt 4, p. 388–9.
34. Williams, statement to Seapower Subcommittee (5 March 1981) p. 16.
35. Mann, *Department of Defense Authorization FY 1980*, Pt 6, p. 2990.

8 Soviet ASW Developments

BACKGROUND

The Soviet Navy or VMF (*Voyenno-Morskoy Flot*) exhibited no great overt interest in ASW prior to the development of American SSBNs.[1] It had no long ocean sea-lanes to protect, and the primary naval concern was to interdict enemy forces approaching the homeland from ocean areas. In the early 1950s US naval carrier aircraft were given a nuclear strike capability, and the Soviet Navy increasingly concentrated on systems and exercises to counter that threat. With the appearance of the *Polaris* missile submarines in the early 1960s, Soviet declaratory policy designated anti-SSBN warfare as a major naval mission.[2] Open-ocean ASW-specialised surface ships, aircraft, and submarines were acquired, and their numbers were sufficiently adequate by 1973 to allow ASW to form a major part of large exercises outside home and near waters.[3]

American tactical nuclear submarine developments reinforced concern for ASW. In the late 1960s the United States contemplated constructing two new SSN classes and, though only one was series-produced, the Soviet Union particularly feared a growing SSN threat to its own new and also growing SSBN fleet.[4] Chapter 4 identifies some of the measures put in hand to deal with the threat, and indirectly they form part of the Soviet Union's anti-US SSBN strategy. This is because any measure which helps to ensure Soviet SSBN survivability helps also to deter the use of US missiles.

Also reinforcing a concern for ASW were British, French, and Chinese ballistic missile submarine developments. Britain has brought four SSBNs into service since 1967, and France six since 1971. Both states have put in hand programmes to modernise their fleets and, in France's case, to augment it as well. In addition, China is expected to have its first operational SSBN in 1985. (An old Chinese diesel-powered ballistic missile submarine is not considered operational.)

Eliminating rather than simply deterring the SSBN threat in war is the preferred Soviet policy, and in the Soviet mind the antecedents to success include considerable 'scientific–technical' progress and the development of 'entirely new principles' of anti-submarine warfare. Col-Gen Lomov, an important General Staff theoretician, wrote in 1973:

> The questions of countering submarines are very important, as submarines hold an important place among the strategic weapons of modern war. Powerful weapons, great range and high manœuvrability comprise the inseparable qualities of this means of modern combat on the sea and ocean theatres of military operations. To parry these qualities in the enemy submarines means to solve a problem of strategic significance, and the possibilities to solve it depend directly upon the acceleration of scientific–technical progress.[5]

Admiral Gorshkov, Commander-in-Chief of the Soviet Navy, wrote in a similar vein three years later:

> The intensive development of submarines, in particular the appearance of missile submarines with atomic power, the fight against which assumed the character of a state task, raised the question of a further and sharp rise in the effectiveness of anti-submarine weapons. Even then it was clear that the solution of this problem was essentially to be sought not by perfecting the available means of combat, the technical possibilities of the development of which were coming close to the limit. The question was one of developing entirely new principles of combating submarines, which also determined the new demands for combating them.[6]

It is impossible for Western analysts to know exactly how far the USSR has come (or predict how far it may go) in developing scientific–technical systems or new principles for ASW. Nevertheless, some assessment, admittedly tentative, is possible of its anti-SSBN potential. Such an assessment must consider both Soviet ASW and US SSBN developments. The former were dealt with in Chapter 7. The latter are dealt with here.

DETECTION SYSTEMS

Like the United States, the USSR deploys a variety of acoustic systems. These include sonars fixed to or lowered from ships, submarines and helicopters as well as small sonobuoys dropped from aircraft. Of potentially greater significance are a fixed bottom-moored area-search system, at least one type of towed array, and self-contained portable listening devices.

There are numerous references in the Western literature to bottom-moored acoustic devices in the Sea of Japan, the Kurile Islands area, the Pacific Ocean east of Kamchatka, the Barents Sea, and possibly parts of the Norwegian Sea.[7] A 'Russian build-up of cable-laying vessels' is offered as evidence that the overall system is being improved and expanded.[8] There are, however, limits to any expansion since Soviet geography is not suitable for setting out long underwater arrays in the Atlantic, the Mediterranean, or in the far reaches of the Pacific, and there are no indications that the coasts of states friendly to the USSR have been used for such purposes. Hence towed arrays and portable self-contained sensors may be particularly attractive for use in remote areas.

A towed-array system has been deployed on the *Victor* III submarine, where it is stowed in a highly visible pod on the boat's after-end, but there is no information as to whether it is useful for broad-area search or more narrow tactical purposes.[9] Portable sensors are already much in use, with some washing up on American coasts near SSBN bases or transit routes, and others fetching up in fishing trawls in areas where SSBNs regularly conduct trials.[10] Press accounts refer to some as 'buoys', implying they float on the water, and to others simply as 'devices', 'bugs', or 'sensors', implying that they may be under-water systems. There is little information about how any are emplaced. The Soviet Oceanographic Research Fleet has been said to play a role, and one device described as 'torpedo-shaped',[11] may have been delivered by submarine. If so, this would be consistent with claims that the submarines, mini-submarines, and bottom-crawlers operating within Swedish waters had as at least one mission the laying of under-water devices.[12]

It is generally accepted that Soviet acoustic sensing is in general not as effective as that of the US, but the US lead seems to be based less on greater understanding of hydroacoustics than on US advances in signal-processing.[13] Admiral Harry Train compared them as follows: the Soviets 'do not have the ability to process acoustic information . . . as we do. There is a vast difference in having a sensor . . . and knowing how to use [it] . . . We have the analytical processing systems that go with them'.[14] Soviet acoustic detection capabilities would presumably increase greatly with the introduction of computer hardware and software equal to that in the United States and possibly available through third countries. American officials have expressed fears to that effect, and presented as evidence Soviet sonar buoys, which have come into US hands, whose operations were guided by electronic chips identical to those manufactured by RCA and by Texas Instruments.[15] This concern has been at least one of the reasons for US efforts to tighten up our technology transfer constraints in CoCom (the Co-ordinating Committee dealing with sales of technology to the Eastern Bloc) and elsewhere.

It is uncertain what an increase in Soviet detection capabilities would mean. It would depend on the location and number of sensors deployed and the adequacy of the communications linking them to processors and to ASW attack forces. It would also depend on the acoustic characteristics of US submarines which, US officials say, American systems have difficulty detecting.[16] Presumably even an upgraded Soviet system would find it no easier.

This last consideration may have spurred Soviet non-acoustic efforts. According to US intelligence officials, the Soviet programme began in the late 1950s and is extremely well-supported and 'broad-based', 'looking at everything that might contribute to the problem'.[17]

Specific evidence of progress is scarce. There are magnetic anomaly detectors on aircraft but, as with those of the US, they would almost certainly sense only at short ranges. Also, like the US, there are deployed technologies which are not particularly useful against submerged submarines which refrain from launching weapons or emitting electronically. These consist of mobile optical, infra-red, radar and signal intelligence sensors as well as fixed OTH radars and SIGINT ground sites.[18] Some of these undoubtedly also gather information useful to acoustic sensing systems. Deployed Soviet oceanographic ships could do so as well.

Some Western writers have alleged the use of experimentation with satellite-based systems for detecting submerged, 'electronically-quiet' boats.[19] Also, as noted earlier, when arguing in the 1970s for development of an extremely low frequency (ELF) system for communicating with deeply submerged submarines, some American defence officials expressed fears of a Soviet non-acoustic breakthrough in the 1980s which could detect shallow SSBNs or their antennæ.[20] As yet, however, no evidence has been presented that satellite-based or wide-area shallow submarine systems have been deployed, though it is certainly not unreasonable to suppose that experiments do take place. It should be clear from Chapters 2 and 3, furthermore, that such systems, especially if carried on a satellite, would be monumentally difficult to bring to fruition as effective wide-area sensors. When the US Chief of Naval Operations indicated Navy willingness in 1981 to forego ELF funding, the implication was that a shallow submarine breakthrough (whatever the platform used) had not materialised and was not expected to do so soon. In fact, Congressional testimony reveals general agreement among relevant US officials and agencies (DoD,

Navy, Air Force, and CIA) that in the foreseeable future the USSR will not deploy a system which will make the oceans (or even its upper reaches) transparent.[21]

In this regard William Perry is appropriately cited since he seems to be one who has presented the best Soviet case (or the worst US case) on future American SSBN detectability. He did so when justifying the M-X land-based missile (as a hedge against a Soviet ASW breakthrough) and the long-range *Trident* SLBM. His FY81 report as Under Secretary for Research and Development characterised the situation as follows: The Soviet Union is 'in the early development phase of new submarine detection systems which by the early 1990s could have some level of effectiveness against our current nuclear submarines'.[22] As will be seen presently, Perry felt it 'extremely unlikely' that the USSR actually would (as opposed to could) deploy a system capable of detecting SSBNs. Nevertheless, he often dwelt on the 'could' side of the issue, and emphasised that 'current' SSBNs, that is, those which needed to be within 2500 NM of their targets, could have problems. This is because, by concentrating on the limited ocean areas that SSBNs must use, by knowing when a submarine left port, by estimating its speed, and by eliminating regions a submarine might avoid (possibly because of shallow water or heavy merchant traffic) the Soviet Union might be able to isolate some SSBN patrol areas and concentrate their ASW search and attack assets there.[23] Perry pushed for US development of a longer-range SLBM to allow SSBNs greater room in which to manœuvre. He summarised his argument as follows:

> The Soviet Union is pressing very hard on submarine detection and anti-submarine warfare . . . To the extent we maintain these patrol areas [accommodating 2500 NM missiles], we allow the Soviet Union, as they expand their ASW capability, to increase their probability of being able to detect us in relatively limited areas.
>
> Therefore the greatest issue in . . . maintaining . . . survivability . . . was increasing the patrol area . . . We therefore maintain the survivability of the submarines even if

the Soviets make . . . order of magnitude improvements in their ability to localize submarines, an extremely unlikely possibility.[24]

A more likely possibility may be that outlined by Dr David Mann, Perry's counterpart in the Navy Department in 1979. He also characterised projected Soviet capabilities in area terms. After briefly outlining (in censored testimony) Soviet improvements in ASW sensors and forces, he said: 'The improvements will give [them] better technical capabilities to detect, track, and attack submarines operating near the USSR . . . in confined waters or . . . transiting choke-points'.[25] This view seems more restrictive than Perry's in the amount of area for which a threat is foreseen, and it must have played a role in the Navy's decision not to retrofit the longer-range *Trident* C-4 missile into all the submarines previously fitted with the 2500 NM *Poseidon* C-3 missile. Twelve submarines were so retrofitted, but nineteen were not because, as one Admiral put it 'we don't see a threat today that could dictate the backfit'.[26]

In short, then, even if one accepts even the most anxious of American official projections, it would still seem that the best which the Soviet Union might achieve in the foreseeable future is an area detection capability limited to specific areas.

It is always possible, of course, that American projections are wrong, and that the USSR area-search ASW threat is more serious than estimated. The 'group-think' syndrome and a psychological need not to feel threatened have caused many nations in the past to dismiss predictable and grave threats. Independent of such factors, present American appreciation of Soviet non-acoustic detection potential could, as some have suggested, be hampered by Soviet secrecy and by gaps in American knowledge, compared with that of the Soviet Union, about one or another non-acoustic possibility.[27] Such gaps may well exist. An official 1981 comparison of each side's basic non-acoustic ASW technology found it impossible to determine which was more advanced,[28] and an earlier review of intelligence enigmas in Soviet military research and development estimated that some of the unexplained activities 'may be directed against our fleet ballistic missile submarines'.[29]

Therefore, it would be wrong to dismiss outright the possibility of US misjudgement about Soviet non-acoustic potential. Yet the analyses in Chapters 2 and 3 throw considerable doubt on the achievement of an area-search non-acoustic breakthrough by *either* superpower in the foreseeable future. Hence, it seems justified to accept US estimates as valid in the absence of compelling evidence to the contrary. In addition, the crucial question – to be discussed in the next chapter – is whether the USSR could make operational any breakthrough so secretly or quickly as to catch the United States off guard.

SOVIET ATTACK PLATFORMS AND WEAPONS SYSTEMS

In 1984 the Soviet Union had about 285 tactical submarines, but of these only the 120 or so nuclear-powered units would have the speed and endurance to seek out and trail SSBNs in broad ocean areas.[30] Of the 120, furthermore, fifty or so are armed with anti-ship cruise missiles and one would not expect them to be much involved in operations directed against the US ballistic missile submarines. Soviet submarine construction for the 1980s, however, seems much more heavily oriented towards producing SSNs for ASW tasks than it was in the 1970s when the primary emphasis was on producing SSBNs. If the most recent trend in submarine-construction is extrapolated into the future, then one should expect about five or so ASW capable SSNs to appear each year.[31]

Present production centres on the *Victor* III and *Alfa* classes. The former, it may be recalled, probably carries a towed array while the latter is reported to be the world's fastest and deepest-diving submarine. Of significance is that either or both presumably provided the basis for American officials concluding that Soviet SSNs may qualitatively equal or surpass those of the US in some areas.[32]

What seems to remain a weak area in Soviet mobile platforms is the rather limited inventory of fixed-wing ASW aircraft. The USSR has about 190 of these, but only about half (fifty or so *Bear* F units [3000–4000 NMi radius] and fifty or so Il-38 *May* units [1000–1500 NMi]) are suited to open-ocean ASW. They carry radars, sonobuoys, magnetic anomaly detectors (though not on all *Bears*), and torpedoes. None but the *Bear* is being produced, and this only in small numbers. There are no indications as to when successor aircraft might appear. Experiments have certainly been carried out with WIG (Wing-in-Ground) airframes, but it remains to be seen if or when these may become operational in any ASW role.[33]

Of 290 major surface combatants in the Soviet Navy, approximately 130 are designated by the Soviets as ASW ships or have ASW as a major capability.[34] Few if any of them would be likely to play any significant role in anti-SSBN warfare unless an SSBN were to approach Soviet home or near waters in war. It is in those waters that the surface ASW combatants will be concentrated, working in conjunction with other forces to find and destroy enemy submarines, regardless of type. However it can be assumed that the primary targets are US SSNs which might be presumed to be searching for Soviet SSBNs.

There are also non-combatant intelligence collection ships (AGIs). They patrol regularly off US SSBN bases and appear in areas where SSBNs conduct trials, but they could not hope to survive in those areas after a war began.[35]

As for weapons, the VMF has torpedoes and depth charges, with nuclear warhead and rocket-propelled variants for both. Western claims that the non-nuclear systems are more powerful than comparable US systems may well be true in view of the Soviet propensity for large warheads and superiority in chemical explosives.[36] There is also an extensive Soviet inventory of sophisticated mines which could be significant if laid off SSBN bases or across SSBN transit routes by submarines, mini-submarines, bottom-crawlers, aircraft or surface ships.[37] Civilian ships and planes could also play a role here. If nuclear barrage is contemplated, the USSR is estimated to have some 7500 warheads available if all their strategic missile launchers (both land- and sea-based) were primed for attack.[38] Additional warheads would be available on missiles kept in reserve at storage facilities. Soviet warheads tend to have much larger yields than those of the US and ten different missile types or variants have yields of 1 MT or larger and two modifications of the SS-18 alone have 20 MT yields. Most of the remainder of the warheads are 300KT or greater.[39] There is no indication, however, that any of the warheads are of the plunging type which would explode only under water.

The average Soviet ASW submarine, aircraft or surface ship may not be as good as its American counterpart; nevertheless, if the Soviet ASW forces know where an enemy submarine is or where it might be, they might have considerable capability to mount – in areas where they would be free to operate – effective barrier or local 'search-and-destroy' operations. Their approach in home and near waters is likely to be one of massing air, surface and sub-surface forces in a labour-intensive campaign.[40] Massing results in quantity making up for any problems in quality but they may get in each other's way and make distracting acoustic noise. Should they attack, their torpedoes or depth charges – if they are as powerful as some believe – would almost certainly destroy any target the weapons encountered.

Finally, the USSR does not seem to have taken advantage or been able to take advantage of access to foreign ports or facilities in the Atlantic or Pacific in order to base numerous ASW forces regularly abroad or establish ASW ground sites. The vast bulk of the ASW forces, be they air, surface, or sub-surface, are based primarily at home and, until the Soviet Union obtains a large-area open-ocean sensor, it probably makes little sense to base many of them abroad.

NOTES

1. See N. Polmar, 'Thinking About Soviet ASW', *US Naval Institute Proceedings* (May 1976).
2. See MccGwire, 'Naval Power and Soviet Global Strategy', pp. 167–9.

3. See D. C. Daniel, 'Trends and Patterns in Major Soviet Naval Exercises', *Naval War College Review* (Spring 1978) p. 37.
4. See M. MccGwire, 'A New Trend in Soviet Naval Developments', *International Defense Review*, no. 5 (1979) p. 676.
5. N. A. Lomov (ed.) *Scientific–Technical Progress and the Revolution in Military Affairs* (translated and published under the auspices of the US Air Force; Washington: GPO, n.d.) p. 276.
6. Gorshkov, *The Sea Power of the State*, p. 207.
7. See Assembly of the West European Union (WEU), 'Antisubmarine Warfare', p. 7; Synhorst, 'Soviet Strategic Interest'; Burns, *The Secret War for the Ocean Depths*, p. 155; Besnault, *'Genèse, Vie et Survie de SNLE'*, p. 39; Tsipis and Forsberg, *Tactical and Strategic ASW*, p. 81; Polmar 'Soviet ASW: Highly Capable or Irrelevant?', pp. 723 and 726; and J. Adelman, 'Soviet ASW–Ahead or Behind', *Defence* (June 1980) p. 436.
8. L. Booda, 'USSR Catching Up in Ocean Technology', *Sea Power* (September 1980). pp. 34–5. See also 'A Soviet Sub Detection System?', *Newsweek* (8 September 1980) p. 15.
9. See picture and description in *Jane's Fighting Ships 1983–84*, p. 497.
10. See 'Weinberger Says Soviet Device Found Near Base', *International Herald Tribune* (27 June 1983) p. 3; 'Soviet Detector Washes Up Ashore', *Washington Star* (6 June 1981) p. 2; S. Talbott, 'The Soviets Stir Up the Pacific', *Time* (23 March 1981) pp. 54–5; E. Mahony, 'Vessel Trawling Off Block Island Snags Soviet Spy Buoy', *Hartford Courant* (4 March 1983) p. 3; 'Keeping High-Tech Secrets', *Newsweek* (25 January 1982) p. 34; and 'Soviets Bug Trident Sub Testing Range', *Chicago Tribune* (24 June 1983) p. 10.
11. Talbott, 'The Soviets Stir up the Pacific', p. 54.
12. See, *inter alia*, 'Sub Shows Soviet Is Over-Confident, NATO Says', *Baltimore Sun* (10 November 1981) p. 5.
13. See Perry, *FY 1982 Department of Defense Program for Research*, p. I-6.
14. Train, Testimony in *Hearings On Military Posture* and *HR 2970*, p. 775.
15. See 'Some of Our Chips Are Missing', *Time* (14 March 1983) p. 32; Statement of Admiral James Watkins, USN, Chief of Naval Operations before The House Armed Services Committee on the FY 1984 Military Posture and Budget of the US Navy (7 February 1983) p. 41; 'Soviets Spy on Sub With US Designed Device', *Chicago Tribune* (27 June 1983) p. 13.

16. See *supra*, pp. 124–5.
17. Shapiro, *Department of Defense Authorization FY 1979*, Pt 9, pp. 6667. See also W. Manthorpe. 'The Soviet Navy in 1979–Part I', *US Naval Insitute Proceedings* (April 1980) p. 115.
18. See Ball, *Can Nuclear War be Controlled*, p. 44; Jansani, *Outer Space*, chaps. 4 and 6 and pp. 135–53.
19. See, *inter alia*, Toth, 'US Reliance on Nuclear Subs' p. 1; H. Bradsher, 'Soviets Push Research to Locate Submarines', *Washington Star* (31 July 1981) p. 6; and 'Salyut 7 and ASW', *Aerospace Daily* (29 November 1982) p. 137.
20. Supra, pp. 169–70.
21. See in particular statement by Admiral Carter to this effect, *Department of Defense Authorization FY 1982*, Pt 7, p. 4037.
22. Perry, *Department of Defense Authorizations 1981*, Pt 3, pp. 10–11.
23. See Congressional Budget Office, *The US Sea-based Strategic Force*, p. 46.
24. Testimony of William Perry in US Senate Armed Services Committee, *Department of Defense Authorization for Appropriation for Fiscal Year 1980*, 96th Congress, 1st Session (1979) Pt 3, p. 1327.
25. Mann, *Department of Defense Authorization FY 1980*, Pt 6, p. 2992.
26. Carter, *Department of Defense Authorization FY 1982*, Pt 7, p. 139.
27. MccGwire, 'Technological and Operational Trends', p. 52–56.
28. Perry, *FY 1982 Department of Defense Program for Research* (20 January 1981) p. II-32.
29. As quoted in Polmar, p. 728.
30. See *Jane's Fighting Ships 1983–84*, pp. 492–505.
31. Ibid, p. 146.
32. See Perry, *FY 82 Department of Defense Program for Research (20 January 1981)* p. II-33 and Under Secretary of Defense R. DeLauer, *The FY 1984 Department of Defense Program for Research Development and Acquisition*: Prepared for the 98th Congress, 1st Session (1983) p. II-18.
33. *Jane's Fighting Ships 1983–84*, p. 549.
34. Ibid.
35. See Testimony of Rear Admiral Sumner Shapiro in US House Armed Services Committee, *Hearings on Military Posture and HR 2970*, 97th Congress, 1st Session (1981) Pt 3, pp. 31–2 and

'Soviet Spy Ship Lurks Offshore to Study New US *Trident Sub*', *Washington Star* (12 June 1981) p. 5.
36. See J. Bussert, 'ASW Weapons Analysis', *Defense Science and Electronics* (March 1983) pp. 52–4 and DeLauer *The FY 84 Department of Defense Program for Research*, p. II–18.
37. See Perry, *FY 1982 Department of Defense Program for Research* (20 January 1981) p. VII-57.
38. *Soviet Military Power*, pp. 19 and 23.
39. IISS, *Military Balance 1984–85*, p. 133.
40. See Shapiro, *Department of Defense Authorization FY 1979*, Pt 9, p. 6665; Harvey, *FY 1978 Authorization for Military Procurement, Research and Development*, Pt 10, p. 6619; Mann, *Department of Defense Authorization FY 1980*, Pt 6, p. 2969; and Mann in US Senate Appropriations Committee, *Department of Defense Appropriations for Fiscal Year 1980*, 96th Congress, 1st Session (1979) Pt 4, p. 378.

9 Soviet ASW and US SSBNs: Conclusions

As with Chapter 6, this Chapter looks at the intersection of Soviet ASW and US SSBN developments to judge whether the former pose a destabilising threat to the latter. Factors enhancing the USSR's anti-SSBN potential are outlined first, followed by a listing of factors degrading it. An assessment is then offered of the USSR's potential with some concluding observations on the issue of a Soviet breakthrough.

FACTORS ENHANCING THE USSR'S ANTI-SSBN POTENTIAL

1. The USSR has a variety of acoustic detection systems ranging from a purported bottom-mounted area search system in the vicinity of the Soviet homeland to different types of portable systems affixed to, lowered from, or delivered by air, surface, and sub-surface platforms.
2. The Soviet Union also has a vigorous, broad-based, and well-funded non-acoustic research programme which has been continuing for over twenty years.
3. The Soviet Navy has been providing itself with open-ocean ASW attack platforms since the mid-1960s. The most impressive developments may be in the nuclear-powered attack submarine fleet. There were seventy SSNs of various types in 1984, and the force should grow numerically in the foreseeable future. In recent qualitative comparisons of superpower 'leading edge'

deployed technologies, furthermore, the US DoD rated the superpowers 'equal' in the SSN category.
4. The Soviet practice of massing available ASW forces in a labour-intensive campaign may result in quantity making up for any shortfalls in quality. It heightens the prospects of mounting successful barrier or localisation and attack operations against known or suspected enemy submarines.
5. Weapons seems to be an area of strength. The Navy has torpedoes and depth charges, with nuclear warhead and rocket-assisted variants for both. If as powerful as some believe, they should certainly incapacitate any target encountered, including single-hulled US SSBNs. The inventory of mines is believed to be the world's largest, and because the US Navy is poor at countering mines they could have significant effect if laid off American SSBN bases by whatever means.
6. To some extent, any drop in US SSBN numbers simplifies the USSR's application of resources to the anti-SSBN task. As *Ohio*-class ships enter service through the early 1990s, they will make up for the retirement in the early 1980s of the *George Washington* and *Ethan Allen* classes of submarines. The long-term trend, however, is for the SSBN fleet to drop again, beginning in 1993, from over forty units to possibly twenty or less before the year 2000.

FACTORS DEGRADING THE USSR's ANTI-SSBN POTENTIAL

1. America's solutions for ensuring the security of its SSBN fleet are not wholly identical to those that the Soviet Union applies to the protection of its own ballistic missile-carrying fleet, but America's dedication to this task is no less. The SSBN Security Programme closely monitors the USSR's ASW developments and conducts experiments to test the feasibility of different ASW search

methods. When appropriate, countermeasures are devised affecting either the design and engineering of the US submarines or their operational practices.

2. An important countermeasure is the low sound propagation of American SSBNs. *Ohio*-class ships, for example, are said to be the quietest in the world, and the US SSBN force is the primary customer of the US Navy's environmental sensing programme, information from which is applied to finding acoustic hiding places. An indicator of the low sound propagation is that American acoustic systems, reputedly superior to those of the USSR because of better signal-processing, are said to have great difficulty detecting US submarines.

3. Another countermeasure, adoption of the *Trident* longer-range missile, has increased to tens of millions of square nautical miles the area that SSBNs can patrol and still strike Soviet targets. The submarines evidently take advantage of the sea-room allowed in individual ocean basins and, when on 'mod-alert', need not remain within range of their targets. The result is that they keep well away from virtually all Soviet acoustic detection systems. The bottom-moored system seems more oriented towards searching for intruders entering home waters than detecting submarines at the distances where US SSBNs can be expected to remain, and there is no indication that the USSR intends to deploy the system out to those distances. From Chapter 3, furthermore, it should be clear that monitoring submarine traffic in large areas of distant waters would require building from many tens to hundreds of towed acoustic array vessels and/or the deployment of tens to hundreds of thousands or more of self-contained listening devices (depending upon their acoustic detection range) such as have occasionally washed up near US SSBN bases. Again, there is no indication that the Soviet Union is preparing to do either of these things.

4. American officials do not foresee a Soviet detection breakthrough (non-acoustic or otherwise) putting the US SSBN force at hazard in the foreseeable future. In

the 'extremely unlikely possibility' that the USSR's advances threaten *Poseidon*-armed submarines, the longer-range *Trident*-armed boats should remain safe.[1]

5. The USSR does not seem to have taken advantage or been able to take advantage of access to foreign ports or facilities in the Atlantic or Pacific to base numerous ASW forces or to develop ground sites. The vast bulk of Soviet ASW assets are found in the homeland and, until the Soviet Union obtains a large area-search sensor for distant regions, it makes little sense to base many attack platforms abroad.

6. Basing substantial forces abroad would also seem to run contrary to the heavy commitment of maintaining a defence perimeter around the homeland. Doing so will place such heavy demands on the Soviet Navy in war that it is difficult to see where it will obtain the assets for significantly challenging American SSBNs operating outside the perimeter. As Secretary Weinberger put it in a citation presented earlier, the Soviet concept for wartime ASW operations calls 'for anti-submarine forces to be concentrated in home waters in support of newer classes of Soviet ballistic missile submarines'.[2]

7. It seems safe to assume that the US Navy acts to ensure that US SSBNs are not being trailed. 55 per cent of the *Lafayette*-class submarines and 66 per cent of the *Ohios* can be expected to be deployed at any one time (resulting in a total of about eighteen SSBNs at sea at all times in 1983). With their own towed-array sonar and quiet operations, each should certainly detect a trailer before the trailer detects the SSBN. By committing modern submarines, such as *Alfa*- and *Victor*-class boats, to protecting Soviet SSBNs, furthermore, the USSR limits the number of modern SSNs available for trail.

8. Barrage seems no more an option for the Soviet Union, now or in the foreseeable future, than it is for the US. There is no prospect that the Soviet Union will develop a system capable of localising all deployed US SSBNs to a small enough area, or to filter out false alarms, to make barrage feasible. There is also no indication that Soviet warheads are of the plunging type.

NET ASSESSMENT AND CONCLUSIONS

Protracted conventional war scenario

Table 9.1 summarises factors enhancing and factors degrading the USSR's anti-SSBN potential. The latter clearly outweigh the former. The Soviet mine inventory could pose serious problems if laid in the vicinity of US SSBN bases and transit routes, but such action would not affect the units which were already at sea prior to mining. Until the SSBN force totals begin to drop again in the mid-1990s, at least eighteen and perhaps as many as twenty-four submarines would presumably always be in the high seas before mines were laid.

A US SSBN might be in difficulty if it were detected and attacked by Soviet ASW units working together, for their combined efforts and the lethality of their weapons could prove decisive, but Soviet units would have to find the submarine first. The prospect for any but random detections in the foreseeable future seem so low as to render impossible the attrition of a destabilising proportion of American SSBNs. This is particularly true if, as argued in the Introduction, only seven-to-nine submarines are sufficient to forestall any US inclination to use rather than lose its SSBNs. Attrition should also be minimal because the vast bulk of Soviet forces, including their most modern ASW units, will be committed to maintenance of the maritime defence perimeter around the Soviet homeland. In short, while any US SSNs entering Soviet near waters would have to face the bulk of what ASW capabilities the USSR possessed, US SSBNs, by staying out of those waters (as they almost certainly would) should evade those capabilities entirely. Wherever located, furthermore, Soviet ASW forces would undoubtedly themselves suffer attrition in the course of a war even though the US Navy, in contrast to its Soviet counterpart, does not seem to have any specific programme for seeking out and destroying enemy ASW units.

TABLE 9.1 *Summary of factors enhancing and degrading the USSR's anti-SSBN potential*

Factors enhancing	Factors degrading
1. Soviet acoustic detection systems range from purported bottom-mounted system in the vicinity of the homeland to a variety of portable systems	1. The Americans are determined to ensure the survivability of their SSBNs, and the SSBN Security Program continually seeks to keep abreast of potential threats and countermeasures
2. The USSR's non-acoustic research programme is extremely well supported and broad-based	2. The low sound propagation of US SSBNs makes any passive acoustic detection very difficult
3. The Soviet Navy has built up an inventory of ocean-going ASW prosecution units, with the most impressive area of development probably being the SSN fleet	3. US SSBN patrol areas widely outflank present and prospective Soviet acoustic area search systems
4. If Soviet ASW forces know where a submarine might be, the chances that they might incapacitate it are strong because of their tendency to mass available forces in a labour-intensive campaign	4. US officials do not foresee a Soviet breakthrough (non-acoustic or otherwise) putting the SSBN force in hazard in the foreseeable future
5. The Navy seems to have an impressive array of weapons which, if as powerful as some believe, should incapacitate any target they encounter	5. The USSR does not seem to have taken advantage or been able to take advantage of access to foreign ports or facilities in the Atlantic or Pacific to base numerous ASW forces or ground sites
6. The long-term trend of a drop in US SSBN numbers may simplify the USSR's application of resources to the anti-SSBN task	6. The Soviet Navy's heavy commitment to maintaining a defence perimeter around the homeland during war makes it difficult to see where it could, now and in the foreseeable future, obtain the assets to challenge significantly American SSBNs operating outside the perimeter

7. In the face of US countermeasures, a Soviet trailing threat to the US SSBN force seems very small

8. Into the foreseeable future, barrage does not seem any more an option for the USSR than it is for the US

Surprise strike scenario

The prospects for destabilising surprise attacks against US SSBNs seem also very low indeed especially if the survival of only one or two US submarines is enough to deter the USSR from contemplating a first strike. The lack of an open-ocean detection and filtering system makes moot any question of nuclear barrage or simultaneous attack with air-delivered conventional weapons. US countermeasures would also seem to eliminate any Soviet prospect for continuous trailing of the SSBNs at sea. Beyond these more narrow considerations are some of the same contextual factors mentioned earlier as restricting any US surprise attack. One is the difficulty of preparing for all-out war without disclosing one's hand. Another is the problem of destroying virtually simultaneously not only SSBNs, but also all other US nuclear retaliatory systems and related command-and-control elements.

Some final thoughts

Only one conclusion is warranted from the above analysis: it does not appear that the USSR will have a destabilising anti-SSBN capability in the foreseeable future. Nevertheless, some respected analysts believe that, while US ASW capabilities at present surpass those of the Soviet Union, it is the USSR which has greater destabilising potential in the long term. They accept that Soviet efforts to protect their own strategic submarines should succeed in preventing the Americans, even if they wanted to do so, from incapacitating a destabilising proportion of Soviet SSBNs. But they also argue that the USSR does have an explicit anti-SSBN policy, that it is devoting considerable resources to a non-acoustic breakthrough, that the US SSBN Security Programme cannot so duplicate the level of Soviet non-acoustic research as to understand fully how far the Soviets have come or what they might achieve; and that, by concentrating so much on reducing noise and increasing the ocean areas where SSBNs can operate independently, the US has paid too little attention to reducing non-acoustic observables and has too readily discounted the possibility of a non-acoustic breakthrough which might threaten unprotected SSBNs in the high seas.[3]

Few would disagree with the first two points, and the last two constitute plausible possibilities against which new evidence must be continually evaluated. Yet, as argued here, there is considerable reason for doubt that either superpower can in fact hope to achieve a non-acoustic area-search breakthrough in the foreseeable future. Should one occur, it would still be subject to environmental conditioning and countermeasures with some of the latter – such as keeping submarines running slowly and deeply – being relatively simple to implement.

The crucial question is whether the US could discover the occurrence and nature of a breakthrough *fast* enough to counter it. The conversion of a breakthrough into an operational, fully reliable, well-exercised capability with destabilising potential should take at least a decade or more,[4] and the closer it comes to fruition, the easier it will be to discover. As a former US Director of Naval Intelligence put it, it is 'difficult . . . to know' about Soviet non-acoustic technology when it is in the planning and laboratory phases, but it 'is easy to collect information . . . when he is operating and testing something'.[5] In the end, full operationalisation would probably require the deployment of many sensors, the activation of data links, the purchase of additional attack platforms, and the exercising of all these systems. In view of the stated ease of collecting information on such activities, the years over which these activities would take place before the USSR had a destabilising potential, and the priority which the US attaches to monitoring Soviet anti-submarine developments, it seems reasonable to assume that enough information could be acquired to allow time for the adoption of appropriate countermeasures.

NOTES

1. See above, p. 181.
2. See above, p. 102.
3. See especially MccGwire, 'Technological and Operational Trends', pp. 52–6.
4. It took the Soviet Union more than a decade, for example, to give themselves the very formidable anti-carrier warfare capability they have today, and carriers are certainly easier to find than submarines. Recall also that the Soviet Navy started in the mid-1960s taking in hand open-ocean ASW prosecution platforms, but it was not until 1973 that ASW was a major part of a major open-ocean exercise.
5. Shapiro, *Department of Defense Authorization FY 1979*, Pt 9, pp. 6666–7.

Part IV
Conclusion

10 Conclusions

This chapter is divided into four parts. The first presents the study's overall conclusions on the stability implications of superpower ASW developments. These conclusions provide an appropriate backdrop for two sets of remarks which are pertinent to the subject. The first set addresses the prospects of negotiated arms control specifically aimed at enhancing strategic stability; the second offers a few general thoughts on the survivability of British and French SSBNs. Finally there are two statements, one from a US and the other from a Soviet official, which seem particularly apt as closing observations.

FINDINGS CONCERNING STABILITY

This study set out to address whether the United States or the Soviet Union will have a strategically destabilising ASW capability in the foreseeable future. In the absence of an unpredictable breakthrough, it does not seem that either could have such a capability before roughly the mid-1990s and doubtful after that. While by definition one cannot predict the unpredictable, it is very hard to see how that judgement could be overturned. The main reason has less to do with any lack of progress in achieving greater ASW capabilities than with the efforts of both states to ensure that their SSBNs remain survivable. The United States, after all, has made and is continuing to make considerable strides in acoustic detection, and it has provided itself with qualitatively impressive attack platforms. The USSR is also much more capable in ASW today than it was twenty or so years ago when it began its massive investment in ASW research, especially non-acoustic, and in open-ocean attack platforms. The important point is that neither superpower ignored the other's ASW advances; rather, actual or anticipated progress spurred each to make changes in the SSBNs themselves and in their operational practice to ensure that these strategically sensitive, enormously expensive, platforms remain survivable.

To a large extent each has gone its own way. The Americans, for instance, have tended to concentrate on noise reduction more than have the USSR, but some or all of Soviet SSBNs may be more capable of countering active acoustic transmissions because of a sound absorbancy coating over their hulls. Their double hulls, furthermore, may make them better able to absorb the effects of an attack.

Similarly, while both superpower SSBN forces are increasingly made up of units which can cover their targets at very long ranges, each has taken advantage of that ability in different ways. The United States has deployed the boats in wide expanses of the deep open-ocean, thereby putting them far beyond the reach of most Soviet sensor systems for years to come. This practice also vastly complicates all phases of the ASW process should the USSR markedly and unexpectedly increase its ability to monitor large areas of ocean far from the homeland. While on patrol, furthermore, a US boat generally receives and desires little or no support from friendly general-purpose forces after it leaves the immediate vicinity of its base. In contrast, the Soviet Union has taken advantage of the long range of its seaborne missiles to deploy submarines near to home and in ice-laden waters which can be defended. In this regard, choke points can be turned into barriers. The clear intent is to outflank American area-search acoustic devices found in the open oceans, thereby partially rendering moot the question of Soviet SSBNs being noisier than those of the US. A second intention is probably to simplify the protective efforts of Soviet general-purpose naval forces, which now have as one of their major missions the attrition of America's ASW capabilities and the defence of Soviet SSBNs. A third intention may be to take advantage of the nearby ice to neutralise nearly all overhead detection sensors and the possibility of being subjected to barrage attack as well as to make trailing by SSNs more difficult.

As for peacetime deployments, the United States maintains both more SSBNs and, because of a smaller fleet, a considerably greater proportion of its SSBN fleet at sea. It thus insures against the deployed boats being caught in port in the event of a surprise attack. The Soviet Union seems to assume that Western preparations for attack could not be hidden and that the boats would have time to move out on warning. As a result they may well feel that the SSBNs most secure in peacetime are those in port and that, if deployed for war, those units and their crews would have the maximum endurance possible precisely because they had not been at sea in the period immediately preceding the warning of war. This would seem to accord with a general Soviet predilection for a 'surge' capacity rather than a high peacetime deployment rate and may say something about Soviet confidence in keeping equipment at a high state of readiness.

Both the US and the Soviet Union have also sought security in numbers, and the trend is expected to continue through the early 1990s. The Soviet SSBN fleet is projected to remain consistently at sixty or so SSBNs at least until the 1990s while the US fleet will grow from thirty-four to over forty. The American force, however, is then projected to drop sharply to about twenty units, all of the *Ohio* class, by the end of the century as a result of the block retirement of submarines which first appeared between 1963 and 1967. The ultimate number of *Ohio* submarines has yet to be decided, however. Twenty is an interim planning figure, and the final number could be less since at least one justification for the purchase of the *Trident* 2 (D-5) missile is that fewer *Ohio* SSBNs would be needed than if they were armed only with *Trident* 1 (C-4) – the missile being placed in them today. This is a potentially worrying development. The reason is the impossibility of predicting today the status of Soviet ASW so far into the future; it may be such that a comparatively large SSBN fleet may be important to ensure stability. As the Scowcroft Commission report put it, 'the prospect of concentrating all of the submarine-launched [ballistic] missiles at sea in a very few large [*Ohio*] submarines raises some concern'.[1] Offsetting this concern, however, is the prospect that the drop in numbers will not begin to occur until the mid-1990s. This gives the United States time to consider and, if necessary implement, alternatives such as the accelerated purchase of *Ohio* submarines or the design of a smaller, less expensive submarine, which can be bought in larger quantities. No less important is the fact that both the Americans and the Soviet Union are arming general-purpose submarines with strategic nuclear cruise missiles. While not necessary intended as an SSBN protection measure, this development will have that effect by significantly increasing the number of strategic missile carriers with which adversary ASW forces will have to contend. Consequently, numbers should continue to provide some security though they will consist of more than just ballistic missile submarines.

All things considered therefore, the SSBN protection measures adopted by or available to each superpower seem well suited for dealing with the other's foreseeable ASW threat. This does not mean that all SSBNs would survive a surprise attack or conventional war attrition, but as argued in Chapters 6 and 9, enough should survive to ensure deterrence and stability for the next ten years or so and probably beyond.

The major factor which could overturn that comforting assessment is an unpredictable ASW breakthrough, but whether and how long it could prove destabilising will again depend on what measures are implemented to counter it. Fortunately for SSBN forces, nearly all submarine observables are subject to natural masking and mimicking, thereby providing scope for limiting detections on the one hand and causing too many 'detections', that is false alarms, on the other. SSBN protection forces would also have the option in war of destroying critical elements of either the breakthrough system or the overall ASW network of which it is a part, thereby negating the system's utility without destroying the system directly.

Of course, how well a state reacts to a breakthrough by its opponent depends on its discovering or anticipating the breakthrough and understanding how it is employed. Again, SSBN forces are fortunate that conversion of a breakthrough into a destabilising operational capability should take a decade or more and is almost certain to involve visible activities – such as deploying new equipment and conducting experiments and exercises. Nevertheless, SSBN protection authorities may not discover that a breakthrough has occurred, or they may react too slowly, incorrectly or not at all, possibly because of cover and deception, poor intelligence-gathering or analysis, a failure of understanding, or simply an unwillingness to accept the undesired prospect of vulnerable SSBNs. The consequence could well be instability were it not for the fact that a state's determination to eliminate the other's SSBNs is not unfettered.

In other words, other concerns temper each superpower's desire to rid itself of the SSBN threat by force. An 'out-of-the-blue' surprise attack against ballistic missile submarines could occur only in the context of initiating a general war, a daunting prospect for any rational decision-maker. In particular, initiating a comprehensive pre-emptive nuclear strike with the aim of eliminating an opponent's land- and sea-based nuclear deterrent is likely to remain impossible because of factors such as timing, co-ordination, secrecy and the uncertainties of firing over the Pole. Should a war begin conventionally instead, either deliberately or accidentally, the overall demands on superpower ASW forces will be heavy. As well as hunting American SSBNs, Soviet ASW forces will remain concerned with establishing a maritime defence perimeter and protecting their own SSBNs. US ASW forces will be unable to ignore the 300 or so other submarines in the Soviet inventory, for some will be threatening the American homeland or Eurasian theatres of war with long-range cruise missiles, others will threaten Western sea control and high-value surface ships, and yet others will directly support Soviet SSBNs.

In conclusion therefore, it seems that American and Soviet ASW capabilities should not be destabilising in the foreseeable future, in the absence of an unpredictable breakthrough, and the main reason is that SSBN forces have undertaken the necessary measures to protect themselves.

An ASW breakthrough could well be destabilising, but a critical determinant will again be the reaction of SSBN protection forces. Should there be a breakthrough with destabilising potential, its impact would be mitigated by the fact that a state's determination to eliminate the other's SSBNs by force is not unfettered.

NEGOTIATED ASW ARMS CONTROL: AN ADDITIONAL MEASURE?

The focus to this point has been exclusively on measures each superpower can implement unilaterally to protect its own SSBNs. It is now appropriate to consider an altogether different type of measure, one based on mutual US–Soviet agreement to help to ensure the survivability of their own and the other's SSBNs through negotiated restrictions on the activities of ASW systems or forces.

There are many proposals to that end found in the published literature, but they fall into four main groups.[2] One group would restrict the number, quality, or deployment of area-search sensors. Examples here include a ban on active acoustic sensors above some agreed power level or a prohibition on the mid-ocean deployment of any acoustic sensor resting on or anchored to the ocean floor. A second group of proposals would restrict the number or the activities of attack forces. Most numerical suggestions concentrate here on the establishment of an absolute or a flexible limit on SSN numbers, the latter being directly linked to the number of adversary SSBNs. Proposals proscribing activities often call for a ban on SSBN trailing, with active acoustic trailing most often mentioned. Some would also outlaw attacks against SSBNs which identify themselves during a non-nuclear war either by surfacing or by emitting a distinctive signal when submerged. A third group of proposals unites elements of the first two by advocating SSBN sanctuaries within which opposing ASW systems or forces would not be permitted to operate. The sanctuaries could be off each state's homeland, possibly near SSBN bases or in isolated areas. The last group of proposals would regulate anti-submarine weapons, and the only specific suggestion yet made would outlaw the testing or deployment of plunging nuclear re-entry vehicles.

If the SALT record is any indicator, the prospects for agreement on negotiated controls are not good. They were evidently not an agenda item in SALT I or II. The USSR did raise the question of controls in general and sanctuaries in particular in SALT II, but only as part of its response to an American attempt to discuss banning of depressed-trajectory SLBMs.[3] (These have a relatively short time of flight and could be an important element of a surprise attack especially against US Command structures or bomber bases.) Neither the US initiative nor the Soviet response was pursued, but while in Vienna in 1979 for the SALT II signing, President Carter did tell President Brezhnev that creation of safe havens for SSBNs might be a possible topic for SALT III.[4] There is no information as to whether the topic came up in START, but continued Soviet interest in safe havens was implied in a speech by President Brezhnev reported on 17 March 1982.[5] Addressing the Soviet Trade Union Congress, he called for 'maximum restraint in the military activity of the two opposing blocs of states', and chose as his example 'a mutual limit on operations of naval fleets. In particular, we would consider it possible' he went on to say, 'to agree that the missile submarines of the two sides should be removed from their present extensive combat patrol areas and that their cruises should be restricted by limits mutually agreed upon'. While Brezhnev's statement spoke of limits on SSBN operations, it did not, however, specifically address limitations on ASW forces.

For a number of reasons, it would be surprising if ASW controls were to be part of any future START agreement. One reason is the lack of impetus for agreeing on this issue. A second is the strong opposition to such controls from groups in both states as well as the lukewarm support which might come even from some arms control advocates. A third is the complexity of the problem of achieving equitable, verifiable and acceptable controls.

Lack of impetus

If, as argued here, SSBNs will not be threatened to a destabilising degree, then there is no compelling force driving the superpowers to reach agreement on anti-submarine controls. The greatest impetus for agreement would come if *both* nations felt threatened simultaneously, for if only one did, the other would have no incentive to negotiate unless it were unambiguously committed to stability or unless it sought to win concessions in other areas of the strategic balance.

Without a destabilising threat to either state's SSBN fleet, the only incentive might be a mutual desire to agree a confidence-building measure (CBM). If confidence is really to be built, an agreement would probably have to be not only negotiable but also obviously beneficial to both sides. A prime candidate here is the outlawing of ocean-plunging RVs or their testing. Since neither side has evidently tested or deployed such weapons, neither should feel it was giving up anything critical. Additionally, the sensitive question of verification should be no great problem if a total test ban of such systems is what is agreed.

Opposition and support for controls

In contrast to the absence of any strong incentive for negotiating controls is the existence of powerful groups which would surely argue against any measure limiting what they do. These are not only the military professionals dedicated to ASW, but also the civilian industrial and research organisations which participate in and benefit from each nation's ASW effort. In addition, spokesmen with damage-limiting perspectives can be expected to argue that absolutely no restrictions should be placed on systems or forces which can counter enemy nuclear delivery systems. Others would surely argue that reducing an enemy's SSBNs during a war could encourage it to cease hostilities and negotiate. (This is the converse of the 'use-or-lose' argument.)

It is appropriate to note that not all proponents of arms

control would necessarily be enthusiastic about attempting to negotiate ASW restrictions. It is easy to imagine some of the same reservations offered by Feld and Rathjens in 1972 being echoed today.[6] They had, in effect, two major concerns, both grounded in the precedent of SALT I. First, they feared that negotiations could lead to undesirable military spending or programmes. One reason is the 'bargaining chip syndrome' where programmes which might not otherwise be approved on their merits are accepted because they support a nation's negotiating posture. A second reason is that negotiations could lead to unwarranted concern about the survivability of the sea-based deterrent, and thus to the approval of unnecessary measures to shore up survivability. A third reason is that in order to win support for an agreement proponents might have to make concessions and themselves support programmes not restricted by an agreement.

Feld and Rathjens expressed another major concern, namely that negotiations could lead to a distortion of priorities in both arms control and strategic weapons programmes. They believed that negotiations could result in a 'disproportionate weight being given to a scenario for the initiation of nuclear war that is presently implausible, and likely to remain so under almost any circumstances – that of a deliberate "first strike" – while we pay far less attention than their seriousness warrants to other problems'. Among the latter they included accidental nuclear war, limited nuclear war and the proliferation of nuclear weapons.

Complexity of the issues

Achieving agreement on nearly all proposals will be difficult in any case because of the many factors that both superpowers will consider when evaluating proposed regimes. One is the impact of any restrictions on the performance of critical tasks unconnected with any desire to eliminate the other side's SSBNs. For example, restrictions on area-search sensors, or on the number and deployment of attack forces, could make more difficult attempts to obtain adequate strategic warning, the collection of other necessary intelligence, the achievement of sea control in general, the protection of high-value surface ships or friendly SSBNs in particular, and the countering of 'nth country' SSBNs – this last being a factor of special concern to the USSR in view of the existence of British and French as well as Chinese ballistic missile submarines. In addition, while the establishment of sanctuaries by agreement may be consistent with Soviet wartime maritime bastion strategy, it would be inconsistent with the intention of the US to ensure open-ocean sea control by putting the Soviet Navy on the defensive close to home.

A second factor that both Superpowers would consider is the perceived equity of each proposal. The asymmetries in the ASW capabilities of both states could make it difficult for them to agree on equipment limitations or operational controls such that each feels equal in what it gives up. This factor is no problem if both agree to forego technologies in common upon which neither is highly reliant – such as large fixed active sonars or plunging RVs – but such measures would have no immediate appreciable impact on SSBN survivability. Even then, one or other superpower might be unwilling to give up an option that it feels may be important later though it may not be so now.

At least six other factors would certainly be considered, but none needs elaboration. Would any restrictions apply to one's own allies or those of the other superpowers? Would they require radical changes to be made in current or planned force postures and research programmes? Is the agreement verifiable and does it allow for timely countermeasures if violations were to occur? Do the negotiations or agreement provisions require the divulging of secret information? Could the provisions of any agreement be readily circumvented or be rendered irrelevant by concentrating on unrestricted technologies or operational options?

The cumulative effect of all these considerations can make the negotiation process very complex and the prospects for success highly questionable. An important consequence is that, if stability is to be ensured in this area of the strategic balance, it may well continue to be due exclusively to unilateral measures taken by both superpowers rather than to bilateral agreement. Within that context, what can be said about the survivability of British, French and Chinese SSBNs in the face of Soviet ASW capabilities?

SOVIET ASW AND THE SSBN FORCES OF BRITAIN AND FRANCE

As noted earlier, Britain and France have ballistic missile submarine fleets which they are modernising, and China will soon begin to operate the first unit of what will probably be a small force of SSBNs. Discussion of the survivability prospects of Chinese units is too premature to be of any value, but two general thoughts can be offered about the prospects for British and French submarines.

Under present circumstances, it seems inconceivable that the USSR would act against any British and French strategic nuclear forces independent of a conflict with the United States. This means that a disarming surprise strike against the British and French deterrents, while theoretically possible, would occur only in the context of a larger attack against the American deterrent, and, as argued in Chapters 6 and 9, the probability of such an attack is in any case extremely low and so the former can be disregarded as a separate case.

In a NATO–Warsaw Pact conventional war, the survivability prospects of British or French SSBNs seem excellent if they reach the open sea (possibly with the aid of friendly forces before or during war), implement anti-trail measures (again possibly with friendly support), otherwise operate carefully, and remain south of the United Kingdom-Greenland-Iceland Gap. A submarine patrolling north of the Gap could well survive, but by patrolling south it lessens considerably the assets the USSR could devote to anti-SSBN warfare. These would consist primarily of Soviet ASW submarines. Unsupported by a wide-area search system and confronted by anti-trail measures, they should be hard pressed to find and prosecute any western SSBN determined to stay out of harm's way.

Remaining south of the Gap should pose no great difficulty for the UK submarines, for their *Polaris* A-3 missiles (with 2500 NMi. range) can strike the USSR's largest cities (Moscow, Leningrad and Kiev) with the submarines remaining in an arc stretching roughly from Gibraltar to the tip of Greenland. In the mid-1990s new British SSBNs will be armed with the *Trident 2* missile (6000 NMi. range), allowing them to attack the same cities from nearly anywhere in the North Atlantic. French SSBNs fitted with the M-20 missile (about 1500 NMi. range) have now to patrol north of the Gap to hit the same targets, but all French SSBNs except the oldest (*Le Redoutable*) are being converted to the M-4 Missile whose range (2200 NMi.) will give them a distant targeting capability roughly comparable to that of the British *Polaris* submarines today.

CLOSING OBSERVATIONS

This study has concentrated on the survivability prospects of superpower SSBNs. Thus, it is appropriate to end with the following observations, one by a former high US defense official and the other by a no less important Soviet spokesman. The American is William Perry, and, as noted in the Introduction, he was an influential spokesman on the issue of SSBN survivability in his capacity as Under Secretary of Defense for Research and Engineering in the Carter Administration. Hence, it seems significant that he wrote after leaving office:

> Both the United States and the USSR are pursuing intensive efforts in submarine detection research and development. During this decade we will likely have a high degree of technical progress in various techniques now under development, but the operational systems resulting from such technological progress do not necessarily pose a threat. Even if they did pose a threat, we probably could devise effective countermeasures . . . In this field the offense will continue to have the advantage over the

defense; that is, strategic submarines should be able to maintain their high degree of invulnerability.[7]

The second observation is from Sergei Gorshkov, the Soviet Navy's Commander-in-chief. Though quoted earlier in this study, it bears repetition because it seems so consistent with Perry's:

> Can submarines, despite constant improvements in the means of anti-submarine defense, achieve strategic goals in a war at sea? The answer to this question demanded much research. All of it invariably confirmed the high effectiveness of submarines when rightly used and given proper combat backing. This conclusion proved particularly convincing in relation to atomic-powered submarines.[8]

NOTES

1. Scowcroft Commission, *Report of President's Commission on Strategic Forces*, p. 9.
2. See, *inter alia*, Garwin, 'Anti-submarine Warfare', pp. 248–59; Feld and G. Rathjens, 'ASW, Arms Control and the Sea-Based Deterrent', in K. Tsipis *et al.* (eds.) *The Future of the Sea-Based Deterrent* (Cambridge: MIT Press, 1973) pp. 121–47; J. Wit, 'Sanctuaries and Security: Suggestions for ASW Arms Control', *Arms Control Today* (October 1980); M. MccGwire, 'Soviet-American Naval Arms Control', in G. Quester (ed.) *Navies and Arms Control* (New York: Praeger, 1980) pp. 44–100; K. Booth, 'Law and Strategy in Northern Waters', *Naval War College Review* (July–August 1981) pp. 3–21; R. B. Byers, 'Seapower and Arms Control: Problems and Prospects', *International Journal* (Summer 1981) pp. 487–514; R. G. Purver, 'The Desirability and Feasibility of Negotiated Controls on Strategic Anti-Submarine Warfare', paper prepared for the 23rd Annual Convention of the International Studies Convention, Cincinnati, Ohio, 24–7 March 1982; and B. McCue, *The Threat to the SSBN: Unilateral and Bilateral Response* (unpublished Master's Thesis; Cambridge: MIT, 1980).
3. S. Talbott, *Endgame: The Inside Story of SALT II* (New York: Harper Colophon Books, 1980) pp. 208–9.

4. R. P. Labrie (ed.) *SALT Handbook: Key Documents and Issues* (Washington: 1979) p. 417.
5. An excerpt from the speech appeared in *The New York Times* (17 March, 1982) p. 6.
6. Feld and Rathjens, 'ASW, Arms Control and the Sea-Based Deterrent', pp. 140–6.
7. Perry, 'Technological Prospects', p. 138.
8. Gorshkov, *The Sea Power of the State*, p. 190.

Index

Abdel-Hady, M.   63
ABM system   4, 8, 117
acoustic detection: sensors 65–70, 83, 85, 119, 126, 145, 146; US superiority in 2, 178, 201; acoustic modelling 119–23. *See also*: arrays, acoustic; hull of submarine; hydrophones; Integrated Undersea Surveillance; Surveillance Towed Array Sensor; noise; RDSS; silencing of submarines; sonar; Sound Surveillance
acoustic indicators and signals   27–36, 49
Acoustic Research Center, Moffet Field   120
acoustic shadows   122
AGIs (Soviet intelligence collection ships)   183
aircraft   3, 9, 19, 47, 60, 61, 67, 71, 72, 76–8, 125, 130–1, 183.   *See also*: airships; helicopters; *Orion*; wing-in-ground
aircraft carriers   101, 150
air-drag on satellites   62, 63
Alfa submarines 102, 182, 192
altimeters   79, 87, 123
anchored sensors. *See* bottom-mounted
antennae   169–70, 179
anti-ballistic-missile system (ABM)   4, 8, 117
Arctic seas, operations in   104–8, 118, 132–3, 146, 149
arms control, negotiated   206–11
Arms Control and Disarmament Agency (ACDA)   166
arrays   119, 122–5, 147
arrays, acoustic, towed   60, 66–8, 109, 125, 132, 166, 177, 192. *See also* Surveillance Towed Array Sensor
Artemis sonar   126
Atlantic, operations in   103, 118, 123–4, 161
atmospheric pressure   48, 74

Ballistic Missile Early Warning System (BMEWS)   117
Baltic states   105
Bangor, Washington   168
Barents Sea   177
barrage   3, 20–1, 136, 148, 149, 155, 166, 183, 192, 195
barrier operations 20, 66, 70, 71, 76, 77, 84–8, 184, 190. *See also* mines
bases   61, 102–3, 105, 168, 183, 184, 192, 194, 206
bathyphotometers   42
bathythermographs   46
beam-forming techniques   69
Bear aircraft   183
Besnault, R.   33
biological luminescence   42–3, 51
blockade   20
bombers   3, 9
bottom of sea, condition of   31, 33, 34, 48
bottom-crawlers   109, 178, 183
bottom-mounted instruments   39, 59, 66, 67, 70, 109, 177, 189, 191, 194, 206
Brezhnev, President   207

British submarines 34, 175, 176, 210, 211
Brown, Harold 20–1, 135–6
bubbles 23
Bundy, McGeorge 6
buoys 45, 46, 66–8, 85, 125, 130, 169, 183

cables 66, 109, 123, 125, 177
calibration of sensor data 73–4
Cann, Gerald 118–19
Captor mine 135, 136, 149
Carrier Battle Group (CBG) 130, 132, 153
Carter, President 4, 207
cavitation 29, 35
Charleston, S. Carolina 168
chemical explosives 183
Chilton *et al.* 72
Chinese submarines 175–6, 210, 211
choke points 20, 104, 181, 202
circulation patterns 48
civil defence 117
Claytor, Graham 137
cloud 73, 74, 76–8, 82, 86, 87
communications 169, 170, 179
computer technology 72, 119, 120, 122, 132, 145
confidence-building measure (CBM) 208
contaminants 43–4, 51, 70, 71, 77, 85
contrast resolution of sensors 75, 78
conventional war 3, 4, 9, 151–5, 205
convergence zones 32–3
convoy duties 130, 150, 153
costs: of building submarines 133, 163; of operations 61, 135; of warheads 165; of silencing machinery 36
countermeasures: to detection 22, 23, 35–6, 69, 83, 84, 109, 147–8, 191, 195; to mines 169, 190
Cox, A. W. 33

crew proficiency in noise reduction 109
cruise missiles 60, 117, 130, 132, 133, 150, 182
currents 32, 40, 42, 46, 48

data processing. *See* processing
data relay satellite 80
Davis, C. M. Jr 70–1
decoys 22, 23, 35, 70, 134, 149, 167, 170
Defense Advanced Research Projects Agency (DARPA) 119, 120, 126, 129, 146
'delousing' 22, 23
Delta submarines 14, 15, 97–9, 103, 148
density of water 46, 48
depressed trajectory SLBMs 207
depth of sensors 67–8
depth of submarines: in barrage 20; effect on detectability 29, 32, 36, 37, 42–5, 49–51, 69, 168, 179; diving depth 84, 86, 134, 182. *See also* layers of water
depth charges 131, 133, 183, 190. *See also* SUBROC
design of submarines. *See* hull
deterrence 1, 3–8, 117, 147, 151, 175, 195, 204. *See also* stability of strategic relationship.
dipoles 70
Doenitz, Karl 38
drilling, effect on ocean noise 33

eddies 32, 36, 121
Einzig, R. E. 70–1
electric field sensors 70
electromagnetic effects 38–40, 49, 50, 130, 146, 179
electromagnetic sensors 72–83, 86, 120
environmental data 72–4, 110, 120–3, 145–7, 167, 191
environmental effects 23, 27, 32, 36, 40, 147. *See also* cloud;

marine life; rain; waves; wind
Ethan Allen SSBNs   163, 190
exercises   170–1, 175
extremely low frequency (ELF) electric fields   39, 40, 49, 50, 169, 170, 179

false alarms and targets   19, 21, 24, 33, 34, 42, 48, 51, 52, 69, 70, 76, 84, 126, 147, 150, 204
Feld and Rathjens   209
fibre, optical   71
Finland   105
fish   31, 40, 43
floating wire antenna (FWA)   169
'flow'   29, 35
forward-looking infra-red (FLIR) systems   77, 86
French submarines   34, 175, 176, 210, 211

galvanic currents   39, 70
Garwin, R.   69, 83
'gatekeeper' forces   22, 23
Geiger, R. K.   121, 122
George Washington SSBNs   163, 190
Gorshkov, S.   102, 103, 154, 176, 212
gradiometers   40, 47
Grechko, A. A.   101
Greenland–Iceland–UK Gap   104, 136
Greenland Sea   103, 104

Hayward, Thomas   118
helicopters   60, 67
Hodara, H.   78
Holy Loch   168
Honhart, D. C.   74
Huh, O. K.   78
hull of submarine: detection of   50, 51, 77, 79, 129; streamlining of   35, 45, 51, 52, 166; anechoic coating of   35, 69, 100, 167, 202; sensors attached to   45, 132;

double   100, 134, 135, 149, 202
hump   44, 46, 49, 51, 77, 79
hydrodynamic displacement effects   44–9
hydrodynamic disturbance. *See* cavitation; 'flow'; hump; Kelvin wake: 'singing'; turbulence; waves
hydrophones   28, 29, 32, 35, 66, 67, 119, 123

ice   36, 104–8, 118, 133, 134, 148, 150, 202
identification, friend or foe (IFF)   24
ILIAC system   120
Indian Ocean   161
infra-red sensors   38, 41, 50, 73–8, 81, 82, 86–7, 123, 127, 170, 179.
integration of data   119, 146
Integrated Undersea Surveillance System (IUSS)   123, 125, 131, 145, 155
intensity of acoustic signals   30
intercontinental ballistic missiles (ICBM)   3, 9, 19, 162. *See also* missiles
International Institute for Strategic Studies (IISS)   2
isothermal water layers   31–2, 36

jamming   23, 35, 100, 109, 134, 150, 170
Japan   105
Japan, Sea of   103–5, 127, 149, 177
Jasani, B.   62

Katz, A.   7
Kelvin wake   45, 51, 79
Kiev aircraft carriers   101
King's Bay, Georgia   168
Kirov battle cruisers   101
Kurile Islands   104, 177

Lafayette submarines 161–3, 166–8, 192
land-based sensors 82–3, 88
LANDSAT 82
large aperture arrays 119
lasers 37, 45, 51, 76, 77, 86, 129
launchers for SLBMs 163–4, 183
layers of water 31–2, 34, 36, 41, 48, 68, 121, 124
Leonardo da Vinci 28
lidars 77
localisation 19–21, 65–6, 69–71, 76, 77, 84–8, 120–21, 124, 127, 145, 150, 167, 190
Lomov, N. A. 176
Los Angeles submarines 132–3, 146
low-light-level image intensifiers (LLLII) 42, 76, 77, 85
lubricants, leaking of 43
luminescence, biological 42–3, 51

MccGwire, Michael 2, 83
machinery noises 29, 35, 36, 166
MacNamara, Robert 117
magnetic field sensors 70–1, 107
magnetic anomalies 39, 40, 51, 71, 107, 128, 130, 179, 183
magnetohydrodynamics(MHD) 39, 47, 49, 50
magnetometers 40, 71, 72
Malinovsky, R. 106
Mann, David 135, 167–8, 171, 181
manpower on SSBNs 165
mapping 47, 72, 122, 170
marine life, acoustic signals generated by 31, 34. *See also* biological luminescence; fish; whales
massing of forces 184, 190, 194
Mediterranean 127, 161
microwave sensors 47, 73, 76, 79, 81, 87. *See also* passive microwave radiometers
mines 20, 24, 104, 132–6, 146, 149, 168–9, 183, 190, 193

mini-submarines 109, 178, 183
missiles: Soviet 5, 97–9, 117; American 161–8, 171, 183–4. *See also* ABM; ballistic missile early warning system; cruise missiles; depressed trajectory SLBMs; intercontinental ballistic missiles; launchers; M-X; *Polaris*; *Poseidon*; range; self-initiating anti-air missiles; submarine-launched ballistic missiles; *Titan*; *Trident*
missile launch and flight, detection of 38, 50, 77, 82, 86, 89, 127, 166
Mission Capistrano 126
models, analytical, for signal processing 72, 119, 120, 122, 123
Mooney, H. McD. 78
moonlight 42, 76
multiple re-entry vehicles (MRV) 5
multi-spectral sensors 76, 78, 79, 81–2, 87
M-X missile 3, 150, 171, 180

NATO operations 165–6
Naval Eastern Oceanography Center 74
navigation 170
Navy Remote Oceanographic Sensing System (NROSS) 123, 146
Nierenberg, William 127
noise: ambient ocean noise 33–6, 107–8, 110, 126; emitted by submarines 28–9, 67, 69, 107–9, 125–6; of Soviet submarines 99, 100, 124–6, 132, 134, 146, 148; of US submarines 166, 167, 178, 191, 194, 202; under ice 107–8; analysis of noise 72, 120–22. *See also* acoustic

detection; acoustic indicators; silencing
non-acoustic indicators 27, 36–54
non-acoustic detection 79–84, 122, 127–30, 146, 148; Soviet 179, 181, 182, 189, 191, 194, 196
North Pole, magnetic effects of 107, 156, 205
Norway 105
Norwegian Sea 103, 104, 177

Oceanographic Research Fleet, Soviet 178
oceanography 72–4, 110, 120–3, 145–7, 167, 191
Ohio submarines 5, 161–8, 171, 190–2, 203, 204
Okhotsk, Sea of 103, 104, 149
optical fibre 71
optical wavelength sensors 76–7, 81, 85, 89, 179
Orion P-3 patrol aircraft 130, 131, 146, 150, 155
over-the-horizon (OTH) B radar 82–3, 88

Pacific Ocean, operations in 103, 123–4, 161, 177
paint, anti-fouling 43
passive microwave radiometers (PMRs) 41, 78–9, 87, 123
patrol areas: of Soviet submarines 103, 106, 148, 183, 207; of US submarines 161, 168, 180, 191, 194, 202
patrol periods 168
Perry, William 3, 21, 37, 47–8, 125, 127, 129, 149, 167, 180, 181, 211, 212
persistence of signals 27, 28, 39, 41–4, 46, 49, 53, 80, 83, 85
photographic systems 73, 76, 86, 128
plume, thermal 41, 77, 86
plunging weapons 20, 150, 184, 192, 207, 208

Podney, W. 40, 72
Polaris missile 175
Polmar, N. 99, 131
Poseidon missile 4, 161–2, 181, 192
ports and harbours 20, 24, 76, 128, 168
power supply to sensors 66, 67
pressure, atmospheric 48, 74
pressure of water 32, 34, 40, 45, 46, 70
probability of detection (PD) and probability of false alarm (PFA) 69-70, 84
processing of signals and data 66–70, 72, 80, 82, 87, 109, 119, 120, 122, 123, 130–2, 145–7, 150, 178
propellor, effects of 29, 35, 39, 45
Proteus 131

radar 37, 38, 50, 73, 79–83, 86–8, 119, 123, 127, 130, 179, 183
radio signals 28, 38, 107
radio-isotopes 43
radiometers 41, 47, 73–5, 78–9, 87, 123
rain 48, 76–7
range: of sensors 66–8, 70–2, 82, 100, 124, 145, 147, 202; of Soviet missiles 98, 99, 102–3, 109, 202; of US missiles 168, 180, 181, 191, 192, 202
Rapidly Deployable Surveillance System(RDSS) 125, 145, 152
Rathjens, J. 209
reactors, nuclear 43, 165
reflectivity of ocean surface 47, 49
refraction of sound 31–3
repairs 168
reverberations 68, 69, 126
Rodionov, B. I. 78, 106, 107

sabotage 109, 150

Sadek, A. 63
Sager, R. 40, 72
salinity 32, 34, 70
sanctuaries 206, 207, 210
Sanguine system 169
satellites 38, 50, 61–5, 73, 74, 77–82, 84, 86, 87, 89, 122–3, 127–8, 146–7, 179
Scowcroft Commission 203
seabed. *See* bottom
Seafarer system 169
search 19: methods of 60–1, 65, 66, 68, 69, 72, 76–9, 83–9, 107, 119, 126–30, 145; integration of data 120, 150; Soviet capability in 177–82, 192, 194. *See also* Sound Surveillance System (SoSuS)
search and rescue 77
SEASAT satellite 79–81
Security Technology Programme 170–1, 190, 194
seismic disturbance 43
self-initiating anti-air missile (SIAM) 170
sensors: deployment of 59–65; characteristics and uses 19, 24, 27, 46–9, 60, 65–89; acoustic 65–70; non-acoustic 70–89, 127–30; portable 177–8, 189, 194; proposed restriction of 206. *See also* Sound Surveillance System
Sèvres, Treaty of 105
shadow zones 32
shear currents 48
ships, surface, 33, 34, 40, 48, 60, 71, 85, 101, 120, 125, 146, 183
Shuttle Imaging Radar-A 81
SIGINT collectors 82, 88, 179
signals and indicators 27; submarine-generated 38, 65–6, 171. *See also* acoustic indicators; non-acoustic indicators; intensity; persistence; processing
signature, acoustic 29–30, 109, 124
silencing of submarines 29, 35, 36, 69, 99–100, 166–7
'singing' 29, 35
size of submarines 35, 45, 133, 148, 165, 167
slicks 47, 48
SOFAR (Sound Fixing and Ranging) 32, 68, 121, 124
solar events 40
sonars 23, 28, 29, 30, 32, 33, 36, 66, 68, 85, 100, 126, 127, 167, 177
sonobuoys 66–8, 85, 130, 183
Sound Surveillance System (SoSuS) 123–5, 145–8, 150, 152
South China Sea 127
space shuttle 63
spacecraft. *See* satellites
spatial resolution of sensors 62, 75, 76, 82
Speed, Roger 61
speed: of sensors 60, 61, 67; of submarines 29, 35, 41, 44, 45, 46, 69, 84, 134, 166
Spitzbergen 105
spoofing 100, 109, 148
'spreading' of signals 30
stability of strategic relationship 1–4, 9, 20, 101, 145, 147, 153–5, 195–6, 201, 203–6
Stand Off Weapon (SOW) 135, 155
Stockholm International Peace Research Institute (SIPRI) 2
Strategic Arms Limitation Talks (SALT) 99, 207
Strategic Arms Reduction Talks (START) 163, 207
submarines: SSBNs, survivability and strategy for deterrence 1, 4, 6–9, 147, 148, 151, 193–6,

203, 204, 208, 211; SSNs in anti-submarine operations. *See also* USA, forces and operations, ASW developments; USSR, forces and operations, ASW developments. *See also* depth; hull; manpower; noise; patrol; propellor; repairs, silencing; size; surface observability; wake; weapons. *See also Alfa; Delta; Typhoon; Victor; Yankee; Ethan Allen; George Washington; Lafayette; Los Angeles; Ohio;* British submarines; Chinese submarines; French submarines
Submarine Inertial Navigation System (SINS)   170
Submarine Launched Ballistic Missiles (SLBMs)   6–8, 147, 207. *See also* missiles
Submarine Launched Mobile Mine (SLMM)   136
SUBROC   133, 135, 146
super-conducting quantum interference device (SQUID)   71–2
surface effects on ocean   47–9, 77, 79
surface observability of submarines   34, 47–9, 128
surface ships. *See* ships
surprise strike   3–6, 155–6, 195, 205, 211
Surveillance Towed Array Sensor System (SURTASS)   125, 145, 150, 152
swath width   37, 75, 78–81
Sweden, territorial waters of 109, 178
synthetic aperture radar (SAR)   79–82, 87
Tactical Development Programme   170–71
technology transfer   178

temperature of water   31–2, 34, 45, 46, 48, 70, 73–5, 77–9, 107, 122. *See also* ice; layers of water; thermal scarring
testing of weapons   208
Texas Instruments   178
thermal infra-red sensors   76–8, 81
thermal plume   41, 77, 86
thermal scarring   40–2, 51, 78, 79, 87, 127
thermocline layer   31, 36, 41
Tierney, J.   121
'time-late' sensor problem   68–9, 80
Tiros-N satellite   79
Titan missiles   150
titanium   40
torpedoes   100, 130, 131, 133, 134, 136, 146, 149, 150, 155, 183, 190
towed decoys   22–3
towed detection devices   22, 45, 46, 60, 66–8, 70, 85, 109, 125, 132, 166, 177, 192. *See also* SURTASS
trace element detectors   44
tracking   3, 19, 21, 65, 66, 70, 71, 77, 85–9, 119, 120, 124,
trailing   19, 20, 22–5, 60, 61, 65, 66, 70, 71, 85–9, 206; counter measures against   149, 155, 166, 168, 192, 195
Train, Harry   178
transducers   28
triangulation   66, 69, 124
Trident missiles   3, 5, 161–5, 167, 168, 171, 180, 181, 191, 192, 203
Tsipis, Kosta   33–5, 69, 108
turbidity   37, 50, 77
turbulence   29, 44–6, 49, 52
Typhoon SSBNs   14, 15, 97–100, 103, 106, 148, 161
Urick, Robert   121
USA: forces and operations   130–7, 148, 161–71, 175, 194,

203, 204; ASW developments and potential 117–37, 145–56, 190–7, 201; strategy 117–18, 156; estimated damage from nuclear attack 6–7. *See also* stability of strategic relationship

USSR: forces and operations 97–110, 117, 123–4, 130, 131, 145–56, 182, 189, 203, 204; ASW Developments 2–3, 126, 175–84, 189–97, 201; home waters of 100, 102–4, 118, 123, 148, 175, 183, 191–4; naval policy and strategy 109, 147, 156, 175–6; estimated damage from nuclear attack 4–5, 8. *See also* stability of strategic relationship

variable depth sonars (VDS) 66, 85

vertical boundaries in water column 32, 34

Victor submarines 102, 177, 182, 192

wake of submarine 37, 40–6, 49, 51, 52, 77, 79, 128

warheads, numbers and yields: Soviet 14–15, 97, 98, 183, 184, 190; US 4–5, 21, 149, 150, 162–6

waste, dumping of 43–4

water. *See* currents; density; eddies; hydrodynamic displacement and disturbance; layers; magnetohydrodynamics; oceanography; pressure; salinity; temperature; thermal plume; turbidity; turbulence; vertical boundaries; waves

Watkins, James, 118

waves 39, 40, 44–9, 51, 52, 73, 80, 81, 129

weapons: US 133–6, 133–6, 148, 149; Soviet 183, 190, 193, 194. *See also* depth charges; mines; missiles; plunging weapons; torpedoes; warheads

Weinberger, C. 102, 192

Wells, W. H. 78

whales 40, 43

whitecaps 48, 77

Wilkes, Owen 2

winds 40, 48, 81

Windsor, E. P. L. 78

wing-in-ground (WIG) planes 61, 183

wrecks 40

Yankee SSBNs 14, 97–9, 103, 109, 148, 153

Zeiberg, S. 128